WALKING IN ROMAN CULTURE

Walking served as an occasion for the display of power and status in ancient Rome, where great men paraded with their entourages through city streets and elite villa owners strolled with friends in private colonnades and gardens. In this first book-length treatment of the culture of walking in ancient Rome, Timothy O'Sullivan explores the careful attention which Romans paid to the way they moved through their society. He employs a wide range of literary, artistic, and architectural evidence to reveal the crucial role that walking played in the performance of social status, the discourse of the body, and the representation of space. By examining how Roman authors depict walking, this book sheds new light on the Romans themselves – not only how they perceived themselves and their experience of the world, but also how they drew distinctions between work and play, mind and body, and republic and empire.

TIMOTHY M. O'SULLIVAN is Associate Professor of Classical Studies at Trinity University in San Antonio, Texas.

WALKING IN ROMAN CULTURE

TIMOTHY M. O'SULLIVAN

Trinity University

CAMBRIDGE
UNIVERSITY PRESS

CAMBRIDGE
UNIVERSITY PRESS

University Printing House, Cambridge CB2 8BS, United Kingdom

Cambridge University Press is part of the University of Cambridge.

It furthers the University's mission by disseminating knowledge in the pursuit of
education, learning and research at the highest international levels of excellence.

www.cambridge.org
Information on this title: www.cambridge.org/9781107475991

First published 2011
First paperback edition 2014

A catalogue record for this publication is available from the British Library

Library of Congress Cataloguing in Publication data
O'Sullivan, Timothy M., 1975–
Walking in Roman culture / Timothy M. O'Sullivan.
p. cm.
ISBN 978-1-107-00096-4 (hbk.)
1. Rome – Social life and customs. 2. Rome (Italy) – Social life and customs.
3. Walking – Rome – History. 4. Walking – Social aspects – Rome – History.
5. Walking – Rome – Psychological aspects – History. 6. Identity (Psychology) – Rome –
History. 7. Group identity – Rome – History. 8. City and town life – Rome – History.
9. Walking in literature. 10. Latin literature – History and criticism.
I. Title.
DG78.O84 2011
937–dc22
2011000385

ISBN 978-1-107-00096-4 Hardback
ISBN 978-1-107-47599-1 Paperback

for Ana

Contents

List of figures		*page* viii
Acknowledgements		x
List of abbreviations		xii
	Introduction	1
1	The art of walking	11
2	Seneca on the mind in motion	34
3	Urban walkers on display	51
4	Cicero's legs	77
5	Theoretical travels	97
6	Walking with Odysseus	116
	Conclusion	150
Bibliography		158
Subject index		176
Index locorum		183

Figures

Figure 1   Odyssey Landscapes, panels 2 and 3. Vatican
            Museums.   *page* 117

Figure 2   Odyssey Landscapes, panels 4 and 5. Vatican
            Museums.   118

Figure 3   Odyssey Landscapes, panels 6 and 7. Vatican
            Museums.   119

Figure 4   Odyssey Landscapes, panels 8 and 9. Vatican
            Museums.   120

Figure 5   Odyssey Landscapes, fragmentary panel. Left: black
            and white sketch reproduced with permission from
            Licia Vlad Borrelli, "Un nuovo frammento dei
            'paesaggi dell'Odissea'," *Bollettino d'Arte* 41 (1956)
            289–300: Fig. 1, p. 290. Right: photograph of original
            courtesy of the Museo Nazionale Romano.   121

Figure 6   Reconstruction (by author) of the Odyssey
            Landscapes as originally arranged. Watercolors of the
            individual panels are reproduced with permission
            from Ralf Biering, *Die Odysseefresken vom Esquilin*
            (Munich 1995). All rights reserved.   123

Figure 7   Close-up of the top left corner of Panel 2 of the
            Odyssey Landscapes, showing the two pillars and
            connecting architrave. Sketch by author.   128

Figure 8   Pompeii: Portico of the Praedia of Julia Felix. Photo
            by author.   129

Figure 9   Rome: House of Augustus, Room of the Masks.
            Photo by Koppermann, DAI-Rom 1966.0024.   131

Figure 10 Rome: House of Augustus, Room of the Garlands.
Photo by Koppermann, DAI-Rom 1966.0031.   131

Figure 11 Odyssey Landscapes (in nineteenth-century
reproduction by H. C. Krohn), Panel 2. From
Woermann, *Die antiken Odyssee-Landschaften*
(Munich 1876), Plate 1.   136

Figure 12 Odyssey Landscapes (in nineteenth-century
reproduction by H. C. Krohn), Panel 3. From
Woermann, *Die antiken Odyssee-Landschaften*
(Munich 1876), Plate 2.   137

Figure 13 Odyssey Landscapes (in nineteenth-century
reproduction by H. C. Krohn), Panel 4. From
Woermann, *Die antiken Odyssee-Landschaften*
(Munich 1876), Plate 3.   138

Figure 14 Odyssey Landscapes (in nineteenth-century
reproduction by H. C. Krohn), Panel 5. From
Woermann, *Die antiken Odyssee-Landschaften*
(Munich 1876), Plate 4.   139

Figure 15 Odyssey Landscapes (in nineteenth-century
reproduction by H. C. Krohn), Panel 6. From
Woermann, *Die antiken Odyssee-Landschaften*
(Munich 1876), Plate 5.   140

Figure 16 Fellini's *Roma*. A documentary film crew explores an
ancient Roman house.   154

Acknowledgements

It gives me great pleasure to thank the many people who helped me as I wrote this book. Kathleen Coleman directed the dissertation upon which it is based, and she has continued to be an incredible mentor and friend long after graduate school has ended. I am also grateful for the support of the other members of my committee, Gloria Ferrari Pinney and Richard Thomas. I have had the fortune of sharing many of the ideas in this book in public talks, and listeners invariably pointed me in some new and welcome direction; thanks to audiences at Columbia, Texas Tech, Trinity, U.T. Austin, Yale, the 2007 APA meeting in San Diego, and the 2009 meeting of CAMWS in Minneapolis. In addition, I've had the pleasure of talking about walking with a number of colleagues over the years, and I would like to thank in particular Diane Favro, Sander Goldberg, Jeremy Hartnett, Eric Kondratieff, Mark Lane, Alex Purves, Alessandro Schiesaro, Jocelyn Penny Small, and Rabun Taylor.

Many colleagues and friends have been extremely helpful in reading various chapters in draft form over the years, and I would like to thank Bettina Bergmann, Robert Germany, Thomas Jenkins, James Ker, Leah Kronenberg, and Andreola Rossi for their generosity. I am particularly grateful to two colleagues and friends who read the entire manuscript in draft form: Kathleen Coleman, who provided pages and pages of comments in the midst of a very busy year, and Erwin Cook, who read every word with his usual insight and acumen.

Research on this book has brought me on two occasions to the Vatican Museums, where Guido Cornini and Claudia Lega graciously led me through the Sala delle Nozze Aldobrandine. I am also grateful to Rosanna Di Pinto at the Vatican and Daria Lanzuolo at the DAI for their assistance with images. In 2007–8, a Loeb Classical Library Foundation gave me the time to write much of this book, and I thank them for the support. At Cambridge University Press, Michael Sharp and Laura Morris have been ideal editors, and Iveta Adams improved the typescript considerably by her careful reading. I am also grateful to the two anonymous readers for the

Press, who offered many valuable suggestions for improvement. Portions of Chapters 4 and 5 are adapted from my 2006 article "The Mind in Motion: Walking and Metaphorical Travel in the Roman Villa" (*Classical Philology* 101: 133–52), and Chapter 6 is adapted from my 2007 article "Walking with Odysseus: The Portico Frame of the Odyssey Landscapes" (*American Journal of Philology* 128: 497–532). I am grateful to the editors of both journals for permission to include the material here.

This project was also generously supported by two Trinity University Summer Stipends, and university research funds enabled a trip to Italy at a crucial moment during the writing. For their support, I am grateful in particular to Michael Fischer, Vice-President for Academic Affairs and Dean of the Faculty, and Diane Smith, Associate Vice-President for Academic Affairs. At Trinity and in San Antonio I have also learned a great deal from my colleagues and friends Stuart Allen, Rubén Dupertuis, Andrew Hansen, Andrew Kania, Patrick Keating, Kelly Lyons, Jessica Powers, and Harry Wallace. I would especially like to thank the many colleagues, past and present, who have made the Trinity Classical Studies department such a wonderful place to be: Joan Burton, Valerio Caldesi Valeri, Erwin Cook, James Gallagher, Robert Germany, Nicolle Hirschfeld, Thomas Jenkins, Lawrence Kim, Dimitri Nakassis, Grant Nelsestuen, Corinne Pache, Sira Schulz, John Stillwell, and Colin Wells (*requiescat in pace*).

On a personal note, I owe a great deal to the loving support of family and friends. Brendan Cully, Justine Heilner, Susan McDonough, Larry Myer, Brett Simon, and Josh Wise have given me the gift of their encouragement and friendship since we were teenagers. My in-laws Ricardo, Harriett, and Carlos Romo welcomed me into their family many years ago and never looked back. My aunt Nuala Outes first introduced me to the idea of historical walking and has always shared with me her love of the past. My amazing sisters Jennifer, Michelle, Pamela, and Courtney O'Sullivan have always kept me laughing. And my parents, Michael and Rose O'Sullivan, have always supported me no matter what – even when I never stopped taking Latin.

Finally, I'd like to thank my wife and daughter. As I was finishing this book, Lily Romo O'Sullivan came into my life, and nothing has been the same since. Although she can't walk yet, I like to think that she has a few things to say on the subject. And my wife, Anadelia Romo, has been my partner in everything these last seventeen years, and I simply could not have written this book without her. She has read every word countless times, talked over every idea, and sustained me in so many ways. I am grateful for all these things – and, yes, for our many walks together.

Abbreviations

Greek and Latin references are abbreviated in accordance with the third edition of the *Oxford Classical Dictionary*; or, where the *OCD* is lacking, in accordance with the *Oxford Latin Dictionary* or Liddell and Scott's *Greek–English Lexicon*. In addition, I have employed the following abbreviations:

Anon. *De physiogn.*	Anonymous, *De physiognomia* (*Scriptores physiognomonici graeci et latini*, ed. R. Foerster, Leipzig)
Aug. *RG*	Augustus, *Res Gestae*
Juv. *Sat.*	Juvenal, *Saturae*
Manilius, *Astron.*	Manilius, *Astronomica*
Mart. *Ep.*	Martial, *Epigrammata*
Perp.	*Passio Sanctarum Perpetuae et Felicitatis*
PHerc	*Papyrus Herculanensis*
Phld. *Ep.* Sider	*The Epigrams of Philodemos*, ed. D. Sider, Oxford
Phld. *Rhet.* Sudhaus	Philodemus, *Volumina rhetorica*, ed. S. Sudhaus, Leipzig
Plut. *De lib. educ.*	Plutarch, *De liberis educandis*
Polemon, *Phys.*	Polemon, *De physiognomia* (*Scriptores physiognomonici graeci et latini*, ed. R. Foerster, Leipzig)
Sen. *Brev. vit.*	Seneca, *De brevitate vitae*
Sen. *Ot.*	Seneca, *De otio*
Sen. *Vit. beat.*	Seneca, *De vita beata*
Strabo, *Geog.*	Strabo, *Geographica*
Tertullian, *De cult. fem.*	Tertullian, *De cultu feminarum*

Introduction

The geographer Strabo preserves an amusing anecdote about the interaction of Romans and "barbarians" on the Iberian peninsula in the first century BCE. Although the Romans had formed a political alliance with the Vettonians, there was inevitably a certain degree of culture clash (*Geog.* 3.4.16):

τοὺς δὲ Οὐέττωντας, ὅτε πρῶτον εἰς τὸ τῶν Ῥωμαίων παρῆλθον στρατόπεδον, ἰδόντας τῶν ταξιαρχῶν τινας ἀνακάμπτοντας ἐν ταῖς ὁδοῖς περιπάτου χάριν, μανίαν ὑπολαβόντας, ἡγεῖσθαι τὴν ὁδὸν αὐτοῖς ἐπὶ τὰς σκηνάς, ὡς δέον ἢ μένειν καθ' ἡσυχίαν ἱδρυθέντας ἢ μάχεσθαι.

When the Vettonians first arrived at the Roman camp and saw some of the generals enjoying a stroll by walking back and forth on the roads, they assumed that they were crazy and tried to lead them down the road into the tents, since they thought that one should either stay seated and at rest or engage in battle.[1]

We are clearly meant to chuckle at the naïveté of the Vettonians. Strabo even puts the entire incident in indirect speech ("they say that..."), reinforcing the impression that the story of the dim-witted barbarians has attained legendary status, and that there is a long history of tellers and listeners who, by joking at the expense of the barbarian other, have affirmed their own status as insiders, part of the cultured elite. And in case it is not abundantly clear to his readers that the Vettonians' reaction to the strolling generals betrays a lack of culture, Strabo follows up this anecdote with further evidence of their outsider status: "Some would also regard the fashion of some of their women as a sign of their barbaric appearance" (*Geog.* 3.4.17: τῆς δὲ βαρβαρικῆς ἰδέας καὶ τὸν τῶν γυναικῶν ἐνίων κόσμον θείη τις ἄν). The geographer goes on to describe the various headdresses of the local women with a level of astonishment rivaling, no doubt unwittingly, that of the Vettonian yokels he has just ridiculed. The

---

[1] Except where noted, all translations are my own.

I

veracity of the Vettonian incident is beside the point; what is significant is the anecdote's promulgation, the zest with which we can imagine its telling, and the way in which Strabo portrays leisurely walking as a shibboleth of cultured (read: Greek and Roman) identity, as something that separates "us" from "them."

The anecdote perfectly conveys the power of the human tendency to categorize and to draw distinctions: even walking, a trait that is more or less universally human, indeed a trait that distinguishes humans from other species, can become the means through which one human marks himself as completely different from another. Nor is this tendency a lost relic of antiquity. H. F. Tozer, commenting on this passage in the nineteenth century, registers precisely the response that Strabo expected (1893, 104):

[T]his view of walking exercise is not surprising in barbarous peoples, whose own life alternates between violent exertion and absolute indolence. Oriental peoples are possessed by the same idea in a somewhat modified form. The French translators remark – "La première chose qui frappe un Turc quand il vient chez les nations policées de l'Europe, est de voir des hommes se promener sans autre but que celui du plaisir ou de la santé."[2]

Strabo and Tozer, for all the distance between them, engage in a similar game. For both, the barbarian other is a man of extremes, either lolling around in luxury or rushing forth to battle with animal heroism. But instead of seeing these mutually exclusive stereotypes as evidence for the inadequacy of all stereotypes, they even blame the barbarian for their own logical flaw, as if the problem were not one of "our" perception but "their" inconsistency. And for both ancient and modern observers, walking a certain way could serve as a touchstone of "cultured" behavior, with insiders and outsiders clearly delineated (or so they insisted) by the way they moved through society.

The subject of this book – a history of Roman walking – would surely have puzzled Strabo and his contemporaries. Yet at the same time Strabo's portrayal of the Vettonian incident suggests an awareness in antiquity that walking could be viewed through an analytical lens. It even suggests an awareness that walking has its own history. Strabo is a Greek author trying to flatter the Romans among his readers, and this anecdote is part of the flattery: let us agree, suggests Strabo, that the Romans, notwithstanding

---

[2] "The first thing to strike a Turk when he arrives among the refined nations of Europe is the sight of men strolling with no other goal than that of pleasure or health." The comments of the French translators (La Porte du Theil, Koraes, *et al.* 1805–19) also appear in the translation of Hamilton and Falconer (1854, 246).

their barbarian past, now fall on the "correct" side of the Greek/barbarian dichotomy – just look at the way their generals stroll like gentlemen, even in camp.[3] In other words, even Strabo seems aware that although the *act* of walking may be a universal human trait, the way we interpret that act is culturally determined. Moreover, there is far more to interpret than we might realize at first glance. In spite of – or perhaps *because* of – its pervasive presence in everyday life, walking is rarely analyzed on its own terms, as a distinct category of investigation; as I hope to show, this neglect is unfortunate, particularly in the case of the Romans. Because of the privileged position that it occupies in human life, walking plays a central role in our relationship to the world around us; it is essential to our experience of place, to the way we see and think, and to our assumptions about identity (of others and our own).

A few recent volumes have begun to investigate the history of walking.[4] Authors both academic and popular have sought to explore the ways in which this most basic human trait has changed over time, and our perceptions, past and present, of what it means when we walk. A particular focus has been those eras when people consciously cultivated an art of walking, such as the Romantic period, when poets like Wordsworth wrote about their rambles through the countryside, or nineteenth-century Paris, where solitary flâneurs roamed through city sidewalks.[5] Artists, too, have begun to investigate the ways in which walking determines our experience of space; most famously, the contemporary British artist Richard Long creates works that are walks through landscape, and viewers can only access the work through his visual or written documentation of that walk.[6]

When scholars and artists seek out ancient prototypes for self-conscious ambulation, they inevitably light upon the world of Greek philosophy, and with good reason. As is well known, two major philosophical schools that arose in fourth-century Athens acquired names that either refer directly to

---

[3] Notice the similar way in which the British Tozer positions himself and the unnamed "French translators" as cultural allies united against the barbarian Turks.

[4] Solnit 2000; Amato 2004; Nicholson 2008. While there have been no book-length studies of walking in Roman antiquity, both Corbeill 2004, 107–39 and Fowler 2007 explore the role that walking played in the larger context of Roman deportment. The forthcoming volume (which I have not seen) on movement in the Roman city, edited by Laurence and Newsome, promises to advance our understanding of the topic.

[5] On the theme of walking in Wordsworth, see Wallace 1993 and Langan 1995; in Romantic literature and culture more broadly: Robinson 1989 and Jarvis 1997; in the modernist European novel: Barta 1996; in twentieth-century American poetry: Gilbert 1991. On flânerie, see Buck-Morss 1989 and Tester 1994.

[6] On Richard Long, see Fuchs 1986; on Richard Long and other walking artists, see Solnit 2000, 267–76.

walking (the Peripatetics) or to an ambulatory setting (the Stoics). More generally, a host of anecdotes from antiquity, from Diogenes wandering the world looking for an honest man to Thales stumbling into a pit while lost in thought, attest to a real connection between walking and Greek philosophical practice.[7] The association has been strengthened by a long history of reception; European philosophers and artists embraced the culture of the pensive stroll, often in self-conscious imitation of Greek culture. Kant's walks were such a regular feature of his day that, according to Heine (1882, 108–9), the natives of Königsberg set their watches by them. Kierkegaard too was famous for his walks through Copenhagen, and at least one scholar has wondered whether the habit was an act of Socratic emulation.[8] Inspired no doubt by both modern and ancient practice, Nietzsche pushes the association between philosophy and walking to its logical extreme:

On ne peut penser et écrire qu'assis [One cannot think and write except while sitting down] (G. Flaubert). – I've caught you, nihilist! Sitting still [das Sitzfleisch] is the very *sin* against the Holy Spirit. Only *peripatetic* thoughts [die ergangenen Gedanken] have any value.[9]

Nietzsche doesn't simply disagree with Flaubert; he seems to accuse him of a laziness both physical *and* intellectual, as if Flaubert's propensity for sitting leaves him more vulnerable to Nietzsche's attack.

Yet the notion that Greek philosophers *only* practiced their craft while on foot is a fiction.[10] And it was the Romans, in a sense, who enabled and promoted this fiction. Thus Nietzsche's objection is a parody of Greek philosophical practice, for as any reader of Plato will know the bulk of the Socratic dialogues favor Flaubert's suggestion.[11] It is certainly true that the Romans inherited from the Greeks the connection between walking and thinking. But as we shall see in this book they did not hand it down to Europe without making their own contribution. Thus it is especially

---

[7] For the image of the wandering Greek sage, see Montiglio 2005; see also Redfield 1985, 98–102, Bremmer 1991, Nightingale 2001, and my Chapter 5 below.

[8] Pattison 2005, 181. On the central place of walking in Kierkegaard's philosophical project, see Solnit 2000, 23–6.

[9] Ridley and Norman 2005, 160 (Nietzsche, *Twilight of the Idols*, Maxims and Arrows 34). I am grateful to Judith Norman for drawing my attention to this passage.

[10] As Montiglio 2005 shows, the connotations of wandering in the Greek imagination are far too complex and polyvalent to allow for any simple equivalence between walking and philosophical practice, despite later stereotypes.

[11] Montiglio 2005, 171–9 explores the symbolism of walking, sitting, and standing in Plato's dialogues, and argues for the greater importance of sitting and standing still as philosophical poses for Plato. See also Solnit 2000, 14–16, who points out that the later appropriation of ancient Greek walking involves a healthy dose of fantasy.

unfortunate that the role of Roman culture in the reception of Greek philosophical walking has been largely ignored.[12] The wholehearted embrace of walking for leisure during the European age of Enlightenment – what Joseph Amato refers to as "the birth of walking by choice" and Rebecca Solnit calls "walking as a conscious cultural act" – had earlier precedents in the villa gardens and public porticoes in ancient Rome.[13] This Roman reception of Greek ambulatory modes has profoundly altered the way we see Greek philosophical wandering, and this reception, I argue, is an essential precursor to the ambulatory reverie of later authors such as Rousseau, Wordsworth, and Thoreau.

Despite this lineage, the two modes of leisurely walking most associated with eighteenth- and nineteenth-century Europe – the urban promenade and the country ramble – seem not to have had much appeal for the Romans, at least not to the same extent that these practices captured later imaginations. Stories of solitary or lonely Roman wanderers through nature are few and far between in our extant evidence. In part, this silence is due to the very different attitude to untamed nature in antiquity. Even those passages that do suggest an interest in the wild often betray a preference for places marked by human activity and even revulsion for the wilderness.[14] Seneca, for instance, mocks elite Romans with too much time on their hands who wander from one spot to the next, unable to escape themselves: "'We should go see uncultivated places: let's seek out the woodlands of Bruttium and Lucania.' Yet amidst these deserted regions they require something pleasant, the sort of thing that might give their immoderate eyes a break from the extensive squalor of those frightful locales" (Sen. *Tranq.* 2.13: "*inculta videantur, Bruttios et Lucaniae saltus persequamur.*" *aliquid tamen inter deserta amoeni requiritur, in quo luxuriosi oculi longo locorum horrentium squalore releventur*). Seneca manages to confirm in the same paragraph both the existence of an interest in untamed nature in antiquity and the typical negative attitude to those places; while this

---

[12] Rebecca Solnit's excellent *Wanderlust: A History of Walking* is a fine example: in her discussion of ancient walking, the Peripatetics get their necessary nod, but the Romans are nowhere to be found. Amato 2004 does include a section on Roman walking (34–9), focusing in particular on the use of Roman roads by soldiers and travelers.

[13] "[W]alking by choice": Amato 2004, 2; see also his Chapter 3 (71–100) on the rise of the promenade in early modern Europe. "[W]alking as a conscious cultural act": Solnit 2000, 14.

[14] A noteworthy exception is Horace's encounter with a wolf during his stroll through the Sabine woods (*Carm.* 1.22.9–12), though the end of the poem, in which the poet confirms his commitment to Lalage even in the remotest of places, confirms (albeit ironically) the unusual nature of this walk. Another exception is Cicero's *De legibus*, in which the orator strolls through the countryside around Arpinum along with his brother Quintus and his friend Atticus; see Chapter 5 below.

extreme mood swing, as it were, is surely meant to evoke the inconstancy of the elites he lampoons, his description of the woodlands as "extensive squalor" is hard to reconcile with modern attitudes to nature.[15]

More generally, what makes Roman walking distinctive from both earlier and later analogues is the clear emphasis on walking as a profoundly *social* activity, both in the private and in the public realm. As we shall see, strolling with friends was a hallmark of villa culture, so much so that the walk became a virtual symbol of time spent together with a good friend. As Cicero confides to Atticus, "And so then I wait for you, I miss your company, I even demand your return. For there are many things that are worrying and distressing me, and if I only had your ear, I feel I could pour them all out in one walk's conversation" (*Att.* 1.18.1: *quare te exspectamus, te desideramus, te iam etiam arcessimus. multa sunt enim quae me sollicitant anguntque, quae mihi videor aures nactus tuas unius ambulationis sermone exhaurire posse*). When Cicero imagines himself reunited with his friend, he imagines them not just conversing together, but *walking* together. For Cicero, the primary benefit of a stroll is the opportunity for conversation and company. Yet he acknowledges the possibility of solitary contemplation even during a walk with friends: "If someone preparing for a trial were to practice to himself on a journey or on a walk, or if he were to ponder something else rather intently, he would not be at fault, but if he were to do the same thing at a dinner party, he would seem rude because of his ignorance of the occasion" (*Off.* 1.144: *ut si qui, cum causam sit acturus, in itinere aut in ambulatione secum ipse meditetur, aut si quid aliud attentius cogitet, non reprehendatur, at hoc idem si in convivio faciat, inhumanus videatur inscitia temporis*). Cicero's qualification presumes that the walk is a standard setting for conversation among friends; he puts it in the same general category as the dinner party, if at a slightly less formal or rule-bound level. His admonition only makes sense in a society in which a walk or a journey was often a social occasion.

So too in the urban setting. We rarely encounter in Latin literature the solitary urban flâneur that has captured the modern imagination.[16] Even

---

[15] Cf. Beagon 1992, 159–61 on the cruelty of nature (particularly the sea) in the thought of Pliny the Elder. Though she argues (161–77) that Pliny's attitude to the land (as opposed to the sea) is generally positive, he is usually referring to land cultivated through agriculture. See also Davies 1971 on the distinct attitude to natural beauty in the works of Cicero.

[16] Walter Benjamin, one of the first to investigate the phenomenon of flânerie, makes this very point (1999, 417): "Paris created the type of the flâneur. What is remarkable is that it wasn't Rome. And the reason? Does not dreaming itself take the high road in Rome? And isn't that city too full of temples, enclosed squares, national shrines, to be able to enter *tout entière* – with every cobblestone, every shop sign, every step, and every gateway – into the passerby's dream?" On the similarities between flânerie and Roman walking, see Larmour and Spencer 2007b, 17–18.

Horace's famous stroll down the Via Sacra (*Sat.* 1.9) is not as solitary as it might seem, despite the poem's introspective opening; it takes the threat of conversation with the pest to reveal to the reader that there was a slave by Horace's side all along.[17] Elsewhere Horace boasts that he is free to wander through the circus and the forum by himself, but here we have the exception that proves the rule; Horace cites his solitary walks as another way he stands out from the crowd of his overly ambitious peers.[18] There were a number of details about urban life – the lack of a real police force, the constant threat of fire, the paucity of consistently enforced building codes, overcrowding – that must have made walking through the city a daunting experience.[19] Yet the ubiquity of personal attendants and bodyguards is a reflection of the very different realities not only of Rome itself but also of a slave-owning society.[20] There is, in other words, a class filter that disguises the true extent of solitary urban walking; we do not hear much from those who had to walk through the city alone.

But the emphasis on walking in groups in Roman culture, I argue, is more than just a response to urban realities or a symptom of a slave society; it is a reflection of the larger truth that walking, for the Romans, was a marker of identity. There is a constant emphasis on the performative quality of Roman walking, and a constant assumption of an audience to appreciate the performance. These viewers see someone walking (or imagine him or her, through literature) and are immediately able to appreciate something about that individual's identity – whether because he is walking alongside others like him; or because he walks at the center of a group of acolytes; or because he walks in a certain place, at a certain time, or on a certain occasion; or because he sits in a litter, and lets his slaves do the walking. Or even because he moves his body in a certain way. Roman walking, in other words, was not only a way of moving through space but also a performance of identity. By looking at how Romans talk about walking, this book sheds light on the Romans themselves, not only how they

---

[17] Horace begins the poem in solitary contemplation, "musing over something trivial, and absorbed in it" (Hor. *Sat.* 1.9.2: *nescio quid meditans nugarum, totus in illis*); a few lines later, we find out he's not alone: "I say something or other into my slave's ear" (1.9.9–10: *in aurem | dicere nescio quid puero*).

[18] "Thus I live more pleasantly than you, illustrious senator, and thousands of others: I walk alone, wherever I want; I ask how much the vegetables and wheat cost; I often wander the deceptive circus and forum in the evening; I stand awhile by the soothsayers; then I go on home to a plate of leeks, chickpeas, and pancakes" (Hor. *Sat.* 1.6.110–15: *hoc ego commodius quam tu, praeclare senator, | milibus atque aliis vivo. quacumque libido est, | incedo solus, percontor quanti holus ac far, | fallacem circum vespertinumque pererro | saepe forum, adsisto divinis, inde domum me | ad porri et ciceris refero laganique catinum*).

[19] Ramage 1983 and Scobie 1986 offer the best guides to the difficulties of daily life in ancient Rome.

[20] On the effect the ubiquity of slaves had on the Roman imagination, see especially Fitzgerald 2000.

perceived themselves and their experience of the world, but also how they drew distinctions between work and play, body and mind, man and woman, "manly" and "effeminate," rich and poor, citizen and slave, emperor and subject, child and adult, philosopher and student, republic and empire. Walking served as a critical tool of categorization. And how the Romans made sense of themselves and their world is, after all, at the heart of what we try to uncover when we study antiquity.

The book's first chapter ("The Art of Walking") examines how the gait functioned as an index of personal and social identity in Roman culture. Latin literature of all periods shows how the act of walking distinguished free men from slaves, men from women, and insiders from outsiders. Yet the classification of individuals by their gaits involved a certain degree of paradox, particularly in terms of gender. The gait was on the one hand an irreducible, visible feature of individual identity, yet on the other hand, in a society where the performance of social identity was so important, was also treated as a technique of the body susceptible to instruction and manipulation. As this chapter demonstrates, categories such as male and female were not dependent principally on the presence or absence of certain sexual organs, but on the quality of the performance of life: you were a man or a woman if you walked like one. The study of the gait therefore gets to the heart of how Romans thought about their bodies, and the relationship of their bodies to their personal identity.

Walking was not just about the body, however. There was a pervasive belief in antiquity that the movement of the body reflected the movement of the mind. The second chapter ("Seneca on the Mind in Motion") uses the work of the younger Seneca to reveal how the gait was understood to be a mirror of the mind of the walker. Seneca's tragedies frequently stage acts of gait interpretation, with the act of walking becoming a unified performance of physical and mental activity. There were precedents for such an association in ancient playwriting, so in one sense Seneca was the heir of a robust dramatic tradition. Yet a careful study of his other writings reveals that the gait had a philosophical meaning as well: as a Stoic, Seneca cared about how people walked. The path, after all, was the principal metaphor for the acquisition of Stoic principles; for students of Stoicism, even walking like a sage helped them advance on the road to virtue.

The Stoic path often led to the heart of the city itself, as Seneca's writings also make clear. The third chapter ("Urban Walkers on Display") examines how Romans making their way through the city were assessed not only by how they walked but also by who walked alongside them. There were a host of ambulatory rituals in Rome; spectacular processions such as the triumph and aristocratic funeral have attracted most of the scholarly attention. This chapter focuses instead on other common types of processions, such as the escort that accompanied aristocrats as they made their way to the forum and around the city. The entourage that surrounded powerful men was a well-known ancient phenomenon; during the Roman republic, it was particularly associated with candidates for office. Yet the phenomenon of the escort persisted long after republican institutions had died, and a consideration of how authors such as Pliny and Tacitus deploy these associations suggests that ambulatory movement through the city could promote an ideological attachment to the past.

The purposeful stride of the powerful man in the city also acquired meaning by its contrast to the leisurely stroll popular among Roman aristocrats at home. The fourth chapter ("Cicero's Legs") investigates the culture of the *ambulatio*, or leisurely walk, in the Roman villa, particularly as described in the letters and philosophical dialogues of Cicero. The Roman *ambulatio* flaunted the economic independence of the walker, who did not need to use his body to earn a wage, and could instead walk back and forth with no particular destination. The regular movement of a walking in a portico, with arms and legs swaying in a more or less consistent rhythm, allowed for an increased focus on the conversation itself, as the body disappeared into its automatic movement. The Roman *ambulatio* was therefore a social and even an intellectual activity, a setting for conversation among social equals.

The intellectual associations of walking for leisure also had an historical explanation, since Romans associated this activity with Greeks in particular. Chapter 5 ("Theoretical Travels") explores in greater detail the intellectual background of the Roman *ambulatio*, particularly in the concept of *theoria*, or traveling to see and learn, which Plato and others adopted as a model for philosophical inquiry. For these philosophers, the mind could travel where the body could not, and retreating into the flight of the mind even involved an abnegation of the body. The notion of philosophical inquiry as metaphorical travel persists in Roman culture, as passages in Varro and Seneca make clear. I argue, however, that Roman *ambulatio* culture represents a further refinement of this idea, embracing the movement of the body as an activation of the notion of *theoria* and travel. The chapter thus reveals the intellectual background necessary to understand the domestic displays of the Roman villa and town house which, as many scholars have shown, encouraged the visitor to think of other places and times as he strolled through.

We are fortunate to have a remnant of just such a domestic decorative ensemble: the Roman fresco known as the Odyssey Landscapes, now housed in the Vatican. The final chapter ("Walking with Odysseus") demonstrates how an appreciation of the culture of Roman walking can alter our perception of one of the most studied artifacts from antiquity. The late republican painting is duly famous for its sensitive rendition of landscape, but less famous for the fictive portico frame that is painted "over" the frieze, dividing it into individual scenes. I argue that this portico would have evoked in the Roman viewer the experience of the *ambulatio,* and thus served an interpretive function in addition to its more familiar narrative function. The painted portico put the viewers in the proper frame of mind to appreciate the intellectual associations of the Odyssey Landscapes, as they walked with Odysseus on a parallel journey to greater insight.

CHAPTER I

The art of walking

In the first book of Virgil's *Aeneid*, Aeneas and Achates separate from their shipwrecked companions and set out to discover where they have landed. They come upon a woman dressed in hunting garb, who explains to them the land they are in and the story of its queen. Only as she turns away does she reveal herself as the goddess Venus, Aeneas' mother (*Aen.* 1.402–5):

> dixit et avertens rosea cervice refulsit,
> ambrosiaeque comae divinum vertice odorem
> spiravere; pedes vestis defluxit ad imos;
> et vera incessu patuit dea.

Thus she spoke. Turning away, she gleamed from her rosy neck, and the heavenly tresses wafted a divine fragrance from her head; her clothes flowed all the way down to her feet, and by the way she walked she was clearly a true goddess.

Venus needs no words to advertise her divinity; her physical presence – the color of her complexion, the smell of her hair, the flow of her garments, and, above all, the nature of her walk – is eloquent enough. The alluring scene perfectly conveys part of the appeal of a religion with anthropomorphic gods: simple, everyday gestures – the turn of the neck, for example – may be depicted with a transcendent, divine beauty that ordinary humans can evoke, but not replicate. But despite the fact that Venus at first successfully conceals her divinity, and fools her own son by adopting a human disguise, there are some physical features that are impossible to conceal. When Aeneas first hears her speak, he suspects that she is a divinity, perhaps even Diana (*Aen.* 1.326–34); only when she walks away, and he sees her move for the first time, are his suspicions confirmed.[1]

---

[1] Wlosok 1967, 85 n. 46 cites *Iliad* 13.71–2 as precedent for a god (Poseidon) being recognized by his gait; it is not quite clear in the Homeric text whether it is his gait in particular that gives Poseidon away, or just his feet and legs (so Janko 1992 ad loc.). A character in Heliodorus' *Aethiopica* (3.12–13), however, cites the Homeric passage in a discussion of the gait of divinities.

Venus is not the only goddess in the *Aeneid* whose stride gives her away. In Book 5, when Iris disguises herself as Beroe and urges the Trojan women to burn their ships, the old nurse Pyrgo is the only one to see through the goddess' disguise. "Observe," she says, "the signs of divine beauty: her shining eyes, her breathing, her face, the sound of her voice, or at least her stride as she moves" (*Aen.* 5.647–9: *divini signa decoris* | *ardentisque notate oculos, qui spiritus illi,* | *qui vultus vocisque sonus vel gressus eunti*). Other gods in the poem have more success in their attempts to impersonate humans, though they still must disguise the way they walk; when Cupid disguises himself as Ascanius in Book 1, two acts suffice to effect his transition from divine to mortal: he sheds his wings and adopts Ascanius' gait.[2] The notion of a distinctive divine gait becomes a topos in ancient literature, so much so that it is parodied by the novelist Heliodorus: a character notes that the gait is the best way to distinguish the gods in our midst because they do not walk, but glide, as the truly wise will know (*Aeth.* 3.13.2).

The frequency with which Latin *incessus* ("gait") is used where we might not expect it in English poses a translation challenge; translators often feel the need to translate *incessus* as "bearing" or "demeanor," when neither the *Oxford Latin Dictionary* nor the *Thesaurus Linguae Latinae* even lists these as possible definitions. Take, for example, the following passage from Cicero's *De finibus*; Cicero is taking Epicureanism to task for using everyday words to express a philosophical meaning that is different from or even contrary to their everyday meaning, and to support his point he appeals to the meaning of bodily comportment (*Fin.* 2.77):

vide igitur ne non debeas verbis nostris uti, sententiis tuis. quodsi vultum tibi, si incessum fingeres, quo gravior viderere, non esses tui similis; verba tu fingas et ea dicas, quae non sentias?

Therefore see that you don't use our words, but your own meanings. If you were to falsify your expression or your gait in order to appear more severe, you would not be true to yourself; so, then, should you falsify words and say what you do not mean?

In the Loeb edition, Rackham translates "*quodsi . . . fingeres*" as "if you assumed an unnatural expression or demeanor."[3] The choice is revealing in that it successfully translates the sense of the Latin for a modern audience by treating *incessus* as a synecdoche for physical self-presentation generally, but, in order to

---

[2] *Aen.* 1.689–90: "Obeying the commands of his dear mother, Cupid sheds his wings and, rejoicing, walks forth with Ascanius' gait" (*paret Amor dictis carae genetricis, et alas* | *exuit et gressu gaudens incedit Iuli*). Cf. Juno's creation of a phantom Aeneas (10.640): "She gives it a voice but no mind, and she reproduces how he walks when he moves" (*dat sine mente sonum gressusque effingit euntis*).
[3] Rackham 1931, 167.

do so, is unfaithful to the literal meaning of the term *incessus*. English "gait," in other words, does not normally stand in for a person's entire physical being the way Latin *incessus* does; the difference is not just semantic, but cultural.

There is a persistent belief in Roman literature (and in Roman culture more broadly) that we might call the rule of the gait: how you walk defines who you are.[4] Such a principle, moreover, quite obviously depends upon the participation of an audience trained in the art of watching others walk. In the passage above, for example, Venus revealed her identity by her gait (*incessu patuit*); the use of her bodily movement as a means of self-disclosure not only conveys the revelatory power of walking but also suggests that there is an audience who can read the movements of the body and make judgments about others based on how they move. This chapter will survey ancient literature for the types of conclusions that Romans were accustomed to draw from their assessment of how others walked. As we shall see, the gait was especially useful as one of the many tools observers could use to distinguish the class and gender of the walker. As many scholars have demonstrated, elite males were expected to advertise their self-control in their very bodies – for if they could not control their bodies, how could they manage to control the state?[5] The intense focus on elite male gaits manifested itself not as a set of positive recommendations but as a set of negative contrasts: elite males were constantly reminded of the importance of *not* walking like a woman, slave, or effeminate male. Likewise, social rules and warnings abound in the evidence for female gaits in Roman literature. This attention to gendered walking reveals one of the central paradoxes of Roman culture itself. For Roman elites, gait was one of the many bodily characteristics that justified their position in the world; there was accordingly great social pressure to talk about styles of walking as if they were natural, innate, and directly reflective of identity and character. As a result of its social importance, however, considerable effort was spent on training young men to "walk the right way," which suggests an awareness that this seemingly "natural" trait was actually an acquired competence.

[4] A number of scholars have made note of the role that walking played in the larger context of Roman deportment; see, e.g., Brown 1988, 11; Edwards 1993, 69; Gleason 1995, 60–2. There are two longer studies of Roman attitudes to gait. Corbeill 2004 includes a chapter (107–39) on the attention paid to how politicians walked in the late republic, in which he argues that popular politicians consciously adopted flamboyant gestures and conspicuous gaits to distinguish themselves from their stiff opponents; the chapter also has much to say about the attention paid to gaits in Roman culture more broadly. Fowler 2007, written before his death in 1999, connects Roman attitudes to dignified walking to the larger discourse of *constantia* so important to Roman male self-image (and to Augustus in particular); his interest is not just in Roman gaits but in how the study of such a topic gets to the heart of what it means to study another culture.

[5] For the discourse surrounding elite male bodies in ancient Rome, see Edwards 1993, 63–97; Gleason 1995; Richlin 1997; Gunderson 1998; Connolly 2007.

FACE AND GAIT

What does your friend look like? If asked this question, we modern observers might first describe facial characteristics, hair color, or build; perhaps we would mention sartorial preferences or other visible aspects of our friend's personality. It is unlikely, however, that we would describe how this friend walks, unless his or her gait were particularly memorable. Ancient sources give quite a different impression. To be sure, in a society filled with busts and ancestor masks, the face was still the primary focus of physical description, just as today; "for the face," in Cicero's memorable formulation, "is a performance and a picture of the whole mind."[6] But as many scholars have shown, bodily comportment was also an important aspect of individual identity in ancient Rome, and therefore keenly observed.[7] In a deeply stratified face-to-face society such as Rome's, the movements of the body conveyed the status of the person no less than facial characteristics.[8] Put another way, if the face was the most important aspect of an individual's physical appearance, it was also a relatively fixed feature of one's identity; indeed the popularity of the portrait in antiquity depended upon its ability to convey what remained more or less visually consistent about a person from one day to the next. The gait, on the other hand, represented identity in motion, the most important aspect of an individual's entire physical reality animated in space and time.

Proof for the importance of this pairing can be found in Latin literature, where we often find the face (*vultus*) and gait (*incessus*) together referring to the sum of a person's physical appearance. In these cases, the word *vultus* includes not only the physical face but also its full expressive possibilities, while *incessus* too not only has a specific reference – the way someone walks – but also, by a kind of metonymy, can refer to the whole of one's physical comportment. The Christian martyr Perpetua, to take one example, demonstrates her willingness to meet her death by walking into the arena with a "shining face and calm step" (Perp. 18.2: *lucido vultu et placido incessu*). In the *Metamorphoses*, Ovid adds a third element when describing the power of Morpheus to assume the likeness of

---

[6] Cic. *De or.* 3.221: *animi est enim omnis actio et imago animi vultus*. On the role of facial expressions in Roman politics and culture, see Corbeill 2004, 140–67.

[7] See, e.g., Edwards 1993, 63–97; Gleason 1995; Wyke 1998; Montserrat 1998; Aldrete 1999; Porter 1999; Miller 2004; Corbeill 2004; Roller 2006; Fowler 2007.

[8] As Maud Gleason puts it in her excellent study of this topic (1995, xxiv); "Deportment matters. It is a shorthand that encodes, and replicates, the complex realities of social structure, in a magnificent economy of voice and gesture."

human beings in dreams: "there is no one more ingenious than he is at capturing someone's gait and countenance and manner of speaking" (*Met.* 11.635–6: *non illo quisquam sollertius alter | exprimit incessus vultumque sonumque loquendi*). Cicero uses the same triad when he describes how the tribune designate Rullus adopted a whole new persona after his election, studiously displaying "a different face, a different tone of voice, a different walk" (*Leg. agr.* 2.13: *iam designatus alio voltu, alio vocis sono, alio incessu esse meditabatur*).[9] It is not the only place where Cicero focuses on the face and gait as constitutive of the whole person, including character.[10] A particularly memorable instance comes in his attacks on Piso and Gabinius in the *Pro Sestio* (17):

quorum, per deos immortalis, si nondum scelera vulneraque inusta rei publicae vultis recordari, vultum atque incessum animis intuemini: facilius eorum facta occurrent mentibus vestris, si ora ipsa oculis proposueritis.

And if – by the almighty gods! – you are not yet willing to remember the crimes of these men, and the wounds they inflicted upon our republic, then at least in your imagination look upon the countenance and the gait of each man: their deeds will come more easily to mind if you have their faces before your eyes.

In a rhetorically deft gesture, he protests that their misdeeds are too grievous to recount openly, but that if the jury recalls what they *looked* like, then their evil deeds will inevitably come to mind as well. It is noteworthy that Cicero first introduces the idea of physical appearance by a reference to countenance and gait (*vultum atque incessum*), and then calls upon the jury to remember their faces (*ora*) in particular. The rhetorical move clarifies what would have been evident to Cicero's audience: by *vultum* and *incessum* he means not only those specific physical features but also their entire appearance, demeanor, and character.[11]

The Cicero passage suggests the possibility of disguising one's gait or adopting a new one – a common topos, as we shall see. The idea of disguise depends upon an equally pervasive notion that individuals have a particular gait that is an irreducible aspect of their physical person – everybody has one. In this sense, the gait is similar to the face: they both convey individual and familial identity. Cleopatra's son Caesarion, for instance, testified to his paternal lineage not only by his name but also by his appearance and his

---

[9] Cf. Cic. *Sest.* 105: "People loved these men [*sc.* popular politicians] – their names, their way of speaking, their faces, their way of walking" (*horum homines nomen, orationem, vultum, incessum amabant*).

[10] I shall have more to say on the Roman tendency to interpret gait as a reflection of mental disposition and character in Chapter 2.

[11] For more on the way that Piso and Gabinius walk, see Corbeill 2004, 118–20.

gait.[12] In this view, the stride was just another bodily trait that could be inherited, like facial features or hair color. According to Seneca's Andromache, Astyanax inherited his father Hector's gait (in addition to his features, bearing, hands, height, brow, and hair).[13] Neither Caesarion nor Astyanax ever knew their fathers; the passages rely upon a general awareness that bodily comportment passed from one generation to another. Indeed, as Anthony Corbeill has noted, the actors in Roman funeral processions were chosen for their physical resemblance to the deceased family member; since these actors wore *imagines* (portraits of the deceased), other physical attributes, such as build and gait, were more important for the actor's success.[14] The funeral parade illustrates the very Roman idea that a "family gait" was no less distinctive than a "family nose."[15]

GAIT AND GENDER: WALK LIKE A MAN

In one of his letters, the younger Seneca cites the Stoic Aristo, who poked fun at the tendency of schoolmasters and grandmothers to instruct their pupils in practical etiquette, rather than teach them one philosophical principle that can be applied to every situation (*Ep.* 94.8–9):

"sic incede, sic cena; hoc viro, hoc feminae, hoc marito, hoc caelibi convenit." ista enim qui diligentissime monent ipsi facere non possunt; haec paedagogus puero, haec avia nepoti praecipit, et irascendum non esse magister iracundissimus disputat.

"This is how you walk. This is how you dine. This is proper behavior for a man. This is proper behavior for a woman. This is proper behavior for a married man. This is proper behavior for a bachelor." In fact the very ones who so carefully offer such

---

[12] Suet. *Iul.* 52.2: "Indeed some Greeks reported that Caesarion resembled his father even in his appearance and gait" (*quem* [sc. Caesarion] *quidem nonnulli Graecorum similem quoque Caesari et forma et incessu tradiderunt*).

[13] Sen. *Tro.* 464–8: "My Hector had these features, he was similar in gait and bearing, he carried his strong hands that way, he was similarly tall in the shoulders, similarly threatening with his grim brow, scattering his long hair on his outthrust neck" (*hos vultus meus | habebat Hector, talis incessu fuit | habituque talis, sic tulit fortes manus, | sic celsus umeris, fronte sic torva minax | cervice fusam dissipans iacta comam*). Cf. Astyanax' steady gait as Odysseus (walking tall) leads him to his death (*Tro.* 1088–91): "Through crowded expanses the Ithacan walks with a majestic gait, dragging the little grandson of Priam with his right hand, and the boy proceeds to the high walls with a steady gait" (*per spatia late plena sublimi gradu | incedit Ithacus parvulum dextra trahens | Priami nepotem, nec gradu segni puer | ad alta pergit moenia*).

[14] Corbeill 2004, 117, where he cites Diodorus Siculus' inclusion of the gait as an imitable trait in the funeral procession (31.25.2).

[15] A number of Latin family names refer to deficiencies of the feet or gait (Atta, Claudius, Crassipes, Pansa, Plancus, Plautus, Valgus, Varus, Scaurus); see Kajanto 1982, 241–2. The many *cognomina* that refer to speed or sluggishness (Agilis, Celer, Citatus, Velox, Lentulus) surely evoked both mental and physical capacities; see Kajanto 1982, 248–9.

instructions cannot themselves perform them. The slave attendant teaches the young boy these things; the grandmother teaches her grandson these things. And the exceedingly anger-prone schoolteacher preaches that one must never get angry.

Aristo may disapprove, but his dismissal inadvertently reveals the prevalence of this sort of instruction. Like the swaddling of infants, teaching children to move and walk the right way was considered an essential part of their formation, and was explicitly gendered.[16] Indeed the philosopher himself, in the course of his objection, places great importance on the notion of gender distinction; his disapproval of old women and slaves teaching young (elite) males suggests that gender, status, and class divisions must be respected and reinforced from an early age. Perhaps this is why there is such emphasis in our sources on the apprenticeship of young men in the forum (the so-called *tirocinium fori*); in the elite male imagination, the "teacher" at this stage of the educational process was finally someone worth emulating.[17] As the young man shadowed his older mentor through the forum he learned not only how to speak and interact with others but also the posture, demeanor, and comportment befitting a statesman.[18] As Maud Gleason puts it, in antiquity masculinity "was a language that anatomical males were taught to speak with their bodies."[19] And walking, the act of putting the body in motion, was an essential part of that language. For the gait conveyed not only the personal or familial identity of the walker, but also gender identity.

So how should a Roman man walk? The answer, of course, depended on the man. Here, as so often, the definition of *vir Romanus* was a question not only of gender but also of status.[20] The Roman man conveyed his status in the way he moved through the city, through his house and gardens, and through his life. Among the many markers by which the elite man distinguished himself from others, particularly from slaves, was his gait. Speed

---

[16] On swaddling and gender, see Gourevitch 1995. For Soranus' advice on the swaddling of infants, see Harlow and Laurence 2002, 42–3.

[17] On the *tirocinium fori*, see Cic. *Amic.* 1.; Tac. *Dial.* 34; Plin. *Ep.* 2.14.10. As David 1992, 333–41 points out, the institution was attractive because it was a natural extension of the father–son relationship.

[18] As Corbeill 2004, 4 suggests. Cf. David 1992, 338–9: "Ces jeunes gens qui s'attachaient à un citoyen illustre devaient le suivre pas à pas, l'observer dans ses attitudes et ses gestes, mémoriser systématiquement les paroles qu'il prononcerait" ("These young people who attached themselves to an illustrious citizen were expected to follow him step by step, to observe his bearing and gestures, to memorize systematically the words that he uttered.") On the *tirocinium fori* and gender, see Richlin 1997, 92–3; on Roman rhetoric and masculinity, see Connolly 2007.

[19] Gleason 1995, 70; see 60–2 for more specific instructions on how to "walk like a man."

[20] On ways in which the "ideal of immobile *constantia*" for the Roman elite male was made manifest while walking, see Fowler 2007 (quote at 6). On the connections Romans made between the gait and both gender and status, see Corbeill 2004, 117–23.

was a particular concern.[21] It is a well-known motif of Roman comedy that slaves run, so much so that the phrase "running slave" (*servus currens*), as Corbeill (2004, 117) notes, is "almost tautological."[22] The notion that men of a certain class should not hurry is spoofed by Plautus in his *Poenulus*, where some freedmen in their attempts at social climbing adopt the exaggerated slow pace of an aristocrat, admonishing the love-crazed Agorastocles for his hurried impatience. "For free citizens," one of the freedmen remarks, "it is more fitting to walk through the city at a moderate pace; I consider it the mark of a slave to rush and run about" (Plaut. *Poen.* 522–3: *liberos homines per urbem modico magis par est gradu | ire, servile esse duco festinantem currere*).[23] The *servus currens* conveys meaning by his evocation (in his very gestures) of societal expectations about the utilitarian approach to slaves' bodies, but he also contributes to the formation of those expectations. The running slave is an obvious example of a process of give and take between reality and representation, especially because the primary way in which that representation would have been received by the Roman audience was not in fact textual, but visual; the connection between the theatrical performance of Roman comedy and the social performance of Roman domestic life would have been all too obvious to the spectators. Quintilian in fact makes a similar connection between stage and real life while instructing his reader that some situations require rapid gestures, while others require more restrained gestures; to prove his point he appeals to the well-known fact that slaves and the lower class walk quickly on stage, while others walk with more dignity (literally "more weightily").[24] Moreover, the lack of any real distinguishing physical features to separate servile and free in the Roman world encourages the development of other marks of servile identity: the hurried gait is a gentler version of the slave collars and brands of the mines.

The notion that aristocrats should walk slowly is of course not unique to Roman culture, and there are similar attitudes in ancient Greek literature, for example.[25] Still, as Fowler (2007, 6) notes, there is something especially Roman about the measured gait: "the ideal of immobile *constantia* was even

---

[21] On the importance of a measured gait in Roman culture, see Corbeill 2004, 122–3; Fowler 2007, 4–15.

[22] On the *servus currens*, see Csapo 1987, 399–401; Fitzgerald 2000, 15. As Erwin Cook points out to me, the common use of the slave name "Dromo" in Roman comedy (Plaut. *Asin.* 441, *Aul.* 398; Ter. *Ad.* 376, *An.* 860, *Haut.* 249; cf. Lucian, *Dial. meret.* 10.2, 12.3, *Timon* 22) is part of the same pattern.

[23] Similarly, the servant Pythias in Terence's *Eunuch* notes the leisurely approach of the slave Parmeno, dubbing him (with considerable irony) a "good man" (*Eun.* 918–19: *virum bonum*).

[24] "The same observation is also true of movement. So in plays, for example, young men, old men, soldiers, and matrons walk with more dignity, while slaves, maids, lackeys, and fishermen move more quickly" (Quint. *Inst.* 11.3.112: *eadem motus quoque observatio est. itaque in fabulis iuvenum senum militum matronarum gravior ingressus est, servi ancillulae parasiti piscatores citatius moventur*).

[25] See Bremmer 1991, 16–20.

more central to Roman conceptions of bodily stance [*sc.* than to Greek conceptions]."[26] The choice of the toga as the dress of state is one sign: the cumbersome garment was held in place with no clasps, only its own weight, thereby requiring that one arm be kept at the side at all times, and forbidding any sort of quick motion. Indeed this inconvenience must have been part of its appeal: don a toga, and it's hard *not* to walk the "right" way.[27] But if walking too fast would suggest an economy of movement inappropriate for an upper-class male, there was also the risk of moving too slowly.[28] A slow gait correctly suggests that others should wait for the elite male, but excessive slowness might convey a sluggishness of mind on the part of the walker, or even an unwillingness to perform his identity as a member of the upper echelon. Or, even worse, as Cicero warns his son, it might make him look like a woman (Cic. *Off.* 1.131):

cavendum autem est, ne aut tarditatibus utamur [in] ingressu mollioribus, ut pomparum ferculis similes esse videamur, aut in festinationibus suscipiamus nimias celeritates, quae cum fiunt, anhelitus moventur, vultus mutantur, ora torquentur; ex quibus magna significatio fit non adesse constantiam. sed multo etiam magis elaborandum est, ne animi motus a natura recedant, quod assequemur, si cavebimus ne in perturbationes atque exanimationes incidamus et si attentos animos ad decoris conservationem tenebimus.

Moreover, we must be careful neither to employ an effeminate lingering in our gait (lest we seem like floats at a parade), nor in our haste to pick up excessive speed; for when that happens our sides heave, our expression changes, our face is twisted: all of which clearly signify that constancy is lacking. But we must take even greater care that the movements of our minds do not lose their natural pace, which we can ensure by being careful not to succumb to agitation or excitement, and by keeping our minds attentive to the preservation of decorum.

Why does Cicero think a slow gait is effeminizing? Is there a perception that women walk, or should walk, more slowly?[29] Perhaps – but the

[26] Both Fowler (2007, 1) and Corbeill (2004, 123) aptly cite Augustus' famous motto "hurry up slowly" (*festina lente*) as another example of the Roman ideal of moderate movement. Caligula later shows his divergence from this Augustan ideal: envious of the attention lavished on a successful gladiator, he hustles away from the spectacle, trips on his toga, and falls down a set of stairs (Suet. *Calig.* 35.3).

[27] As pointed out to me by Sander Goldberg. On the restricted movements imposed by the heavy imperial toga, see Stone 1994, 20–1. Quintilian (*Inst.* 11.3.138) speculates that the change in dress over time has altered gesture as well; see Stone 1994, 16.

[28] On the "golden mean" of Roman walking (not too fast, not too slow), see Corbeill 2004, 118–20; Fowler 2007, 11–15.

[29] Cicero also suggests that a woman should walk more slowly than a man in a joke preserved by Macrobius (*Sat.* 2.3.16, as emended by Housman 1918, 163–4): when Cicero saw his son-in-law Piso walking too softly and his daughter too quickly, he said to his daughter "Walk like your husband," <and to his son-in-law, "Walk like your wife"> (*Cicero . . . cum Piso gener mollius incederet, filia autem concitatius, ait filiae "ambula tamquam vir," <at genero, "ambula tamquam uxor">*).

comparison to the floats at a procession is telling.[30] Pliny the Elder makes
a similar leap of thought (from feminine display to floats) in a passage
about *luxuria*, in which he compares the jewelry worn by Lollia Paulina to
the luxurious spoils carried on *fercula* in a triumphal parade (*HN* 9.118).
The point of comparison is different, but the overall connection is similar:
a slow walk, like excessive jewelry, is an affectation that attracts attention
to itself. Languid movements and shiny pearls attract male desire, but, as
objects of desire, should not be characteristics of the male subject. As
Corbeill (2004, 129) has remarked, the ideal male gait (and body) draws no
attention to itself; the male body should act as a transparent conduit to the
moderate mind of its bearer. This, too, is why a quick gait is undesirable;
not only does it liken the walker to a slave or worker, but it also distorts his
body, thereby drawing unwanted attention to it. Cicero moves with ease
from the movements of the body to the movements of the mind, for, in his
view, the ideal male body reveals nothing about its physicality, reflecting
only the mind and character of the male. The body that draws attention to
itself automatically excludes its bearer from the ranks of the upper-class
male, and a particularly conspicuous or expressive gait – whether too fast
or too slow – is an easy way to draw such attention.[31]

The ideal male gait, then, exhibits moderation, a synthesis of body and
mind, and a clear and visible control of both. This measured pace is what
the Romans understood to be "natural" and "proper" for free-born males;
it is the performance of the ideal of moderation epitomized in the golden
mean. Catiline, for example, testifies to his deviation from this aristocratic norm by the way he walks, sometimes fast and sometimes slow: his
gait is no less fickle than his mind.[32] Gleason (1995, 61) traces the
philosophical ideal back to Aristotle, whose *megalopsuchos* advertises his
status in his slow movements.[33] In the centuries that followed, the development of the art of physiognomy – deducing character from physical
characteristics – turned these sorts of physical observations into a

---

[30] *ut pomparum ferculis similes esse videamur. fercula* are used not only in public processions (carrying
      spoils or images of the gods in triumphs and other parades) but also to carry in food at a dinner party,
      hence the need for the explanatory *pomparum* here.

[31] Compare Apuleius' use of the very rare word *gestuosus*, which we might translate as "expressive," in
      conjunction with the gait of one of the priests of Isis: "one of the blessed attendants, expressive in his
      gait" (*Met.* 11.11: *unus e ministerio beato gressu gestuosus*). He also uses the word to refer to the boys and
      girls who enter "with an expressive gait" (10.29: *incessu gestuosi*) to perform a Pyrrhic dance on stage.

[32] "He had a bloodless pallor, his eyes were repulsive, at times he walked quickly, at times slowly; on his
      face and in his expression there was derangement" (Sall. *Cat.* 15.5: *igitur colos ei exsanguis, foedi oculi,
      citus modo, modo tardus incessus: prorsus in facie voltuque vecordia inerat*).

[33] Arist. *Eth. Nic.* 1125a. See also Bremmer 1991, 19.

comprehensive system.[34] In these texts we find rare instances where the assumptions of a culture are organized and made explicit; Gleason (1995, 55) calls the work of the second-century sophist Polemon, the most famous of the ancient physiognomists, "a highly elaborated operations manual for a technology of suspicion that was indigenous to his culture." As we might expect, gait was a legitimate sphere of inquiry for the practicing physiognomist (Polemon, *Phys.* B39, trans. R. Hoyland):

Know that length of stride is an indication of loyalty, good counsel, extensive ability, strong-mindedness, and anger. They are a people who excel in being with kings. Shortness of step indicates that its owner can hardly complete an action that he has begun, and it also indicates anger and bad disposition.

Throughout the works of the physiognomists, the ideal male walks slowly, with total control, his head and shoulders upright and confident, metaphorically towering over those beneath him.[35]

In a culture where control itself was gendered male, for a man to walk ostentatiously was to mark himself as effeminate and powerless. Here is where the bulk of the physiognomists' efforts are spent: on teaching the male how to spot the *cinaedus* in their midst, and how, implicitly, to avoid being mistaken for one. *Cinaedus* is commonly defined as the male recipient of anal sex, though, as Williams (1999, 175–8) argues, the word has a broader reference than, e.g., *pathicus*. The word is directly borrowed from Greek *kinaidos*, which "primarily signifies an effeminate dancer who . . . adopted a lascivious style, often suggestively wiggling his buttocks in such a way as to suggest anal intercourse" (Williams 1999, 175). The *cinaedus* was marked, in other words, by how he moved his body, so gait was a particularly good way to identify him.[36] The difference could be as subtle as a tilt to one side or the other (Polemon B40, trans. Hoyland):

If you see that when he walks he moves his sides and shakes his joints, associate him with fornication, for this is the walk of women. It is the same if there is an inclination to the right side in his stature when he moves. As for the one who inclines in the direction of the left, judge for him ignorance and stupidity.

[34] The relevant texts are gathered in Foerster 1893; Polemon's treatise on physiognomy (known principally through later Arabic and Latin translations) has been newly edited and discussed in Swain 2007a. See also Evans 1935 and 1969; Barton 1994, 95–131; and Gleason 1995, 29–37 and 55–81.

[35] On the analysis of gait by physiognomic authors, see Gleason 1995, 60–2; and Swain 2007b, 185–7.

[36] On the *cinaedus*' gait, see Corbeill 2004, 120–2 (with ancient evidence assembled in n. 64). On the figure of the *kinaidos*, see Winkler 1990; Davidson 1997, 197–82. On the *cinaedus*, see Richlin 1993; Williams 1999, 172–208 (and *passim*).

The physiognomists present themselves as experts in spotting "degenerates" by the way they walk, but there were also plenty of amateur detectives. "The gait," says Seneca, "gives the unchaste man away" (*Ep.* 52.12: *impudicum et incessus ostendit*).[37] In Phaedrus' account, Demetrius of Phaleron assumes that Menander is a *cinaedus* when he sees his anointed body, his flowing garments, and his "voluptuous and languid gait" (5.1.13: *gressu delicato et languido*). Softness of gait is an often cited characteristic, part of the same metaphor of softness that usually designates the effeminate male: "If a man is effeminate, isn't his softness apparent in his very gait?" asks Seneca (*Ep.* 114.3: *si ille effeminatus est, in ipso incessu apparere mollitiam?*).[38] The symptoms of the effeminate gait are all defined in opposition to the positive traits of a "real" man's gait, as deviations from an ideal norm. The clearest example is the occasional use of "fractus" (literally "broken," metaphorically "effete" or "exhausted") to describe the effeminate body.[39] The *cinaedus'* deviation from "real" manliness is so complete that his entire body is not simply broken, but "fake"; according to Manilius, "a gait feigned to softness pleases" the effeminate male (*Astron.* 5.153: *fictique placent ad mollia gressus*).[40] In the next section, we shall see that there was an ideal feminine gait as well, one that exhibited some of the flowing "softness" of the effeminate gait, but which also suggested a sense of that control and moderation expected of elites of either gender.

WALK LIKE A WOMAN

In the Roman mindset, a woman's way of walking was no less fundamental an aspect of her identity than it was for men. For women, too, the gait was indistinguishable in some important sense from her person: Catullus tells his verses that they will easily recognize his "disgraceful adulteress" (42.3: *moecha turpis*) because she "walks disgracefully" (42.8: *turpe incedere*). Just as the physical ("ugly") and moral ("disgraceful") senses of *turpis* are indistinguishable, Lesbia's stride and character are one and the same. Yet, as we might assume, the expectations for women's bodily comportment were quite

---

[37] See Gleason 1999, 75; Corbeill 2004, 114.

[38] On the symptoms of *mollitia* in Roman culture, see Edwards 1993, 63–97.

[39] Petronius for example in his mock-epic has a catalog of the world; the Persians are marked by the "broken gait characteristic of an enervated body" (*Sat.* 119.1.25: *fractique enervi corpore gressus*). Quintilian observes that "a smooth body, a broken gait, and womanly clothes" are often taken to be "the signs of a soft and deficient man" (*Inst.* 5.9.14: *corpus vulsum, fractum incessum, vestem muliebrem ... mollis et parum viri signa*). On the latter passage, see Williams 1999, 189.

[40] Cf. Anon. *De physiogn.* 74, where the anonymous author (paraphrasing Polemon B38) claims that all movements of the body can be grouped into four species, of which one is true and natural (*vera et naturalis*) and the other three are feigned and contrived (*fictas et simulatas*). See Repath 2007, 602–3.

different than the expectations for men, and were intimately connected to larger societal perceptions of gender roles.[41] Typically, the expectations are expressed as polar opposites and in particularly moralizing terms: idealized *exempla* of good and bad women with their good and bad gaits.

By way of example, let us examine the portraits of a pair of Roman women who inhabit either side of the continuum of expectations. First: the positive role model. An appropriate gait was such a desirable feature that it could be mentioned on a tombstone, as in the well-known case of the second-century BCE noblewoman Claudia (*CIL* 1² 1211):

> hospes, quod deico paullum est, asta ac pellege.
> heic est sepulcrum hau pulcrum pulcrai feminae.
> nomen parentes nominarunt Claudiam.
> suom mareitum corde deilexit souo.
> gnatos duos creavit. horum alterum
> in terra linquit, alium sub terra locat.
> sermone lepido, tum autem incessu commodo.
> domum servavit. lanam fecit. dixi. abei.

Wayfarer, what I have to say is brief, so stop and read it through. This is the not so pretty grave of a pretty woman. Her parents called her Claudia. She loved her husband with all her heart. She gave birth to two boys: one of them she leaves above, the other one she buried below. She had a delightful way of speaking, and moreover she had an agreeable way of walking. She kept her home; she spun wool. I have finished speaking; you may leave.

Claudia's pleasing gait and conversational skills are as important to her memory as her happy marriage, her two sons, and her homemaking. As we saw in descriptions of the elite male body, the elite female should comport herself with moderation; *commodus* conveys a sense of the viewer's pleasure at seeing everything in proportion, in its right place, observing the appropriate limit (*modus*). Claudia's walk is *commodus* because it advertises her "moderation" more generally. The physical characteristics of this gait are left unspoken, surely because the reader can imagine how she walked based on the entire picture of her life. In this sense, the choice of words in the epitaph is significant. At first glance, the description of Claudia's gait may seem like an afterthought, with *tum autem* ("and besides") introducing an additional trait that has just occurred to the mind of the writer. But *tum autem* may also serve as a slight corrective to what has just preceded (hence my translation "and moreover"). After all, Claudia's forays into the world of conversation could have been perceived as forays into a setting more appropriate for men, particularly the context of public

---

[41] On women's bodily comportment in antiquity, see Bremmer 1991, 20–2; Corbeill 2004, 70–2.

speech. The addition of her modest gait clarifies for the Roman reader that Claudia's penchant for conversation observed the requisite sense of feminine restraint and respect for traditional gender roles, as her bodily conduct generally, and her gait specifically, also made clear.[42]

The highly gendered portrait of Claudia's attributes on her tombstone finds a negative corollary a century or more later in Cicero's description of her clanswoman, Clodia (*Cael.* 49):

> si quae non nupta mulier domum suam patefecerit omnium cupiditati palamque sese in meretricia vita collocarit, virorum alienissimorum conviviis uti instituerit, si hoc in urbe, si in hortis, si in Baiarum illa celebritate faciat, si denique ita sese gerat non incessu solum, sed ornatu atque comitatu, non flagrantia oculorum, non libertate sermonum, sed etiam complexu, osculatione, actis, navigatione, conviviis, ut non solum meretrix, sed etiam proterva meretrix procaxque videatur: cum hac si qui adulescens forte fuerit, utrum hic tibi, L. Herenni, adulter an amator, expugnare pudicitiam an explere libidinem voluisse videatur?

> If any unmarried woman opens her home to anyone's desire and quite openly lives like a prostitute; if she proceeds to employ as dinner dates men she doesn't even know; if she acts this way at Rome, in her gardens, and among the crowds at Baiae; if indeed she behaves in such a way – not only in the way she walks, but also in her getup and in her choice of companions; not only by her brazen eyes, not only by her wanton talk, but also by her embraces, by her kisses, by her yacht parties, by her sailing trips, by her dinner parties – if indeed she behaves in such a way that she seems to be not just a prostitute, but a rather forward and provocative prostitute: if any young man happened to be with such a woman, tell me, Herennius, would you think that he wanted to be an adulterer, or just her lover? That he wanted to violate her chastity, or simply to fulfill his own desires?

Cicero's horrified portrait of the wanton woman further elucidates the ideological content of Claudia's tombstone. Whereas Claudia protects her home (*domum servavit*), Clodia opens hers up for public pleasure (*domum suam patefecerit omnium cupiditati*). Claudia ventures out in public, but knows her place, as reflected in her lovely conversation and her agreeable walk (*sermone lepido . . . incessu commodo*); Clodia, on the other hand, has a loose tongue (*libertate sermonum*), and reveals her true shamelessness by her getup (*ornatu*), by her companions (*comitatu*), and even by the way she walks (*incessu*). Cicero's evocation of Claudia's tombstone is in one sense accidental, but in another sense predictable, because both texts

---

[42] The adjective *lepidus* also contributes to the picture, since, as Krostenko 2001, 64–7 demonstrates, it was often associated with feminine physical characteristics, particularly by Plautus. He also investigates its use on the Claudia epitaph (71–2), where he notes that the noblewoman's manner of speaking and walking provides a pictures of her "social attractiveness."

participate in the construction of societal expectations for feminine behavior.[43]

Notice that none of these texts is particularly clear about *how* each woman walks; we would be hard-pressed, for example, to describe precisely Claudia's *incessus commodus*. It is simply assumed that the audience will share a general sense of the right and wrong way for a woman of a particular standing to walk. Moreover, it is not surprising that the gait becomes a focal point for the judgment of female bodily comportment, and indeed for the judgment of women themselves. For her gait, we might say, is the physical symbol of a woman's movement through society, and in patriarchal societies there is *always* a sense of heightened anxiety about a woman's public place. A sense of anxiety about a woman's movement through society, in other words, translates into a sense of anxiety about her motion, and about the movements of her body.

We see this anxiety most powerfully expressed by Christian authors, who adapt this inherited ideology of feminine comportment to a more fully realized sense of the sexual dangers posed to women as they walk through the city. Or perhaps we should speak of the sexual dangers posed to men. As Tertullian makes clear in his famous work on the dress of women, female modesty (now a more specific trait than Roman modesty, and principally about the avoidance of sex) is as much about men as it is about women.[44] Christian women must advertise their modesty in their bodily gestures, lest they give the impression that they are available for sex. The danger, in other words, is male misreading of female bodily deportment. In his introduction to the second book of *De cultu feminarum*, which begins with the importance of a modest gait for Christian women, Tertullian makes the point rather well: "Your salvation, by which I mean the salvation not only of women but also of men, is based on your demonstration of sexual modesty (*pudicitia*) in particular" (*De cult. fem.* 2.1.1: *ea salus, nec feminarum modo sed etiam virorum, in exhibitione praecipue pudicitiae statuta est*).[45] *Pudicitia* is a trait of both men and women in Roman society (see Langlands 2007), so in one sense,

---

[43] Moreover, as James Ker points out to me, there may be more pressure on members of the Claudian clan to mind their steps because of the inevitable etymological play with *claudere/claudicare*, "to limp." For a more extended comparison of these two passages, see Geffcken 1973, 29–34.

[44] For a rehabilitation of Tertullian's misogyny, see Church 1975. On sexual renunciation in the early Christian church, see Brown 1988.

[45] In the next paragraph, Tertullian clarifies the relationship between a proper walk and feminine *pudicitia*: "But for now [we will speak] not about sexual modesty ... but about things that pertain to it, that is, how you should walk" (*De cult. fem.* 2.1.2: *sed modo nos non de pudicitia ... verum de pertinentibus ad eam, id est qualiter vos incedere oporteat*).

Tertullian notes that both men and women must observe sexual modesty to attain salvation. But his sentence, particularly in the context of a pamphlet about the proper deportment of women, also implies that male modesty is contingent in some basic way on female modesty: if women are not careful to deny their bodily allure, how can men be expected to control themselves in their presence?

Some two centuries later, Jerome takes as his target women who would reject this system (*Ep.* 22.13):

hae sunt, quae per publicum notabiliter incedunt et furtivis oculorum nutibus adulescentium gregem post se trahunt ... purpura tantum in veste sit tenuis, et laxius, ut crines decidant, ligatum caput, soccus vilior et per humeros maforte volitans, strictae manicae bracchiis adhaerentes et solutis genibus fractus incessus: haec est apud illas tota virginitas.

These are the women who walk conspicuously in public and by means of the furtive nods of their eyes drag a flock of young men after them. ... They may have only a thin bit of purple on their clothing, their head may be loosely veiled so their hair falls down, their footwear is somewhat cheap and the shawl flies off their upper arms, the tunic is drawn back and clings to their forearms and they may have a loose-kneed exhausted gait: this is the sum total of their virginity.

According to Jerome, the gait is as much an index of sexual availability as a woman's gestures and her clothing.[46] For the gait is in some way gesture in motion, and the danger, for Jerome, is that the wanton woman may turn into a pied piper of sexual allure, taking flocks of upstanding Roman men with her. Moreover, the metaphors used to describe the gait share in the same hierarchical positioning of women and men, employing the same terms that distinguished the gaits of "real" and "effeminate" males. The lax knees of the so-called virgins renders their gait "exhausted" or more literally "broken," clearly a lapse from some ideal "unbroken" gait and a physical indicator of their compromised sexual standards. This description does not just suggest that there is a "broken" female gait and a "whole" one: rather, dissolute females (and effeminate males) as a whole are susceptible to a type of gait that is deformed or broken vis-à-vis the male gait.

We have already seen this idea when examining the characteristics of male gaits that were perceived to be "feminine." The female gait, not surprisingly, shares a number of characteristics with the gait of the effemi-nate male. A passage of Seneca brings together a number of the common metaphors for effeminacy (*Tranq.* 17.4):

---

[46] For a survey of references to gait and footwear in Jerome and the other church fathers, see Adkin 1983.

Scipio triumphale illud ac militare corpus movebat ad numeros, non molliter se infringens, ut nunc mos est etiam incessu ipso ultra muliebrem mollitiam fluentibus, sed ut antiqui illi viri solebant inter lusum ac festa tempora virilem in modum tripudiare, non facturi detrimentum, etiam si ab hostibus suis spectarentur.

Scipio used to move his triumphant soldier's body to the beat. He didn't bend himself with a soft pliancy, as is now customary for men who flow by, surpassing the softness of women even in the way they walk. Instead, he danced the way the men of old used to do during games or holidays: in a manly way, with no loss of reputation, even if their enemies saw them.

"Even in the way they walk": today's men betray their failure in the basic way they move through the world. Unlike Scipio or the men of old, they do not dance only when appropriate, during the special moments when the entire society strengthens its commitment to its norms by transgressing them for a circumscribed time and occasion. Instead, they dance even when they walk.[47] Seneca seems to suggest that by conveying their effeminacy in their very manner of walking their failure is complete, as if the gait is somehow the most basic or fundamental gestural act of the human body. If the gait is effeminate, then all is lost. But the metaphors he uses go beyond the metaphor of weakening or breaking that we saw earlier. These men "flow" softly and thus exclude themselves from masculinity itself. Men are rigid and hard; women are soft and flowing. The metaphorical world of ancient discourse about the gendered body is a way of talking about sexual difference – or rather, of talking *around* sexual difference. These metaphors allow the speaker to avoid talking about sexual organs; they transform biological difference and biological functions (erections, menstrual flow) into an ideological pattern that serves to establish and reinforce strict gendered norms.

The use of the female gait as a point of contrast for male deportment does not preclude the gait from being used to draw social distinctions. As we saw above, Claudia's modest walk suggests a middle point between extremes. A woman's walk should be graceful, but not ostentatious; there is an *art* of walking, as the *praeceptor amoris* of Ovid's *Art of Love* makes clear (*Ars am.* 3.297–306):

> omnibus his, quoniam prosunt, inpendite curam:
>   discite femineo corpora ferre gradu.
> est et in incessu pars non temnenda decoris:
>   allicit ignotos ille fugatque viros.
> haec movet arte latus, tunicisque fluentibus auras
>   accipit, expensos fertque superba pedes:
> illa velut coniunx Umbri rubicunda mariti

---

[47] On the dancing gait of *cinaedi*, see Edwards 1993, 71; Corbeill 2004, 120–2.

ambulat, ingentes varica fertque gradus.
sed sit, ut in multis, modus hic quoque: rusticus alter
motus, concesso mollior alter erit.

All of these things are useful, and worth the effort: ladies, you should learn how to carry
yourselves with a feminine step. Even in your gait you should not ignore the importance
of looking good: it can attract or put off potential boyfriends. One woman swings her
sides artfully, taking in air with her flowing tunic, and she haughtily takes measured
steps. Another woman plods like the sunburned wife of an Umbrian farmer, and takes
huge, straddling steps. But as in so many things, there should be a middle ground here
too: one gait is uncultured, the other more dainty [lit. "soft"] than necessary.

It is appropriate that Ovid offers the most complete extant example of teaching
women how to walk; he offers women a form of instruction akin to that which
Cicero offered his son (*Off.* 1.131), fitting for his "feminist" third book. But
nowhere in the first two books does he actually teach men how to walk (though,
memorably, he tells them where to walk to find girls – in public porticoes
[*Ars am.* 1.491–6]). Ovid may omit this type of instruction for men because they
already get plenty of it elsewhere (as we shall see in the next section of this
chapter). Yet his silence also reflects a tendency to associate the art of training and
transforming the body with women more than men; indeed the passage immediately preceding this one expresses wonder at the ability of women to cry at any
moment in any situation. As Myerowitz (1985, 135) puts it, "As an *artifex* Ovid
even affects to envy the advantages which women have over men in applying *ars*
to their own person. Women, claims his *praeceptor*, have greater scope for *ars* to
repair natural imperfections as well as the social license to use it (*Ars am.*
3.159–68)." Ovid's ideal walk for women is not necessarily a natural one, but
something learned or acquired. (This is what the *et* of *et incessu* conveys: even in
your gait – though you may not realize it – you can convey your mastery of my
love instruction.) Ovid's construction of the feminine ideal as something
composed and artful puts additional pressure on the art of walking taught to
young men. If using art to control the body has an air of femininity about it, then
any attempt by a man to manipulate his gait courts the charge of effeminacy;
recall Manilius' claim that "feigned" gaits (*ficti … gressus*) please effeminate
males (*Astron.* 5.153).[48] Yet the very notion that a man's walk "should" be one way
or another implies that it is something that can be acquired, practiced, and
nurtured. As we shall see in the next section, the paradox of gait instruction is
especially threatening to the ideology of "naturally" masculine behavior.

---

[48] Cf. Petron. *Sat.* 126, where the slave girl Chrysis assumes Encolpius is an effeminate prostitute
because of his "artfully arranged gait" (*incessu arte compositus*).

GAIT INSTRUCTION

In his biography of Claudius, Suetonius includes three letters that the emperor Augustus sent to his wife Livia about her grandson, the future emperor. The precise nature of Claudius' physical condition is unknown to us today, but it was clearly a matter of concern for the imperial family.[49] Augustus seems to believe that the boy showed some promise, despite his physical appearance; other relatives, according to Suetonius, were less forgiving. Nonetheless, even the sympathetic Augustus will not allow Claudius to sit in the imperial box at the circus, citing the public scrutiny of the imperial family as the reason (Suet. *Claud.* 4.3). In another letter, he confides in Livia that he believes Claudius might well be fit for public life, if only he could find a mentor to teach him to walk and move with dignity (Suet. *Claud.* 4.5):

rursus alteris litteris: "Tiberium adulescentem ego vero, dum tu aberis, cotidie invitabo ad cenam, ne solus cenet cum suo Sulpicio et Athenodoro. qui vellem diligentius et minus μετεώρως deligeret sibi aliquem, cuius motum et habitum et incessum imitaretur. misellus ἀτυχεῖ: nam ἐν τοῖς σπουδαίοις ubi non aberravit eius animus, satis apparet ἡ τῆς ψυχῆς αὐτοῦ εὐγένεια."

And in another letter: "Indeed while you are away I will invite young Claudius to dinner every day, so that he does not have to dine alone with his beloved Sulpicius and Athenodorus. I do wish that he would be more diligent and less airheaded about latching on to somebody whose movements and bearing and gait he could imitate. The poor little guy is just unlucky; for in serious discussions, when his mind doesn't wander, the noble excellence of his soul is clear enough."

Young Claudius is more than just a public relations problem for the imperial family – it is genuinely baffling to Augustus that this young nobleman should evoke his ancestors in name but not in body. The somewhat untranslatable εὐγένεια captures this paradox perfectly. Ideally, nobility and excellence are indistinguishable: if a man is well-born, he is excellent, and vice versa. Claudius is certainly well-born, though less obviously excellent in intellect, but his body fails to convey his heritage, and thus threatens to expose the entire system as an ideological construct. At the same time, Augustus recognizes the possibility that a noble gait can be acquired: if Claudius did not have the good fortune to be born with the physical bearing that is his birthright, then at least he could have the good sense to learn how to adopt it.[50]

---

[49] Cerebral palsy is the most common explanation; Levick 1990, 13–15 surveys the ancient evidence.

[50] As Erwin Cook points out to me, Augustus' own experience as a sickly youth may also have informed his handling of his step-grandson. Claudius' gait is also a focus of his physical condition in Seneca's *Apocolocyntosis* (5.3); when Hercules sees Claudius walk in with his "unusual gait" (*incessum insolitum*), he thinks that his thirteenth labor has arrived.

The recognition that the apparently "natural" synthesis of bodily deportment and social identity actually has a learned component raises some obvious questions. If the gait is an "essential" and "natural" trait of both individual and social identity, how can it be a learnable behavior at the same time? Is the constructed nature of deportment just an aristocratic secret that we can see here because of the private nature of this letter from Augustus to Livia? To be sure, the possibility that physical and moral character were not passed on automatically from parent to child was a special source of anxiety when it came to educating the young. Compounding the difficulty was the habit of entrusting the education of upper-class children to slaves and freedmen; as Bloomer puts it (2006, 73), "an upper-class slaveholder would no more educate his son than he would change a diaper, plow a field, or set the table." In a way such a system lets aristocratic parents hedge their bets in the age-old contest between nature and nurture: they can claim all the credit when things go right, and shift all the blame to their social inferiors when things go wrong. Indeed one could rightly argue that modern parents still play this game; but what might surprise a contemporary audience is the extension of this contest to walking itself.

In his discussion of the importance of having morally upstanding slaves watch over young children, Plutarch cites a proverb about walking (*Mor.* [*De lib. educ.*] 3f–4a):

οὐ τοίνυν οὐδὲ τοῦτο παραλιπεῖν ἄξιόν ἐστιν, ὅτι καὶ τὰ παιδία τὰ μέλλοντα τοῖς τροφίμοις ὑπηρετεῖν καὶ τούτοις σύντροφα γίγνεσθαι ζητητέον πρώτιστα μὲν σπουδαῖα τοὺς τρόπους, ἔτι μέντοι Ἑλληνικὰ καὶ περίτρανα λαλεῖν, ἵνα μὴ συναναχρωννύμενοι βαρβάροις καὶ τὸ ἦθος μοχθηροῖς ἀποφέρωνταί τι τῆς ἐκείνων φαυλότητος. καὶ οἱ παροιμιαζόμενοι δέ φασιν οὐκ ἀπὸ τρόπου λέγοντες, ὅτι "ἂν χωλῷ παροικήσῃς, ὑποσκάζειν μαθήσῃ."

Futhermore, it is also worth mentioning the following: regarding the young slaves who will serve the master's children and grow up alongside them, one must above all seek out those who have excellent habits. At the very least they should be Greek and well-spoken, or else the children, tainted by barbarians and people of useless character, might pick up some of their vulgarisms. Those who cite proverbs do not speak unreasonably when they say that "if you live with a cripple, you'll learn to limp a little."

One could hardly ask for a clearer indication of the importance that ancient popular wisdom ascribed to nurture in human development. All the more so since the proverb is, strictly speaking, not true: physical disabilities are not contagious. The saying appeals to Plutarch and his contemporaries in part because it participates in the marginalization of the "abnormal" so common in antiquity (as catalogued in Garland 1995); the larger context of the proverb suggests that a physical handicap had moral implications. But the proverb also appeals because of the moral importance of walking the right way, whether by nature or by training.

CONCLUSION

An awareness of the power of the "performative body" leaves little doubt that the ideal elite body, like elite speech, and indeed like elite power more broadly, involved a great deal of work to establish, learn, and maintain. Furthermore, hierarchies within the elite ensured that bodies were categorized along gendered lines. As Maud Gleason has documented so well, ancient masculinity was "an achieved state."[51] Categories such as male and female were largely dependent on the quality of the performance of life: you were not a man or a woman unless you walked like one. The paradox, of course, is that the ancients preserved and encouraged a robust essentialism in their representations of the gait even as they recognized its performative quality. As with all constructionist versions of reality, the Romans happily paraded their social distinctions as fully grounded in nature – the very definition of ideology.[52] To quote Gleason (1999, 67): "The cultural reproduction of social superiority (male over female, aristocrat over commoner) is a project that presents a double face to the world, representing itself as natural and inevitable to outsiders, but stressing to insiders the importance of nurture and the vulnerability of the entire project to lapses of taste and self-control."

The role that walking plays in this delicate balance between natural and artificial can be seen in a passage from the younger Seneca (*Q Nat.* 7.31.2):

levitate et politura corporum muliebres munditias antecessimus, colores meretricios matronis quidem non induendos viri sumimus, tenero et molli ingressu suspendimus gradum – non ambulamus sed incedimus – exornamus anulis digitos, in omni articulo gemma disponitur.

In shaving and smoothing our bodies we surpass feminine grooming. We men wear whorish colors that indeed respectable women must not wear. With a delicate, soft gait we lighten our step – we don't walk, we parade. We adorn our fingers with rings, and a gem is arrayed on every joint.

[51] Gleason 1995, 159; the entire book is a demonstration of this phenomenon.
[52] Thus, the study of the relation of gaits to individual and social identity speaks to larger debates about essentialist versus constructionist attitudes to the body in Roman antiquity. The principal venue for this debate has been writings on sexuality, particularly male homosexual acts and their relationship to identity markers in Greece and Rome. Halperin 2002 is a particularly useful survey.

Seneca's hyperbolic description of pervasive effeminacy betrays a contradiction at the heart of Roman attitudes to masculinity and femininity. On the one hand, femininity is portrayed as adornment, something that conceals or decorates masculinity, like garishly dyed vestments or gem-encrusted rings. On the other hand, femininity is achieved by subtraction, not addition, and the feminine lurks below the masculine exterior, as men who remove too much body hair reveal to the world. As we have seen in this chapter, the metaphors used to define effeminate gaits exhibit a similar inconsistency. On the one hand, we have seen how the effeminate gait is a "broken" version of its masculine counterpart; in this view, a virile gait is a starting point for men, and the adoption of feminine movements conceals or breaks this ideal. (Again, recall Manilius' characterization of this type of walking as feigned.) On the other hand, the effeminate gait is the "real" way a *cinaedus* moves; any virile qualities are contrived and external. We can explain this confusion away as yet more evidence for moderation as a masculine trait: the Roman male must walk a fine line between feminine extremes. But we may want to preserve the confusion, and leave the question comfortably unresolved, as Seneca (and Roman culture) seems to do: is the effeminate gait the choice, and the masculine gait the "natural" norm? Or must certain men consciously work to avoid the soft seduction of a "natural" feminine gait?

Throughout this chapter I have been surveying the various ways in which Roman authors refer to the gait in order to draw distinctions within their society, distinctions between slave and free, male and female, insiders and outsiders. But the Seneca passage draws our attention to yet another distinction, albeit unintentionally: the gap between the ancient world and our own. Our distance from the ancient world in general, and from ancient bodies in particular, is irrecoverable: we can never fully appreciate Seneca's claim because we can never have the same level of access to the gaits themselves, only their representations.[53] In this sense, the slight inscrutability of his distinction *non ambulamus sed incedimus* ("we do not walk, we parade") is rather appropriate: scholars have struggled to define the difference Seneca draws here between two verbs – *ambulare* and *incedere* – that typically refer to walking in an unadorned, unmarked sense.[54] The difficulty

---

[53] On the epistemological issues that arise in the study of a "peculiarly concrete form of knowledge" such as how to walk correctly, see Fowler 2007, 3–4.

[54] For this reason Horsfall 1971 accepts Leo's suggestion, reported in the apparatus criticus of Gercke's Teubner, that the phrase *non ambulamus sed incedimus* is an interpolation. Though I agree with Horsfall's larger point that *incedere* often refers to walking in an unmarked sense, the existence of a parallel use of *incedere* (also noted by Horsfall) to refer to a woman walking in a stately manner (Juno at *Aen.* 1.46, with further comments by Servius ad loc.) makes the Senecan passage less anomalous.

of fully recapturing the ancient perception of different types of body movements is symbolized by the difficulty of understanding the distinction
between *ambulare* and *incedere* – we are forever on the outside.

Or are we? Or, rather, is *anyone* really on the inside? As Corbeill (2004, 1–2)
has argued, our distance from Roman deportment actually *helps* our understanding in some ways, since we as outsiders are in a better position to see the
cultural forces at play in movements that seem natural and instinctual to
insiders. This sort of analysis is more difficult in the case of walking, which is
more aggressively naturalized than other forms of gesture. There is a sense,
however, in which we have much the same level of access to the interpretation
of Roman walking as Seneca does, paradoxical as it may seem. Take his
mysterious statement again: *non ambulamus sed incedimus*. We are forced to
interpret *incedere* as "parade" based on the context: the word alone is insuffi-
cient.[55] But every act of interpretation, even Seneca's estimation of the
effeminate stride, depends on contextualization. Seneca's interpretation of
his fellow Roman as he walks must appeal to the larger context: who the
walker is, what he is wearing, what Seneca wants us to think of him. Seneca's
use of *incedere* to mean "to parade" is itself a performative act, perhaps even
more so than the effeminate display he denounces. Our distance from Roman
walking, in other words, is simply a more dramatic and obvious instance of the
distance that separates anyone from anyone else's body, that separates one
human from another: we can walk in another man's shoes, but we can never
adopt his walk, no matter how convincing the emulation.

(Cf. also Cynthia parading in Coan silks at Prop. 2.1.5.) Furthermore, postulating an interpolation
here still means that the interpolator (in addition to Servius) clearly had access to a marked meaning of
incedere.

[55] Cf. Horsfall 1971, 146: "Thus, if an *incessus* can be either good or bad, we must look to the context in
each separate instance for the word's colouring, which is usually supplied explicitly."

CHAPTER 2

Seneca on the mind in motion

In a well-known letter to Lucilius about the unity of rhetorical style and personal attributes, the younger Seneca argues that mind, body, and literary style are all interconnected (*Ep.* 114.3):

non potest alius esse ingenio, alius animo color. si ille sanus est, si compositus, gravis, temperans, ingenium quoque siccum ac sobrium est: illo vitiato hoc quoque adflatur. non vides, si animus elanguit, trahi membra et pigre moveri pedes? si ille effeminatus est, in ipso incessu apparere mollitiam? si ille acer est et ferox, concitari gradum? si furit aut, quod furori simile est, irascitur, turbatum esse corporis motum nec ire sed ferri? quanto hoc magis accidere ingenio putas, quod totum animo permixtum est, ab illo fingitur, illi paret, inde legem petit?

It is not possible for someone's literary style to be colored one way, and his mind a different way.[1] If the mind is healthy, well ordered, serious, and moderate, then the style is also dry and sober. If the mind is tainted, then the style is also infected. If someone's mind lacks vigor, don't you see how his limbs drag and his feet move lazily? If his mind is effeminate, how its softness shows up in his very gait? If it is passionate and headstrong, how his steps are quick? If his mind is insane or angry (which is just like being insane), don't you see how his body's movement is agitated, how he does not move but rather is carried along? So don't you think this is even more true of his style, since it is entirely intermingled with his mind, since it is shaped by his mind, obeys it, gets its rules from it?

Seneca's aim in this letter is to convince Lucilius that a man may be judged by his state of mind, by his bodily comportment, or by the style of his speech or writing – to know one part of the man is to know the whole. (Famously, he goes on to use as his primary example Maecenas, whose writing was as loose as his tunic.) To this end, he constructs for his young understudy an argument a fortiori: the state of mind clearly affects how we walk, so it must also affect how we write and speak, since these acts are even more directly connected

---

[1] On Seneca's use of *ingenium* to mean specifically literary style or ability, see Graver 1998, 612–14. On *Ep.* 114, see Graver 1998; Möller 2004, 167–262; Habinek 2005, 205–7.

with our minds. Seneca takes for granted a cultural assumption that will be at the heart of this chapter: the walking body renders visible the movements of the mind.[2] His argument depends on the readiness of his readers to intuit from the gait the disposition of the walker's mind.

The mechanics of this art of deduction are already familiar from the previous chapter, where we encountered ample evidence for the Roman tendency to characterize people by the way they walked. Here, however, Seneca introduces a slightly different aspect of this process by focusing on states of mind in addition to gender and social identity. To be sure, we should not insist too strongly on the difference between mindset and identity, since ancient psychological theory was often inclined to see dispositions of the mind not as subjective states but as manifestations of character types.[3] In fact the close connection between individual identity and psychological state explains why, for instance, the elite male was expected to walk with a slow, steady gait: it advertised the considered and cautious mind that was his birthright.

This chapter will employ Seneca as a guide to the dynamics of the Roman association between the movement of the mind and the movement of the ambulatory body. The relationship between gait and mindset is a recurring theme in Seneca's oeuvre, despite the variety of genres in which he wrote; as we shall see, his different guises as an author and statesman gave him a unique and valuable perspective on the communicative power of walking. As a playwright, he was attuned to the eloquent possibilities of movement and gesture. As a philosopher, he was the spokesman for a specific set of beliefs about the relationship between body and mind. And as a powerful member of the imperial court who fell in and out of favor with more than one emperor, he was well aware of the importance of watching his step in the presence of the princeps.

DRAMATIC WALKING

The notion that the gait can express the mindset of the walker is, of course, not unique to Seneca. Much of Latin literature makes clear that it was perfectly normal to judge others by the way they walked. "Look at me," the servant Chrysis remarks in the *Satyricon*, "I don't know omens, and I don't usually worry about astrology, but I can infer people's characters from their faces, and once I've seen someone walking, I know what he's thinking" (Petron. *Sat.* 126: *vides me: nec auguria novi nec mathematicorum caelum curare*

[2] On the Roman use of physical space and movement as metaphors for mental activity, see Short 2008.
[3] See especially Gill 1996.

soleo, ex vultibus tamen hominum mores colligo, et cum spatiantem vidi, quid cogitet scio). Chrysis' boast reflects the popular consensus that the mind "moved" just as surely as the body, and that the movements of arms, legs, and eyes reflected unseen psychological activity.[4] Walking was therefore a physical and observable analog of mental movement. A number of authors connect variations of pace, for instance, with an unstable mind. The poet Horace in his persona as moralizing satirist condemns the inconstancy of a local celebrity: "There was nothing consistent about that man: often he would run about as if he were fleeing an enemy, and just as often he would inch along like someone carrying Juno's sacred vessels" (*Sat.* 1.3.9–11: *nil aequale homini fuit illi: saepe velut qui | currebat fugiens hostem, persaepe velut qui | Iunonis sacra ferret*). Horace goes on to list other indicators of the man's inconstancy: sometimes he walks with ten slaves, sometimes with two hundred; sometimes he lives like a king, sometimes like a pauper. His inconsistent gait, in other words, is just the most basic or obvious physical evidence of a more general mental inconstancy that pervades all aspects of his life.[5]

The Roman stage was a particularly vibrant venue for deciphering the meaning of physical movement, and this tradition is another important influence on Seneca's interest in modes of walking. The use of masks in ancient drama presumably made the language of the body even more important in distinguishing moods, since the expression of the face was fixed. The precise referents of this physical language are now mostly lost to us, not only because we are distant from the gestures themselves, but also because they were more often an aspect of the play's production rather than of the text itself.[6] Still, we have the scripts of these performances, and characters remark often enough on the gaits of their fellow actors to suggest that the manner of walking was an important aspect of dramatic characterization.

Comedy in particular shows an acute interest in the staging of gaits. As a fragment of Turpilius puts it, "Do you see the way that Phrygian is walking? He's so cocky!" (fr. 102: *viden tu Phrygis incessum? quam est confidens!*).[7] Like the eyes, the gait is a window to the soul; that his step is so confident and

---

[4] See, for example, Sen. *Tranq.* 2.11: "For the human mind is by nature agile and prone to motion" (*natura enim humanus animus agilis est et pronus ad motus*). On the connections between "*motiones* of the soul" and physical movement, see Kuttner 2003, 103–4.

[5] Cf. Catiline's erratic gait (Sall. *Cat.* 15.5), which we encountered in the previous chapter. As Fowler 2007, 11–12 demonstrates, an inconsistent manner of walking is an affront to the Roman ideal of *constantia*.

[6] On the role of non-verbal communication and actors' bodies on the ancient stage, see e.g. Taladoire 1951; Taplin 1978, 58–76; Graf 1991; Valakas 2002.

[7] Wright 1974, 158–9 collects other instances in Roman comedy where a character takes exception to the cocky pose or gait of a slave.

that *he* is so confident amount to the same thing. Furthermore, comedy's interest in gaits often manifests itself in especially self-conscious or meta-theatrical ways; comic characters frequently impersonate others, in part by adopting appropriate body language. In such cases, the body of the actor (or, properly speaking, the character) functions as a sort of second mask. In the *Asinaria*, for example, the slaves Libanus and Leonida have concocted a plan to steal 20 *minae* from an assdealer by impersonating Saurea, to whom he owes that amount. Before this passage, the assdealer has asked Libanus to describe Saurea, just as Leonida, impersonating Saurea, comes storming in (Plaut. *Asin.* 403–6):

LIBANUS: atque hercle ipsum adeo contuor, quassanti capite incedit.
  quisque obviam huic occesserit irato, vapulabit.
MERCATOR: siquidem hercle Aeacidinis minis animisque expletus incedit,
  si med iratus tetigerit, iratus vapulabit.

LIBANUS: By god I see the man himself coming this way; his head is shaking as he walks. Whoever happens to get in the way of this hothead is in for a beating.
ASSDEALER: By god even if he walks brimming with the menace and spirit of Achilles himself – if the hothead touches me, the hothead is in for a beating.

The scene depends upon a mistaken identity or, more specifically, identity deception. Leonida takes on the persona of Saurea by adopting his gait; no doubt we should imagine him walking with exaggerated importance. Saurea apparently walks like a hothead, because in comedy, such a trait signals elite status: important men often have an angry air, and are willing to demonstrate their superiority by threatening violence to others, particularly slaves. Saurea, whom Leonida impersonates, is actually a high-status slave himself, but that is part of the joke: Leonida imitates the overseer Saurea, who himself imitates the angry walk of elite slaveowners in order to assert his importance.[8] The hierarchy of power on stage is represented by the body's vulnerability to violence, and a "violent" gait suggests that a character is a producer of violence, not its recipient.[9]

Given the possibility that Senecan tragedy was recited and not performed, we might suppose that instances of gait interpretation by the characters are less necessary, and therefore less frequent.[10] Yet precisely the opposite is true:

---

[8] Cf. Slater 2000, 50: "Leonida blusters in, playing to the hilt the role of angry overseer."
[9] On the function of violence (specifically threats of torture) in Plautus, see Parker 1989. On the social dynamics that underlie such discourse, see Saller 1994, 133–53.
[10] The classic work arguing that the tragedies were recited and not performed on stage is Zwierlein 1966. More recently the tide has turned in favor of performance; see e.g. Kragelund 1999. For useful summaries of the debate, see Fitch 2000; and Schiesaro 2003, 6 n. 9.

Senecan characters regularly make note of each other's gaits, and the frequency of these moments may in fact argue all the more strongly for the recitation of these plays. How else are we supposed to picture what is going on, if the characters themselves do not tell us? Seneca often provides this sort of observation at entrances and exits in particular, as a type of stage direction or scene setting.[11] As the chorus in the *Phaedra* announces (989–90), "But what news does that messenger bring with his hurried step, wetting his mournful face on his sad cheeks?" (*sed quid citato nuntius portat gradu | rigatque maestis lugubrem vultum genis?*). The characters onstage see a new character rushing in, and the entire audience knows that this new messenger has something on his mind. A fast gait indicates a desire to move the action along, to speed up the forward progression of events with the speed of movement through space. So too with slow gaits, which might indicate concentrated thought or fearful hesitation, as Thyestes displays when he returns to Argos to accept his brother's invitation (Sen. *Thy.* 418–22):

THYESTES: ... nunc contra in metus
    revolvor: animus haeret ac retro cupit
    corpus referre, moveo nolentem gradum.
TANTALUS: pigro (quid hoc est?) genitor incessu stupet
    vultumque versat seque in incerto tenet.

THYESTES: Now I revert again to fear. My mind sticks and wants to turn my
    body back, but I move an unwilling step.
TANTALUS: What is this? My father is paralyzed by a sluggish gait, and he turns his
    face this way and that; he is stuck in uncertainty.

The face is of course particularly adept at conveying mood, but the gait too has its own vocabulary. When one character comments on another's walk, he participates in the classification of body movements that is a regular feature of everyday life. In this scene, for instance, Tantalus' strong reaction to Thyestes' entrance clearly reflects a concern about his father's mental state, but he is also clarifying for the audience that his sluggish gait is a sign of hesitation and not effeminacy, the usual meaning of a slow stride in Roman culture (as we saw in the previous chapter).[12]

---

[11] For other examples of "descriptive periphrases accompanying the entrance of a new character," see Ferri 2003, 249. He also observes (322) that this sort of help is even more vital if the works were indeed not performed. As Sutton 1986, 2–3 points out, such descriptions could never conclusively prove either the recitation or the performance theory, since ancient dramatic authors commonly incorporated these sorts of stage directions into their texts.

[12] Recall too Seneca's use of *pigre* ("lazily") to describe the gait of someone with a dull mind (*Ep.* 114.3), cited at the beginning of this chapter.

Like their dramatic predecessors, Seneca's plays showcase characters who guide the audience in their interpretation, and who act as intermediaries between the world of the stage and the audience. But I would like to suggest that, for Seneca, these intermediary characters are not merely a dramatic device; their interpretive powers make a larger philosophical point about the relationship between inner and outer selves. This system of knowledge empowers these characters, and may by extension empower the audience as well, if they are careful to learn.[13] We can see the system at work, for example, in Seneca's *Trojan Women*, where Odysseus' famed wisdom reveals itself in his acute reading of deportment, including gait. The audience has just seen Andromache hide her son in Hector's tomb, and though she attempts to *look* as if she is grieving, her walk tells Odysseus that something else is going on (*Tro.* 615–18):

> scrutare matrem: maeret, illacrimat, gemit;
> sed huc et illuc anxios gressus refert
> missasque voces aure sollicita excipit:
> magis haec timet, quam maeret.

Examine the mother. She grieves, she cries, she moans. But she bears anxious steps here and there and catches every word with an anxious ear: she fears more than she grieves.

Odysseus demonstrates his ability to ferret out secrets from the smallest physical signs. Both grieving and walking are physically observable traits, but the ability to read the latter in this case confers a kind of power that Odysseus has and average mortals lack. Notice, too, how Odysseus characterizes her steps as "anxious"; Andromache's state of mind is such that her physical movements must be described in psychological terms.[14]

As a Stoic, Seneca is particularly interested in this intersection between mental and physical characteristics. Thus the characters onstage who read the mental from the physical are appealing to Seneca in another sense: they act as Stoic instructors, clarifying Stoic psychology for the audience of students.[15] When Odysseus elides the difference between the physical and

---

[13] For other readings of Senecan characters as embodying authorial power, see Schiesaro 2003, 26–69 on the way in which Atreus asserts authorial control in the *Thyestes*, and Star 2006 on how characters in Senecan tragedy employ the Stoic method of self-command toward decidedly un-Stoic ends.

[14] Elsewhere too the perceived union of physical and mental activity results in the gait itself acquiring attributes more commonly associated with the activity of the mind. Caesar's anxiety to get moving and start the war with Pompey is reflected in his "worried gait," according to Lucan (5.508: *sollicito . . . gressu*), while Petronius' parody has the leader crossing the hostile Alps in anticipation of his invasion of Italy with "carefree steps" despite the weather and circumstances (*Sat.* 123.1.204: *securis . . . gressibus*).

[15] There is a vast literature on the influence of Seneca's Stoicism on his tragedies. See e.g. Rosenmeyer 1989; Boyle 1997, 32–3; Schiesaro 2003; Star 2006.

the psychological in his description of Andromache's stride, he also subtly conveys the Stoic notion that the mind and body must be one, since all of nature is one. Hercules, another Stoic hero, makes the philosophical point explicit (Sen. *Her. F.* 329–31):

> sed ecce saevus ac minas vultu gerens
> et qualis animo est talis incessu venit
> aliena dextra sceptra concutiens Lycus.

But look – here comes Lycus, fierce and carrying threats on his face. His walk is just like his mind. He's shaking somebody else's scepter in his right hand.

Hercules represents the view of the author Seneca in two ways – not only does he "help out" by introducing the main character of the next scene, and telling the audience what his mindset (and gait) is, he also represents the authoritative Stoic voice, for the Stoic truly knows the unity of body and mind and can reveal it to his fellow man.[16]

Even Odysseus, who himself can uncover hidden meanings in the gaits of others, betrays his state of mind by the way he walks. As he enters in the *Trojan Women*, an old man announces his approach (*Tro.* 517–18, 522–3):

SENEX: cohibe parumper ora questusque opprime:
gressus nefandos dux Cephallanum admovet.
ANDROMACHE: . . . adest Vlixes, et quidem dubio gradu
vultuque: nectit pectore astus callidos.

OLD MAN: Control your mouth for a moment and suppress your laments: the leader of the Cephalonians moves his impious steps this way.
ANDROMACHE: . . . Odysseus is here, and indeed with a hesitant step and face: he is putting together clever tricks in his chest.

By now the easy union of face and gait will be familiar, as will Andromache's extrapolation of Odysseus' mental activity from these external cues. His character permeates his entire body, and "characterizes" the parts as much as the whole: he is *nefandus*, so his gait must be as well. As we shall see in the following section, it is not enough to explain this away as a transferred epithet or poetic license. Odysseus' steps really are as abominable as he is, for Seneca's Stoicism will have it no other way.

---

[16] On Odysseus and Hercules as proto-Stoics, see Sen. *Constant.* 2.1: "our own Stoics have regarded Odysseus and Heracles as wise men, since they were unconquered by labors and despised pleasure and conquered all lands" (*hos* [sc. *Ulixem et Herculem*] *enim Stoici nostri sapientes pronuntiaverunt, invictos laboribus et contemptores voluptatis et victores omnium terrarum*). Hercules' behavior in the *Her. F.*, however, has traditionally been read as un-Stoic, though Motto and Clark 1981 defend the character from such claims. Fitch 1987, 40–4 cautions against insisting too strenuously on a Stoic reading of Hercules in the tragedy; he moreover notes (at 43) that even in his philosophical works Seneca's assessment of Hercules is not as positive as it might seem at first glance.

SENECA'S STOIC WALKS

Since Seneca's references to gait in his tragedies raise key philosophical issues, it will come as no surprise that he also explores the relationship between walking and state of mind in the rest of his oeuvre. Let us take as an example the dialogue *De tranquillitate animi* ("On the tranquility of the mind").[17] The work begins with the equestrian Serenus confessing to his friend Seneca that despite his commitment to Stoic frugality his mind sometimes wavers when he sees the luxury that surrounds him. The wealth of his fellow Romans meets his gaze wherever he turns, from the gold-embroidered clothes on their slaves to the splendor of their houses.[18] Confronted by such conspicuous consumption, Serenus goes home dejected: "And so I return home not a worse man but a sadder one, and I no longer walk past my worthless things with my head held high. A silent stinging hesitation creeps in; perhaps those other things really are better" (Sen. *Tranq.* 1.9: *recedo itaque non peior sed tristior, nec inter illa frivola mea tam altus incedo tacitusque morsus subit et dubitatio numquid illa meliora sint*). The problem, in other words, is the way in which the external world jars his mind off course. And when his mind is disturbed, his body follows: even the way he walks through his house is disrupted.[19]

The turbulence of his mind also affects Serenus' walks through the city. He is a good Stoic and tries to participate in public life.[20] But when the usual difficulties of a political life arise and his mind is buffeted, he quickly retreats: "I turn back to retirement and, as is also true of tired herds, my walk home is a bit faster" (*Tranq.* 1.11: *ad otium convertor et, quemadmodum pecoribus fatigatis quoque, velocior domum gradus est*). Once home, however, his studies make him long to run back to the forum, and get involved again.[21] Serenus' body testifies to his inability to keep his mind on an even

---

[17] On the work, see André 1989, 1764–72; Motto and Clark 1993, 133–54.

[18] "But my resolve is weakened by the magnificence of some hall used to train slave attendants; by slaves adorned in gold and dressed more carefully than participants in a public procession; by a host of gleaming servants; now by a house where even the part you walk on is expensive and the ceilings themselves gleam with riches scattered about in every nook and cranny" (Sen. *Tranq.* 1.8: *praestringit animum apparatus alicuius paedagogii, diligentius quam in tralatu vestita et auro culta mancipia et agmen servorum nitentium, iam domus etiam qua calcatur pretiosa et divitiis per omnes angulos dissipatis tecta ipsa fulgentia*).

[19] On the ways in which the *animus* "functions as a sort of synecdoche for the whole person" in Seneca's writings, see Tarrant 2006, 11–13.

[20] Literally, he "decides to go into the middle of the republic" (*Tranq.* 1.10 *placet . . . in mediam ire rem publicam*).

[21] "But when a powerful passage has elevated my mind and when noble stories of exemplary behavior have planted their sting in me, I feel the desire to rush into the forum" (Sen. *Tranq.* 1.12: *sed ubi lectio fortior erexit animum et aculeos subdiderunt exempla nobilia, prosilire libet in forum*).

keel, as he runs home to his private sanctuary and then rushes back again to reenter the public fray.

In his response, Seneca tries to reassure his friend by reminding him of the true meaning of tranquility (*Tranq.* 2.4):

ergo quaerimus quomodo animus semper aequali secundoque cursu eat propitiusque sibi sit et sua laetus aspiciat et hoc gaudium non interrumpat, sed placido statu maneat nec attollens se umquam nec deprimens: id tranquillitas erit.

Therefore we are trying to discover how the mind may always move on a steady and favorable course; how it may be well-disposed toward itself and look on its own state with gladness and not interrupt this joy; how it may stay in a peaceful state, never lifting itself up or sinking: this will be tranquility.

The tranquil mind moves calmly; inability to control the mind not only makes tranquility impossible but also results in perpetual motion of the body. As evidence for the latter Seneca points to those leisure-rich elites who cannot be satisfied with one place, but are always seeking some new adventure, traveling around Italy but unable to escape themselves.[22] Similarly, on a more quotidian level, he ridicules at some length those who lack tranquility in their daily lives, running around for no good reason (*Tranq.* 12.2–4):

circumcidenda concursatio, qualis est magnae parti hominum domos et theatra et fora pererrantium: alienis se negotiis offerunt, semper aliquid agentibus similes. horum si aliquem exeuntem e domo interrogaveris "quo tu? quid cogitas?" respondebit tibi "non mehercules scio; sed aliquos videbo, aliquid agam." sine proposito vagantur quaerentes negotia nec quae destinaverunt agunt sed in quae incucurrerunt; inconsultus illis vanusque cursus est, qualis formicis per arbusta repentibus, quae in summum cacumen et inde in imum inanes aguntur: his plerique similem vitam agunt, quorum non inmerito quis inquietam inertiam dixerit. quorundam quasi ad incendium currentium misereberis: usque eo inpellunt obvios et se aliosque praecipitant, cum interim cucurrerunt aut salutaturi aliquem non resalutaturum aut funus ignoti hominis prosecuturi aut ad iudicium saepe litigantis aut ad sponsalia saepe nubentis et lecticam adsectati quibusdam locis etiam tulerunt; dein domum cum supervacua redeuntes lassitudine iurant nescire se ipsos quare exierint, ubi fuerint, postero die erraturi per eadem illa vestigia.

We must cut back on all this running around done by the vast majority of people, wandering lost through houses and theaters and fora. They offer themselves up for other people's business, always giving the impression that they're doing something. If you ask one of these people as he leaves his house, "Where are you heading? What's your plan?" he will answer, "By god, I don't know, but I'm sure I'll see some

---

[22] A common topos in Seneca; see e.g. Garbarino 1996, 268–74; Montiglio 2006, 564.

people and do something or other." They wander around without purpose looking for something to keep them busy. Nothing they do is by design; they just do whatever they stumble upon. Their course is unplanned and meaningless, like ants crawling around a tree, which make their way to the top and then mindlessly go back to the bottom. Most people lead a similar life to these ants – you could with good reason call it busy inactivity. You will surely take pity on some of these people running as if to a fire; they are always crashing into anyone in their way, knocking themselves and everyone else to the ground, when in the meantime they have run around trying to greet someone who will not greet them back, or trying to escort the funeral procession of someone they don't even know; or they have run to the courtcase of someone who is always litigating or to the engagement party of someone who is always getting married; or they have escorted a litter – indeed on some occasions they have even carried one. Then returning home with an empty weariness they swear that they don't know why they went or where they were – though the next day they will retrace those very same footprints.

The paradox of "busy inactivity" is perfectly captured by their walking; though they "roam those very same footprints" every day (like an ancient performance of *Groundhog Day*), they are truly lost. It is not enough, Seneca says, to know where you are going in some trivial, physical sense; if your mind is not following a clear path, then it is all worthless. Get your mind straight, and your body will follow. So these men exhibit all the signs of the incorrect gait that we saw in the first chapter: they run, they wander back and forth, they crash into other people in their haste to go nowhere. They even stoop to escorting or even carrying the litter of some V.I.P. – as sure a sign of servitude as you could ask for in antiquity. Their lives are wasted in a tragicomic performance of meaningless and frenetic activity.

These are the people Serenus risks being associated with if he does not get his mind under control. Seneca urges his friend to stay on the true path: "Have faith in yourself and trust that you are moving on the right path; don't be diverted by the crossing footsteps of many people running in every direction, some of them even wandering around the same path" (*Tranq.* 2.2: *ut fidem tibi habeas et recta ire te via credas, nihil avocatus transversis multorum vestigiis passim discurrentium, quorundam circa ipsam errantium viam*). Here we begin to see another reason for Seneca's interest in walking: it is not only a reflection of the mind's movement but also a metaphor for the journey to virtue that every Stoic travels.[23] Serenus' frantic racing to and fro is

---

[23] On the Stoic path to virtue see, for instance, Sen. *Ep.* 8.3: "The right way, which I came to know late and weary from wandering – I show it to others" (*rectum iter, quod sero cognovi et lassus errando, aliis monstro*). On Seneca's use of the journey as a metaphor for Stoic practice, see Chambert 2005, 157–65 (and 149–57 as a metaphor for life in general). The connection between travel and philosophy and its relation to Roman walking will be explored further in Chapter 5 below.

a sure sign that his mind is not tranquil, but is also perilously close to the behavior of those clueless unphilosophical types who get in our way (literally and metaphorically) as we travel the Stoic path.[24] The path may be a metaphor, but walking offers Stoic students a rare opportunity to see the metaphor in action.[25] And at times it even seems unclear whether Seneca is being literal or metaphorical, such as in his observation that the ideal Stoic wise man (*sapiens*) does not need to worry about how he walks (*Tranq.* 11.1):

huic [*sc.* sapienti] non timide nec pedetemptim ambulandum est; tanta enim fiducia sui est ut obuiam fortunae ire non dubitet nec umquam loco illi cessurus sit.

The sage does not need to walk timidly or one step at a time; for his confidence in himself is so great that he does not hesitate to go against Fortune herself nor will he ever give way to her.

Everything the *sapiens* does as he moves through life is virtuous by definition; he can *only* walk the right way.[26] But where does that leave Stoic students who are still traveling the road to virtue, modeling their actions on the normative ideal of the wise man?[27] They may well wonder whether Seneca is being literal or metaphorical here. Is he commending the sage's actual gait, or is he more concerned with his confident approach to life in general? The answer is both – and that is the whole point.

The literal and metaphorical use of walking raises another philosophical question: if Serenus corrects his mind, then his body will surely right itself, but is the opposite also true? Can he move closer to virtue by walking the right way? Clearly not without *any* attempt to repair his mind; as the last word (and the title) of the dialogue emphasizes, it is Serenus' mind that is slipping, not his body: none of Seneca's advice can be of use, he tells his friend, "unless intense and constant vigilance surrounds the erring mind" (*Tranq.* 17.12: *nisi intenta et adsidua cura*

---

[24] On the image of bustling urban crowds distracting Stoics from the true path, see also Sen. *Vit. beat.* 1.

[25] A number of scholars have demonstrated the ways in which Seneca frequently collapses the distinction between literal and metaphorical journeys. Henderson 2006 explores the metaphorical implications of Seneca's journey through the tunnel between Naples and Puteoli (throat, *nekuia*, Plato's cave) in *Ep.* 57. Montiglio 2006 nuances the traditional view that Seneca (in keeping with orthodox Stoicism) disapproves of travel.

[26] Cf. *Ep.* 66.5, where Seneca highlights a modest gait (*modestus incessus*) as one of the Stoic goods. Later in the same letter (66.36), he suggests that walking per se is, in the Stoic framework, an absolute indifferent, but that "prudent walking" (*prudenter ambulare*) is a good insofar as it is a characteristic act of a virtuous person: see Inwood 2007 ad loc.

[27] On Panaetius' reorientation of Stoic ethics to focus more on so-called progressors to virtue than on the ideal sage, see Long 1974, 213–16. On the Stoic notion of moral progress (προκοπή), see Roskam 2005, 15–136. On Seneca's divergence from orthodox Stoic views on moral improvement, see Cooper 2006.

circumit animum labentem).[28] An insistence on walking a certain way without any emphasis on correcting the mind runs the risk of turning ethical instruction into a pedantic lesson on good manners, which Seneca may want to avoid.[29] Elsewhere he introduces the idea of teaching someone the correct way to walk as patently ridiculous (*Ep.* 15.7, translation lightly adapted from Gummere 1918):

nec tu intentionem vocis contempseris, quam veto te per gradus et certos modos extollere, deinde deprimere. quid si velis deinde quemadmodum ambules discere? admitte istos quos nova artificia docuit fames: erit qui gradus tuos temperet et buccas edentis observet.

You need not scorn vocal exercises; but I forbid you to practice raising and lowering your voice by scales and specific intonations. What if you should next propose to take lessons in walking! If you consult the sort of person whom starvation has taught new tricks, you will soon have someone to regulate your steps and watch every mouthful as you eat.

As Gleason (1995, 111–12) observes in her analysis of this passage, Seneca's objection is social, not philosophical; bringing in so-called experts to critique the use of their bodies threatens to expose the whole system of elite deportment as a construct and even to grant non-elites access to that system. Yet, as we have seen in his essay on tranquility, Seneca *does* advocate walking a certain way, even if he finds the idea of a user's manual on the subject a bit distasteful.[30] For ordinary Stoics, whose mind and body do not yet enjoy the perfect unison exhibited by the sage, control of the body can encourage control of the mind. As Long (1974, 215) puts it in his introduction to Stoic ethics, "The truly good man acts on the basis of knowledge, which is not reducible to a set of specifiable moral rules. But moral rules can set a man on the right road." For Seneca, walking the right way is one of these moral rules; Seneca thus

---

[28] On the mind as the source of proper walking, see also *Ep.* 114.22: "Let [the mind] be your concern: from it comes our perception, our words, from it comes our deportment, our face, our walk. When it is healthy and strong our speech is also robust, strong, manly; if it sinks down, everything else follows its fall" (*ideo ille* [sc. *animus*] *curetur: ab illo sensus, ab illo verba exeunt, ab illo nobis est habitus, vultus, incessus. illo sano ac valente oratio quoque robusta, fortis, virilis est: si ille procubuit, et cetera ruinam sequuntur*).

[29] For a thoughtful essay on the place of manners and appearance in Seneca's ethics, see Sherman 2005. Cf. Roller 2001, 70–97 on Seneca's efforts to emphasize internal qualities in the context of traditional Roman ethics, which allowed a greater role for the moral value of external characteristics.

[30] Raising the specter of a gait instructor may have been a common way to ridicule practical instruction more generally, as Seneca's citation of Aristo suggests (*Ep.* 94.5 and 94.8; see above, Ch. 1). Though Seneca writes the letter to defend the utility of practical moral instruction, he never specifically responds to Aristo's condemnation of walking lessons, perhaps for the same social reasons Gleason cites. There is a vast bibliography on *Ep.* 94 and 95 and their relation to the Stoic stance on practical advice and ethical instruction; see, most recently, Schafer 2009.

encourages his friend to stop running around the city doing nothing, and even implies that a more careful pace will bring some order and clarity to his thoughts.[31] A tranquil gait will restore tranquility to his mind, and walking like the *sapiens* will help Serenus advance on the road to virtue.[32]

POLITICAL WALKING

Seneca's interest in virtuous walking was a response to political as well as philosophical dilemmas. As is well known, he was exiled by the emperor Claudius, recalled to Rome by Agrippina, and, after an initial stage in which he effectively served as co-regent, eventually ordered to commit suicide by his former pupil Nero.[33] In addition to his own complex relationship with the Roman imperial family, he also wrote in the context of a relatively young monarchy still working out the role of the former aristocracy. As many scholars have argued, the surfeit of men excluded from power fueled Stoicism's rise; although the philosophy valorized public service, it also promoted the idea that the entire cosmos was a second republic that its students could serve if their native land was hostile to great men.[34]

Indeed, despite his complicated political trajectory, Seneca did not advocate a complete withdrawal from imperial Rome. The tranquil mind knows that great men are not always welcome or appreciated by their country. But a hostile reception should not mean an immediate retreat: the aspiring sage can still teach others of the glories of the Stoic life by his example, or by giving advice to youngsters, even if he is not a leading politician. And he used the example of Socrates during the reign of the Thirty Tyrants to show the continued role that those excluded from power could play. Despite the severe limitations on his political voice, in Seneca's view, he was able to remain politically active: "Socrates was still at the center of it all; . . . he went around as a great example for those willing to emulate him when he walked as a free man in the midst of the thirty masters"

---

[31] Near the end of the work (*Tranq.* 17.8) Seneca recommends taking walks outdoors to refresh and strengthen the mind, further confirmation that the actions of the body (and walking in particular) can have a positive effect on the mind.

[32] Cf. Long 1974, 202: "Imitation of the sage or actual good men cannot ensure virtue, but it can certainly set a man on the right road to secure it."

[33] On Seneca's political career, see Griffin 1976, 29–171. On his death(s), see Ker 2009.

[34] See e.g. Shaw 1985, who compares the popularity of Stoicism in imperial Rome to the birth of the philosophy under similar social circumstances in Hellenistic Greece; and Roller 2001, 97–124, who focuses in particular on the ways in which Seneca promoted Stoic ethics as a way for aristocrats to reclaim some of the power they had lost under the Julio-Claudians. On the Stoic "second republic," see Sen. *Ot.* 4 (with Williams 2003).

(Sen. *Tranq.* 5.2: *Socrates tamen in medio erat ... et imitari volentibus magnum circumferebat exemplar, cum inter triginta dominos liber incederet*). Those difficult days put Socrates in a position not so different than his own, Seneca implies. In such times, the example the good man sets as he walks through the city is itself a form of political engagement: even if the odium of the emperor prevents the Stoic from participating in politics he can still set a good example as a private citizen by his temperance at banquets and his loyalty to his friends.[35] Indeed, "the work of a good citizen is never useless: he benefits others just by being heard and seen, by his face, his nod, his quiet resistance, and by his very manner of walking" (*Tranq.* 4.6: *numquam inutilis est opera civis boni: auditus visusque, vultu nutu obstinatione tacita incessuque ipso prodest*). Even if he cannot talk freely, the good man's walk will be of public (and political) service: his body itself bespeaks his opposition to tyranny.

In addition to Socrates, Seneca could have cited Roman precedents for the political implications of walking under the shadow of tyranny. A few generations earlier, during the turbulent transition to autocracy at the end of the republic, Cicero also saw the walk as a political statement. He however feared that his opposition to the regime would be *too* obvious in his gait, and impossible to conceal. Cicero had long shown himself to be a firm believer in the ways that comportment could reveal the truth more clearly than words or deeds. Indeed, as Corbeill has shown, his vocal opposition to popular politicians included objecting to the way that they walked.[36] Now, with the collapse of the republic, Cicero worries that his gait will be the object of scrutiny. In a letter to his friend Atticus, Cicero confesses his apprehension about returning to Rome in the uncertain days after Caesar's assassination; Antony is jostling for control of the state, and his supporters are amassing: it is becoming dangerous even to *seem* opposed to his authority (*Att.* 15.5.3):

Varro autem noster ad me epistulam misit sibi a nescio quo missam (nomen enim delerat); in qua scriptum erat veteranos eos qui reiciantur (nam partem esse dimissam) improbissime loqui, ut magno periculo Romae sint futuri qui ab eorum partibus dissentire videantur. quis porro noster itus, reditus, vultus, incessus inter istos? quod si, ut scribis, L. Antonius in D. Brutum, reliqui in nostros, ego

---

[35] "Let's say it is dangerous for him even to step into the forum: in homes, at shows, at banquets let him play the role of a good comrade, a faithful friend, a moderate banqueter" (Sen. *Tranq.* 4.3: *periculosum etiam ingressu forum est: in domibus, in spectaculis, in conviviis bonum contubernalem, fidelem amicum, temperantem convivam agat*).

[36] See Corbeill 2004, 118–20; the entire chapter (107–39) offers abundant evidence that the gait was a marker of political identity in the late republic. In particular, he argues (133–7) that popular politicians consciously adopted flamboyant gestures and gait as a way of distinguishing themselves from the *optimates*, making clear to the people that they were not like other politicians.

quid faciam aut quo me pacto geram? mihi vero deliberatum est, ut nunc quidem est, abesse ex ea urbe.

Our dear Varro has sent me a letter that somebody or other had sent him (he erased the name), in which it is written that those veterans who are being rebuffed (for some of them have been discharged) are saying rather brazenly that Rome will be a dangerous place for anyone who even seems to dissent from their faction. What, then, about my comings and goings among these people, the way I look and walk? And if, as you write, Lucius Antonius plans to speak out against Decimus Brutus, and others against our friends, what am I supposed to do, how am I supposed to act? Indeed it's my considered plan, at least as things are now, to stay away from Rome.

It is not just a slip of the tongue that Cicero fears, but a misstep: he will have to continually come and go among men who he knows will be watching his every move, and his feelings would inevitably be expressed not only on his face, but in his step. In ancient Rome the way a statesman looked when he walked could be a matter of life and death, as Cicero was himself to discover in the following year.

In some ways, then, the turn to autocracy intensified the examination of gaits. Cicero must be careful not to betray his disagreement in the movements of his body. But the gaze shifted in the opposite direction as well. Maintaining a dignified physical comportment at all times was essential to any member of the Roman aristocracy, but with the rise of a principate, there was special attention paid to the public appearances of the first family. The restriction on frank speech and public debate meant that this physical language was observed ever more intently. Tacitus, for example, frequently mentions the inscrutability of Tiberius' facial expressions.[37] At the death of Germanicus, Tiberius and Livia do not mourn; Tacitus argues that if they had, the Roman people, intently watching their every expression, would have seen through their insincerity.[38] Vitellius faced the same problem; despite his ascent to the top spot, one could see even in his walk that he was not ready for prime time (Tac. *Hist.* 3.56):

sed praecipuum ipse Vitellius ostentum erat, ignarus militiae, improvidus consilii, quis ordo agminis, quae cura explorandi, quantus urgendo trahendove bello modus, alios rogitans et ad omnis nuntios vultu quoque et incessu trepidus, dein temulentus.

---

[37] For the relevant passages, see Evans 1935, 54–5. On the dangers of misreading Tiberius' demeanour, see O'Gorman 2000, 78–89. On the relationship between facial expression and dissimulation (including in Tacitus), see Corbeill 2004, 144–65.

[38] "(They did not mourn), either because they deemed it unworthy of their station to lament in public, or because they would be understood to be faking it, since the eyes of the people were examining their faces" (Tac. *Ann.* 3.3: *inferius maiestate sua rati, si palam lamentarentur, an ne omnium oculis vultum eorum scrutantibus falsi intellegerentur*).

But the most obvious bad omen was Vitellius himself: ignorant of military matters and completely lacking good judgment, he was always asking other people what the order of the troops was, what the use of spy missions was, how much he should press on or hold back his troops in battle; and with every new report he would reveal his anxiety in his expression and in his step, and then he would get drunk.

Presumably, a proper leader would have received bad news more gracefully, or at least hidden his concern. Vitellius' successor Vespasian restores normalcy, and even his right-hand man Licinius Mucianus walks with the confidence of an emperor (Tac. *Hist.* 4.11):

sed civitas rimandis offensis sagax verterat se transtuleratque: ille unus ambiri, coli. nec deerat ipse, stipatus armatis domos hortosque permutans, apparatu incessu excubiis vim principis amplecti, nomen remittere.

But the Roman people, who are skilled at finding faults, had changed their minds and shifted [to Mucianus]; he was the only one whom they solicited and courted. Nor did he fail to rise to the occasion: he was thronged with armed guards, he moved from house to house and villa to villa; with his getup, his gait, and his security detail, he embraced the power of an emperor, but conceded the title.

Mucianus had assumed the power of the *princeps*, if not the name, and one could tell that not only from his actions, but from his very attitude, and the very way he walked. But of course the fact that an unelected crony of the emperor can acquire the sort of armed guard that was the privilege of heads of state in earlier times reveals how far things have changed since the republic – and demonstrating this change is of course Tacitus' goal.[39]

As in Cicero's time, the gait still matters – indeed we might see Seneca's words as a response of sorts to Cicero's question about how to behave during the reign of the triumvirs: "What, then, about my comings and goings among these people, the way I look and walk?" Seneca, with more experience under an autocrat, answers Cicero. If he is unable to voice his opposition publicly, his walk can still demonstrate his commitment to virtue in bad times. Yet at the same time both Cicero and Seneca reveal the extent to which the *res publica* has changed. More often than not the good man cannot do much more than benefit others by his noble stride, so far has power shifted to one man and one family. Both writers take it for granted that the way they walk will reveal their state of mind and even their political leanings. Cicero opts to stay at home, but his subsequent political miscalculations – and his public speeches in particular – would bring about the assassination that he feared. Seneca, on the other hand, lived in a time when a speech along the lines of

---

[39] On Mucianus' power in the early years of Vespasian's reign, see Rogers 1980, 86–9.

Cicero's *Philippics* was unthinkable; no wonder he saw the urban walk as one of the few remaining forms of political protest. While Stoics may have comforted themselves by viewing an urban stroll as a political act, other Roman aristocrats may have pined for the days when good men could benefit others with more than just the way that they walked.

CHAPTER 3

Urban walkers on display

The poet Martial often takes aim at his fellow citizens as they go about their lives in the city, hunting for dinner invitations, relaxing in the baths, or, as here, strolling through streets and colonnades (*Ep.* 2.57):

> hic quem videtis gressibus vagis lentum,
> amethystinatus media qui secat Saepta,
> quem non lacernis Publius meus vincit,
> non ipse Cordus alpha paenulatorum,
> quem grex togatus sequitur et capillatus
> recensque sella linteisque lorisque:
> oppigneravit modo modo ad Cladi mensam
> vix octo nummis anulum, unde cenaret.

That man you see – the one walking slowly here and there; the one who makes his way through the Saepta Iulia dressed in amethyst; the one who in mantle-wearing surpasses my dear Publius and even Cordus himself, numero uno of the cloak-wearers; the one who is followed by a flock of toga-wearing clients and long-haired slaves and a litter with brand new linen curtains and leather straps – just a second ago at Cladius' counter he pawned his ring for barely eight cents, so that he could eat dinner.

Readers of Martial will no doubt recognize as characteristic of his poetry the dissonance between appearance and reality and the last-second defla-tion of a pompous target. But Martial's critique reveals more than just a Roman obsession with hypocrisy or moral consistency. In a status-based society such as Rome, where not only social privilege but even legal protection varied depending on social or economic status, the perform-ance of identity mattered. The poem's preoccupation with clothing, for instance, reflects the larger truth that clothes were not merely a fashion statement in Rome, but also an identity statement.[1] The pretender's fancy

---

[1] A passage in Ulpian (*Dig.* 47.10.15.15) claims that the dress of an upper-class woman mitigated the charge against her sexual assailant – a reduced charge if she were dressed as a slave, and a much lesser offense if dressed as a prostitute; see Frier and McGinn 2004, 468–9.

clothes may mark him as a luxuriant fop, but they also convey a level of status beyond that of his fellow citizens; so too are his clients marked by their devotion to the toga, no doubt because many of them, as freedmen or immigrants, are the first in their generation to earn that privilege. The unnamed pretender, by contrast, no longer needs to advertise his citizenship by donning the toga; he has progressed to a different level of sartorial aspiration.

Clothes make the man, but so does his manner of walking. How Martial's target walks (slowly and aimlessly), where (in a popular portico), with whom (with a retinue of dependants, free and slave) – all mark this unnamed stroller as a man of importance.[2] Even his litter follows behind him.[3] Martial's critique, in essence, is that this man is not as high-status as his ambulatory display would suggest; the poem depends upon the reader's awareness that walking is part of the performance of everyday life. Yet if the poem assumes an audience trained in the art of reading ambulatory displays, so too does the unnamed pretender; his performance of his status does not, strictly speaking, require him to walk around, but by doing so he ensures more spectators for his display.[4]

The focus of this chapter is the literary representation of these sorts of ambulatory performances, and the display inherent in even the most quotidian forms of movement through the city. The recovery of such a spectacle in its full array is of course difficult; though we have occasional hints of what a walk through the city would have been like for the average citizen, literary references to urban walking come primarily from literature written by and for an elite audience.[5] Discussions of movement through the city typically focus less on the everyday forms of movement that would have been the norm and more on formal or exceptional processions, such

---

[2] Like his fancy clothes, his slow gait also runs the risk of courting a charge of effeminacy, which may lie below the surface here; on the feminine associations of walking slowly, see Chapter 1.

[3] Here, in the controlled space of the Saepta Iulia, the man strolls; when he leaves to return home on the busy city streets, he is no doubt conveyed in his litter. Martial also refers to people strolling in the Saepta Iulia at 2.14.5 and 9.59.

[4] So Williams 2004, 193. Note, too, that the sauntering phony's performance has the potential to compete with more traditional performative modes, such as poetry itself; Martial, after all, is also attempting to move up in society by impressing others, though by writing rather than by walking. For a similar move (whereby Martial calls attention to the crass economic motives of another man's stroll, as negative foil for his own proper attitude toward his patrons), see e.g. 2.11, 2.14, and 3.20.

[5] See e.g. Juv. *Sat.* 3.236–48; Mart. *Ep.* 5.22.5–8. The disruption caused by lictors and slaves who cleared the way for elites is a common complaint; see e.g. Sen. *Ep.* 94.60; Juv. *Sat.* 1.37–9. On population density and traffic congestion in Rome, see Tilburg 2007, 119–25. A number of archaeologists and architectural historians have begun to shed light on the pedestrian experience in ancient Rome and Campania; see e.g. Laurence 1994, 88–103; Favro 1996, 24–41 and 252–80; Kellum 1999; Ellis 2004; Hartnett 2007.

as the elite Roman funeral and the Roman triumph.[6] Although neither will
be the focus of this chapter, their prominence in the Roman aristocratic
imagination rendered them an ideal standard against which other more
routine processions were judged. In both cases, the destination (in the case
of the funeral, the rostra in the Roman forum, and in the case of the triumph,
the temple of Jupiter Optimus Maximus on the Capitoline) is only part of the
story; the parade itself conveys meaning, particularly as a display of status and
power. Indeed, the didactic function of such rituals has been a point of
emphasis since at least the second century BCE, when Polybius wrote his
famous description of an aristocratic funeral (*Hist.* 6.53.9–10). Virgil's parade
of heroes in *Aeneid* 6, clearly an evocation of an aristocratic funeral, highlights
the role of movement, casting the Roman funeral procession and its parade of
deceased ancestors as a living, moving statue gallery that generated a narrative
for the stationary viewer.[7] Similarly, the Roman triumphal parade included
the display of placards, paintings, and perhaps even actors, all of which
combined to educate the Roman viewers about the extending reach of their
empire.[8] In short, the triumphal parade was a mobile narrative of contemporary history, while the funeral procession was a mobile narrative of the past.

Given the topic of this book, we should of course note that in neither the
funeral procession nor the triumphal parade did the honorands actually walk.[9]
Yet these rituals nonetheless made use of the symbolic power of walking. For
one thing, it is significant that the honored person in each instance does *not*
walk. In the funeral procession, the guest of honor, as it were, no longer has
the ability to walk in his own funeral. The triumphant general, on the other
hand, still has that option, and instead rides in a chariot that comes to be part
of what Beard calls the "emblematic shorthand" of the ceremony itself.[10] The
significance of that chariot is highlighted by its absence from parallel rituals;
one of the ways in which the lesser triumph, the *ovatio*, was distinguished

---

[6] On the elite Roman funeral, see Nicolet 1980, 346–52; Hopkins 1983, 201–2; Flower 1996, 91–158;
Bodel 1999; Sumi 2005, 41–6. On the triumph, see Versnel 1970; Beard 2007. On the similarity of
Roman triumphal and funeral processions, see Versnel 1970, 115–29; Bodel 1999, 261.

[7] On the similarity between the parade of heroes and the funeral procession, see Skard 1965, 60–5;
Bettini 1991, 145–7. On the parade's evocation of a statue gallery, see Leach 1999, 126.

[8] The triumph thus reenacted for the urban audience the acquisition of new territory by parading it
(both in metaphorical terms, in the guise of representations, but also in metonymic terms, in the form
of slaves and spoils) in the capital of the empire. On this aspect of the triumph, see Beard 2007,
107–86; Östenberg 2009.

[9] Furthermore, in Polybius' account (6.53.8), the actors wearing ancestor masks ride in chariots, though
Diodorus Siculus (31.25.2) mentions their attempt to evoke the gait and bearing of the men they
brought to life (see Corbeill 2004, 117, cited in Chapter 1).

[10] On the importance of the chariot in triumphal imagery (literary and visual), see Beard 2007, 222–4
("emblematic shorthand" at 220).

from its big brother, the full-fledged triumph, was that in the *ovatio* the honored general either rode a single horse or proceeded on foot.[11]

More importantly, in all of these rituals, the size and character of the retinue walking with the man of honor was part of the display.[12] These two types of procession therefore acquired meaning by their contrast to more quotidian forms of procession that advertised the status of the Roman aristocrat, such as the escort that accompanied Roman nobles as they made their way through the city. Put another way, the daily movements of noblemen through the city were rehearsals for grander occasions, such as their final procession through the city on the day of their funeral. On that day, the men who walked in their cortège conveyed the power of the deceased; so too in the more "everyday" forms of procession. The manner in which a nobleman moved through the city was a point of focus in both the republic and the empire; in what follows, we shall see how Romans were trained in the discipline of examining urban walkers not just by their gaits but by the circumstances of their stroll: where they walked, when, why, and with whom.

DEDUCTIO IN FORUM

Juvenal's first satire uses movement through the city to generate its very narrative. The narrator stands still, on a street corner, and records the Roman scene that files past him: "Couldn't you just about fill an empty notebook while you stand on a street corner " (*Sat.* 1.63–4: *nonne libet medio ceras inplere capaces | quadrivio*). We stand on the corner with Juvenal, observing through his eyes the spectacle of the Roman street, shoved aside by the attendants of obese lawyers, men who rat on their friends, shameless legacy-hunters, and guardians who corrupt their wards (1.30–48). Not all of these characters walk, of course; as the undeserving *nouveaux riches* sway past on their litters and sedans, the slaves beneath them walk, not the rich.[13] Yet Juvenal presumes that anyone wanting to comment on the vagaries of

---

[11] Aulus Gellius (*NA* 5.6.27) preserves the dispute: while some of his sources claim that generals celebrating an *ovatio* entered the city riding on a single horse, one source insists that they entered on foot. For other evidence that the general celebrating an *ovatio* entered the city on foot, see Richardson 1975, 55 n. 40. On the *ovatio*, see Richardson 1975, 54–6; Beard 2007, 62–3 and 291.

[12] As Beard 2007, 240–1 notes, people paid attention to who walked with the triumphant general, and where.

[13] Cf. Juv. 7.139–43, where the author complains that men hiring lawyers nowadays look not to their oratorical ability but to their wealth, "whether you have eight slaves and ten companions, whether there is a sedan behind you and toga-wearers in front of your feet" (*an tibi servi | octo, decem comites, an post te sella, togati | ante pedes*).

Roman life should walk down to the corner (even if it is only conceptually) to watch the parade of public life as it passes by. The city is as it walks. And here the spectacle is not the monuments observed by walking viewers, but the walkers and litter-riders themselves.[14]

If ordinary, unmarked movement through the city is a means to an end, then a procession draws attention to itself as both means and end: the movement itself, as much as the destination, is the point of the ritual. And in Rome, even everyday walks could take on a processional quality. By his movement through town, the walker could advertise his or her status or change in status for the urban audience. One such occasion is the quasi-ritual known in the modern sources as the *deductio in forum*; during the republic, the Roman aristocrat who had spent the morning in his *domus* greeting guests (the so-called *salutatio*) would descend on foot to the forum for the afternoon's business, accompanied by various friends, clients, and slaves.[15] The best description from the point of view of the escorted aristocrat comes from Cicero (*Att.* 1.18.1):

nam illae ambitiosae nostrae fucosaeque amicitiae sunt in quodam splendore forensi, fructum domesticum non habent. itaque, cum bene completa domus est tempore matutino, cum ad forum stipati gregibus amicorum descendimus, reperire ex magna turba neminem possumus, quocum aut iocari libere aut suspirare familiariter possimus.

Those phony political friendships of mine have a certain shine in the forum, but they bring me no personal pleasure. Yes, my house is quite crowded in the morning, and I go down to the forum accompanied by herds of friends, but out of that entire crowd I can find no one with whom I can joke freely or sigh intimately.

Cicero makes clear that he takes this walk for political reasons, and not for the sake of a leisurely stroll.[16] Even these men whom he must call friends because they are his social equals (or close enough) walk beside him out of a sense of obligation, not enjoyment. Why? So they can all shine in the reflected light of the forum's "public splendor" (*splendore forensi*). This walk is explicitly for public consumption, and its destination is the forum, the place with the biggest and most important audience for men like Cicero. In fact, despite the occasional use of the phrase *deductio ad forum* in the

---

[14] On the theme of movement in Juvenal 1, see Larmour 2007, 178–91. On movement through Rome as a figure for desire in Horace, Ovid, and Juvenal, see Miller 2007.

[15] On the escort of prominent men in the Roman republic, see Nicolet 1980, 356–61; Morstein-Marx 1998, 270–2; Bell 2004, 214–20. On the *deductio in forum*, see Deniaux 1987, 283–4. On the *salutatio*, see Saller 1989, 57–8.

[16] In a similar vein, Horace cites his ability to walk through the city by himself as one of the benefits of his lack of political ambition; see *Sat.* 1.6.107–15.

modern literature most of the ancient sources use the formula *deduci in forum*.[17] It is no small difference: the important aspect of this journey, as the preposition suggests, is the entrance *into* the forum, where the public man displays, in the heart of the city, his status in motion.

So important was this ambulatory display of status that the entrance of a young man into the forum on the day he assumed his toga of manhood was a climax of his initiation into public life.[18] It was a father's duty to orchestrate this performance, soliciting as many friends as possible to be seen by his son's side as he strode into the forum for the first time. If a boy could attract this much support on his first day, how powerful could he become if his natural abilities should match his inherited connections? It was a time for calling in favors, even from those a few rungs higher on the social ladder. Cicero memorably commiserates with his audience about such obligations in the course of justifying the large escort that came out to greet Murena (*Mur.* 69):

num aut criminosum sit aut mirandum, qua in civitate rogati infimorum hominum filios prope de nocte ex ultima saepe urbe deductum venire soleamus, in ea non esse gravatos homines prodire hora tertia in campum Martium, praesertim talis viri nomine rogatos?

In a society where we are in the habit of often going, when asked, to escort the sons of men of lower rank than us from the farthest point in the city while it is still almost dark, surely it would seem neither criminal nor surprising that people would not feel overburdened to turn out to the Campus Martius at the third hour, especially when invited in the name of such a man?

Cicero's willingness to go all the way out to the edge of town rather than meeting the escort halfway suggests that, along with the forum, the family's *domus* was a focal point of this ritual; the procession unites the two most important spaces in a Roman aristocrat's life. So powerful was this ceremony that the act served as a shorthand for entry into public life: entering or, literally, stepping into the republic: *ingredi in rem publicam*.[19] Nor did the symbolic movement through town end on that first day. As we saw above in

---

[17] The modern use may have been influenced by Cicero's use of *ad forum* at *Mur.* 70, a sort of *locus classicus* for the ritual. In addition to the passages collected in this section, see also Cic. *Mur.* 44, *Phil.* 2.112, *Fam.* 15.4.16 (metaphorical); Varro, *Sat. Men.* fr. 259 (*in forum conducere*); Livy 38.50.10; Aug. *RG* 3; Val. Max. 3.7.1e; Sen. *Ep.* 4.2; Suet. *Aug.* 26.2, *Tib.* 15.1; Quint. *Inst.* 12.6.6; Fronto *Ep.* 1.10.1.

[18] The majority of references to *deductio/deduci in forum* are in reference to this first entrance (e.g. Aug. *RG* 3 of Gaius and Lucius). Since most of the references to initiation involve members of the imperial family, the persistence of the ritual may be an imperial appropriation of a republican tradition. On the donning of the *toga virilis*, see Dolansky 2008.

[19] The unknown author of the *Bellum Africum*, for instance, has Cato rebuke the younger Pompey for his hesitation; his father did not exhibit such fear as a young man, even though "he stepped into the republic without the gift of such a large clientele and a famous name" (*B Af.* 22.4: *neque tantis clientelis*

Chapter 1, the young man's initiation into public life involved an extended internship of sorts (the *tirocinium fori*) whereby the young man followed an older family friend around the forum. According to Quintilian, the young man who has finished his theoretical education should receive a practical education in the public setting by choosing an orator "to follow around and imitate" (*Inst.* 10.5.19: *quem sequatur, quem imitetur*).

The power of the elite male *deductio* was certainly not lost on Augustus: as is well known, he declined the consulship after 23 BCE, save for 5 and 2 BCE, when his grandsons Gaius and Lucius came of age and put on the *toga virilis*. As Suetonius implies (*Aug.* 26.2), the entire point of Augustus' holding office in those years in particular was to endow his grandsons' introduction to public life with the powerful spectacle of the consular procession.[20] On their first day as Roman *viri*, Gaius and Lucius strode into the forum escorted by the princeps himself and his lictors: no ordinary *deductio* indeed, and a clear sign to the populace of the high hopes invested in these young men, who had, after all, already been designated for the consulship themselves. The spectacle was yet another way in which Augustus endowed a traditional republican institution with a new imperial meaning, and was part of a larger imperial turn to ceremony that would become more and more important as the Roman system of government adopted the traditional guise of monarchy.[21] Nero, for instance, marked himself out as heir to the throne during his *deductio in forum*, securing the allegiance of the people and soldiers through donatives and popular displays on his first day of public life.[22]

Since the *deductio* served as an introduction to political life, a life that was the exclusive province of males in republican Rome, the assumption of the manly toga and subsequent procession put the creation of adult men on display for the city. The ceremony was thus quite literally a rite of passage and marked the first instance of what would be a regular occurrence, the dramatic procession of the great man from his home to the forum. As such,

---

nominisque claritate praeditus in rem publicam est ingressus). For other uses of the phrase *in rem publicam ingredi*, see Cic. *Prov. cons.* 40 and *Vat.* 161. Cf. Quint. *Inst.* 7.2.54: *ituris in forum* ("for those about to go into the forum"); Tac. *Dial.* 33.2: *ingressuri forum* ("those about to step into the forum").

[20] Similarly, Suetonius elsewhere notes (*Aug.* 53.2) that Augustus usually went around the city on foot in the years that he was consul, and in a covered sedan when he was not. Presumably this practice avoided the awkward decision about how much of a retinue to employ in those years where he had declined the consulship.

[21] On the transition from republican to imperial ceremony, see Sumi 2005; on later imperial ceremony, see MacCormack 1981.

[22] Suet. *Ner.* 7.2: "After he was led into the forum as a novice he proposed a gratuity for the people and a donative for the military; after formally proclaiming a military display, he carried his shield in front of the praetorians in his own hand. Next, he gave thanks to his father in the senate" (*deductus in forum tiro populo congiarium, militi donativum proposuit indictaque decursione praetorianis scutum sua manu praetulit; exin patri gratias in senatu egit*).

it is a useful contrast to another rite of passage, that of the marriage ceremony, which also involved a *deductio* of the bride from her father's home to the home of her new husband.[23] But of course whereas the young man's *deductio* was the first of many processions, merely the inauguration of a ritual that would become a daily rite, the female *deductio* was a different sort of rite of passage. In ideal terms, it was the only incursion of the young woman into public life, her simultaneous introduction and retirement, as she was led through the streets from one domestic space to another.

The gendering of these mirror *deductiones* becomes even more obvious when we examine occasional instances of female incursions into public space that simultaneously break the mold and harden the ideological distinction between male and female rites of passage. The story of Verginia, for example, emphasizes her escort into the forum by her father.[24] The decemvir Claudius lusted after the freeborn girl, and used his judicial powers to declare her the slave of one of his cronies. After the trial, her father took matters into his own hands (Val. Max. 6.1.2):

atque haec inlatam iniuriam non tulit: Verginius plebei generis, sed patricii vir spiritus, ne probro contaminaretur domus sua, proprio sanguini non pepercit: nam cum App. Claudius decemvir filiae eius virginis stuprum potestatis viribus fretus pertinacius expeteret, deductam in forum puellam occidit pudicaeque interemptor quam corruptae pater esse maluit.

And she [i.e. Chastity] did not endure the committing of an injustice: Verginius was a man of plebeian stock but patrician courage. So that his household would not be contaminated by a shameful act, he did not spare his own flesh and blood. For when the decemvir Appius Claudius, relying on the power of his authority, was coveting rather insistently sex with his virgin daughter, Verginius escorted her into the forum and killed her. He preferred to be the murderer of a chaste girl rather than the father of a fallen one.

By rights, Verginia's one and only *deductio* should be her marriage procession; by adopting the language of the male rite of passage, Valerius Maximus clarifies the full disgrace for Verginius and his family. Not only does her *deductio* turn into a *deductio in forum*, so that it perverts a male rite of passage into adulthood, but it is also a perversion of a funeral procession, ending with her dramatic and public death.[25] Livy's much

---

[23] Notionally, at any rate: weddings did not need such ceremonies to be valid, and there was considerable variety in the possible manifestations of the marriage *deductio*. See Treggiari 1991, 166–7.

[24] Feldherr 1998, 203–12 has a particularly useful discussion of the Verginia episode in Livy's narrative.

[25] Greek tragedy frequently conflates the rituals of funeral and marriage; see Rehm 1994. On the perversion of marriage in the Verginia story, see Feldherr 1998, 211.

longer narrative also lays more explicit emphasis on the inversion of the male *deductio in forum* (3.47.1):

at in urbe prima luce cum civitas in foro exspectatione erecta staret, Verginius sordidatus filiam secum obsoleta veste comitantibus aliquot matronis cum ingenti advocatione in forum deducit.

Back in Rome it was daybreak, and the entire city was standing in the forum, on edge with anticipation. Covered in dirt, Verginius escorted his daughter into the forum, dressed in shabby clothing, with a few matrons as her companions and a large group of advocates.

Like the male rite of passage, this procession takes place in the morning, in the forum, as crowds of spectators look on. Livy, Verginius, the crowd itself – all are versed in the particulars of Roman ritual, and the contrast with the usual steps of the male ritual are obvious, and consciously designed to elicit sympathy (from the viewers and from the readers). Verginia is escorted by matrons, rather than noblemen, and her clothing is worn and shabby – not the shining white *toga virilis* the young man would wear on such occasions, nor the saffron dress she might have been expected to wear on her wedding day, the occasion for what should be her first public procession. Verginia had of course been out in public before – the decemvir's henchman had seized her on the way to school in the forum – but never as the focus of a large retinue. The public quality of her dramatic entrance signifies that something is not right; this procession will in fact be her first and last foray into public life – not in the ideal sense, as a bride, but, rather, as the occasion for her death and funeral.

REPUBLICAN ESCORTS

The *deductio in forum* (both as a daily ritual and as a rite of passage) was part of a larger system of political competition and display in the Roman republic, where one measured the greatness of a man by the size of his retinue.[26] The *locus classicus* for the political importance of the escort is the *Commentariolum petitionis*, the *Little Handbook on Electioneering* purportedly written by Quintus Tullius Cicero to his more famous brother Marcus as he prepared to run for consul in 64 BCE. Candidates for political office need to pay particular attention to their attendants, according to Quintus, because the number of these men functioned as an "an estimate of how

---

[26] On the political importance of the escort, see Nicolet 1980, 356–61; Morstein-Marx 1998, 270–4; Yakobson 1999, 71–8; Bell 2004, 214–15.

much strength and support you will have at the polls" (*Comment. pet.* 34: *nam ex ea ipsa copia coniectura fieri poterit quantum sis in ipso campo virium ac facultatis habiturus*).[27] Quintus goes so far as to create a typology of attendants, distinguishing between *salutatores*, men who greet the candidate at his *domus* in the morning, *deductores*, who accompany the candidate as he makes his way to the forum for his daily business, and *adsectatores*, men who serve as an escort at other times of the day.[28]

The more obvious problem of authorship of this handbook aside, we might question whether the distinctions that Quintus draws, particularly the distinction between *deductores* and more general *adsectatores*, would have been obvious to the average Roman; predictably, the handbook describes the political and social value of the escort from the perspective of the man being escorted.[29] But we can also find evidence for the other perspective, such as in Cicero's defense of Murena during his consulship in 63 BCE. The charge was *ambitus*, and included the accusation that Murena had bribed men to act as *adsectatores*.[30] In the course of defending Murena, Cicero makes a number of comments that reveal the inner logic of the escort, including a brief consideration from the point of view of the men acting as the entourage (*Mur.* 70–1):

homines tenues unum habent in nostrum ordinem aut promerendi aut referendi benefici locum, hanc in nostris petitionibus operam atque adsectationem. neque enim fieri potest neque postulandum est a nobis aut ab equitibus Romanis ut suos necessarios candidatos adsectentur totos dies; a quibus si domus nostra celebratur, si interdum ad forum deducimur, si uno basilicae spatio honestamur, diligenter observari videmur et coli; tenuiorum amicorum et non occupatorum est ista adsiduitas, quorum copia bonis viris et beneficis deesse non solet.... ipsi denique, ut solent loqui, non dicere pro nobis, non spondere, non vocare domum suam possunt. atque haec a nobis petunt omnia neque ulla re alia quae a nobis consequuntur nisi opera sua compensari putant posse.

Poor men have only one place to earn or pay back a service to our order: this effort of providing an escort during our candidacy for office. It is neither possible nor is it expected that Roman knights or men of our order could follow their own candidates

---

[27] Yakobson 1999, 72–5 is an essential guide to this passage; he rightly notes that the author of the *Comment. pet.* implies that the candidate is more dependent on his attendants than the other way round.

[28] Morstein-Marx 1998, 270–1 collects other evidence for the threefold distinction of attendants, which he argues roughly corresponds to a distinction in social status (with *deductores* ranked higher than *salutatores*, and *adsectatores* at the bottom).

[29] For a useful summary of the authenticity debate, see Morstein-Marx 1998, 260–1. As he points out, whether or not Quintus is the author, the work is "so well informed that it remains a first-rate source for late-Republican electoral politics" (261).

[30] See Yakobson 1999, 75–8.

to whom they are closely connected every day; if these men fill our house, if they occasionally escort us to the forum, if they honor us with one lap of the basilica, we appear to be carefully respected and looked after. That constant attention is the task of poorer and less busy men, and a plentiful supply of these men is usually at hand for good and generous men . . . They themselves, then, as they put it, cannot speak on our behalf, they cannot stand surety for us, they cannot invite us to their home. And yet they ask us to do all these things, and they believe that they cannot pay us back for the things which they gain from us with anything other than this service.

As Cicero reveals, the escort was part of a system of exchange, whereby members of the lower orders repaid their patrons for services rendered – representation in court, sustenance at table.[31] The client, without the grand *domus* where he might entertain his patron, resorted to the place that was *his* domain: the street itself. The point, of course, was that others witness this spectacle and deduce from it the power of the man being escorted; without the audience of the street, the spectacle was meaningless. Both the clients doing the escorting and the man being escorted were acting out their status as they walked through the city, and the audience for this narrative were the city denizens, the potential voters at the next election.

Passages such as this one have encouraged some scholars to see the escort as one of the quasi-democratic institutions of the late republic that have been the focus of so much recent debate.[32] Claude Nicolet, for example, interprets the escort as one of the "alternative" institutions emerging in the late republic that offered the people a "means of self-expression" (1980, 356). In this reading, the entourage was an empowering phenomenon whereby average Romans could vote with their feet. In this way, the escort was a less threatening form of mass movement than other ambulatory possibilities, such as the *secessio plebis*, which was a mass movement without aristocratic approval, or a clear aristocratic leader.[33]

Whether or not we see it as a sign of democracy, it is clear that the escort was associated with the political process of the republic, and with elections in particular. Yet there is a potential dissonance here, since the spectacular power of the retinue was also a feature associated with autocrats and kings. Cicero deems it noteworthy that during his stay in Rome Antiochus was allowed to go around the city with almost his full regal train (*Verr.* 2.4.67), while Livy recounts an amusing episode during the Third Macedonian War in which the Macedonian king Perseus and the Roman Q. Marcius Philippus haggle over the size of the entourage that will be permitted to accompany the king during

[31] On Roman patronage, see especially Saller 1982; Wallace-Hadrill 1989b.
[32] See especially Millar 1998; Yakobson 1999; Mouritsen 2001; Hölkeskamp 2004; Morstein-Marx 2004.
[33] On the history of the *secessio plebis*, see Raaflaub 1986.

their negotiations (Livy 42.39).[34] The lictors and other displays of power that accompanied republican magistrates as they walked through the city only escaped the charge of autocratic showiness so long as power was successfully shared. Yet ultimately the same respect for displays of authority that enabled the elaborate entourages in the late republic also enabled the armed gangs that became a regular venue of discord in the same period. Much of the violence of the Roman revolution was not open warfare but the far more ambiguous and hard to define street fights between competing entourages of powerful men.[35] Thus the stakes are real for those who compete to define the nature of such escorts. In the *Pro Murena*, for instance, Cicero relentlessly denies that his client's large retinue has any autocratic or demagogic overtones. A generation later, however, he adopts the opposite tack, going out of his way in the *Philippics* to turn Antony's *comitatus* into a private army (2.108):

qui vero inde reditus Romam, quae perturbatio totius urbis! memineramus Cinnam nimis potentem, Sullam postea dominantem, modo Caesarem regnantem videramus. erant fortasse gladii, sed absconditi nec ita multi. ista vero quae et quanta barbaria est! agmine quadrato cum gladiis sequuntur; scutorum lecticas portari videmus.

What a return to Rome! What a disruption of the entire city! We remember Cinna's excessive power, then Sulla's domination, and just recently we saw Caesar's reign. Well there were swords then too, I suppose, but at least they were kept hidden and not so numerous. But how large and barbarous that display of his! His men follow with their swords, in rigid battle formation; they carry shields along on litters.

Antony doesn't walk through the city; he marches.[36] Even his shields get their own litters. But is the *comitatus* a military or a political institution? It can be one or the other or both, depending on who gets to define it. This ambiguity is a facet not only of the messy reality of everyday life but also of the elision of military and political in Roman public life.

The full spectrum of processions through the city thus posed a series of problems for the Roman audience. A triumph was obviously a triumph: the senate had to approve it, the people had to vote on it. But how did the Romans assess the less formal yet still marked forms of movement through

---

[34] On the *comitatus regius*, see also Livy 1.48.4 (of Servius), 32.39.7 (of Attalus), and 44.43.1 (of Perseus). On the tension between Roman republican and Hellenistic regal institutions, see Rawson 1975 and Bell 2004, 151–7.

[35] On the fine line between escorts and organized gangs in the late republic, see Lintott 1999, 74–85.

[36] Cf. Cic. *Phil.* 13.19: "With what an escort he entered the city! Or rather, with what an army! As the Roman people groaned he threatened homeowners right and left, he singled out houses, he promised his own men quite openly that he would divide up the city" (*ingressus urbem est quo comitatu vel potius agmine, cum dextra sinistra, gemente populo Romano, minaretur dominis, notaret domos, divisurum se urbem palam suis polliceretur*).

the city? Or rather: how did Roman walkers control how the average viewer interpreted their processions? For, in the case of informal modes of procession, contesting viewpoints becomes a real problem. As a final example, let us take Livy's account of Scipio Africanus' march to the Capitoline during his trial in 184 BCE.[37] Scipio descends to the forum and, as Livy tells us, "no other person before – not even Scipio himself when he was consul or censor – was ever escorted into the forum by a bigger crowd of people of every type than he was as a defendant that day" (Livy 38.50.10: *nec alius antea quisquam nec ille ipse Scipio consul censorve maiore omnis generis hominum frequentia quam reus illo die in forum est deductus*). It is hardly unusual for a defendant to call in favors and show the extent of his influence and support by surrounding himself with as many supporters as possible. But Scipio's next move was more memorable still. Pointing out that it was the seventeenth anniversary of his subjugation of Carthage, he announced that he would ascend the Capitoline to perform a *supplicatio* to Jupiter Optimus Maximus, inviting those who would do the same to follow him. Predictably, the entire forum left with him, leaving the accusing tribunes alone with only their attendant slaves (Livy 38.51.12–14):

ab Rostris in Capitolium ascendit. simul se universa contio avertit et secuta Scipionem est, adeo ut postremo scribae viatoresque tribunos relinquerent, nec cum iis praeter servilem comitatum et praeconem qui reum ex Rostris citabat quisquam esset. Scipio non in Capitolio modo, sed per totam urbem omnia templa deum cum populo Romano circumiit. celebratior is prope dies favore hominum et aestimatione vera magnitudinis eius fuit, quam quo triumphans de Syphace rege et Carthaginiensibus urbem est invectus.

He went up from the Rostra onto the Capitoline. At the same moment the entire assembly turned and followed Scipio, so that in the end even the secretaries and the couriers abandoned the tribunes, and no one stayed with them other than their personal escort of slaves and the official who was announcing the defendant from the Rostra. Scipio visited all the temples of the gods with the Roman people, not only on the Capitoline, but throughout the entire city. That day was almost more widely celebrated, considering the goodwill of the people and the genuine estimation of his greatness, than the day on which he entered the city in triumph over King Syphax and the Carthaginians.

Livy makes the logic of Scipio's move clear: he awards himself a spontaneous triumph, the pinnacle of any Roman's career, a day when he moved through the city as if he were Jupiter himself. Livy even has him process with the

---

[37] On Livy's version of the trials of the Scipios, see Jaeger 1997, 132–76 (and 149–53 on the procession in particular). The date is controversial, as is the veracity of the trial itself; Scullard 1973, 290–303 deals with the historical problems. For more on Scipio as an "object of spectacular attention" on the streets of Rome, see Bell 2004, 34–6.

people in a *supplicatio* of more than one temple, to reinforce the image of a triumphal procession through the city. On the actual day of his triumph he was undoubtedly conveyed in a chariot, in a more formal ceremony; but this spontaneous triumph, undertaken on foot, without any of the planning or pomp or circumstance, carried every bit of the honor and esteem.

Yet Scipio's march is not without risk, no matter how great and populous. Since it is informal, it is open to interpretation by others. The accusing tribunes persist in their accusations, and reveal that the triumphal implications were not lost on them (Livy 38.52.3–5):

ubi dies venit citarique absens est coeptus, L. Scipio morbum causae esse, cur abesset, excusabat. quam excusationem cum tribuni, qui diem dixerant, non acciperent, et ab eadem superbia non venire ad causam dicendam arguerent, qua iudicium et tribunos plebis et contionem reliquisset, et, quibus ius sententiae de se dicendae et libertatem ademisset, his comitatus, velut captos trahens, triumphum de populo Romano egisset secessionemque eo die in Capitolium a tribunis plebis fecisset.

When the day [*sc.* of his trial] arrived and he began to be summoned in his absence, Lucius Scipio pleaded on his behalf that his sickness was the reason why he was not there. The tribunes who had chosen the date of the trial did not accept this excuse, and they argued that he had not come to plead his case because of the same arrogance he had shown by abandoning his first trial, and the tribunes, and the entire assembly. On that day, accompanied by those men whom he had deprived of the right and freedom of sentencing him, indeed dragging them along as if they were captives, he had celebrated a triumph over the Roman people and had performed a secession onto the Capitoline away from the tribunes of the plebs.

If this was indeed a triumph for Scipio, say the tribunes, then the Roman people were the captives led in his train.[38] Better yet – this was not a triumph, but a *secessio*: they may have fled to the Capitoline rather than the Aventine, and the crowd may have included patricians as well as plebeians, but Scipio is resorting to the same filibustering tactics that the enemies of the plebs feared for so many centuries. Yet, as Livy makes clear, the tribunes lose this framing battle. The power of Scipio's flight to the Capitoline is that it cannot, no matter how hard the tribunes try, be recast as a *secessio*, because the group that accompanies him represents all orders of Rome (indeed, in Livy's telling, *all* of Rome, though that is surely an exaggeration). Scipio's procession is an idealized body politic on the move through the city – a republic in motion, visiting its monuments, giving thanks to its gods.

---

[38] As Beard 2007, 253 notes, it is "a more shocking paradox in Latin than in English translation."

PLINY AND TACITUS ON THE REPUBLICAN POWER
OF THE ESCORT

However "democratic" the republican escort may have appeared to some, it is clear that it was associated with the mechanisms of republican politics, and the contestation of power in that period. These associations become even clearer in the early principate, where the various types of Roman escorts continued to be relevant precisely *because* of their republican associations.[39] Pliny and Tacitus were especially adept at employing republican institutions for praise and blame, and their use of escort imagery is no exception.[40]

For Tacitus, the republican connotations of the escort are convenient: the escort becomes yet another institution sullied by the emergence of the principate. In particular, Tacitus draws attention to the connection between official escorts and the imperial family as an indication of the new modes of power that result from the transition to monarchy. The rise and fall of Messalina's political ambitions, for example, are tracked through the size of her escort. When she is at the height of her power and intriguing with Silius, perhaps in treasonous plot, she is accompanied by numerous attendants (*Ann.* II.12: *multo comitatu*). But once Messalina's political ambitions are dashed, Tacitus once again draws attention to her diminished state by homing in on the diminishment of her attendants as she walks across the city "with only three companions – so sudden was her isolation" (*Ann.* II.32: *tribus omnino comitantibus – id repente solitudinis erat*). A similar rise and fall applies to Agrippina's escort. At the height of her power, just after Claudius' death, the senate endows her with two lictors, an honor that typically was only granted to women who were Vestal Virgins (and which Tiberius had explicitly denied to Livia).[41] But when her political ambitions become too much for Nero to handle, he attempts to diminish her power by reducing her escort (*Ann.* 13.18):

tribunos et centuriones comiter excipere, nomina et virtutes nobilium, qui etiam tum supererant, in honore habere, quasi quaereret ducem et partis. cognitum id Neroni, excubiasque militaris, quae ut coniugi imperatoris olim, tum ut matri servabantur, et Germanos nuper eundem <in> honorem custodes additos degredi iubet. ac ne coetu salutantium frequentaretur, separat domum matremque transfert in eam quae Antoniae fuerat.

---

[39] On the continuing relevance of patronage under the emperors, see Saller 1982, 41–78; Wallace-Hadrill 1989b, 78–84.

[40] On allusions to the republic in Tacitus' *Dialogus* and Pliny's *Panegyricus*, see Gowing 2005, 109–31.

[41] Agrippina's two lictors: Tac. *Ann.* 13.2; Tiberius refuses lictors to Livia: Tac. *Ann.* 1.14. On the granting of lictors to Vestal Virgins, see Beard 1980, 17.

Agrippina obligingly took tribunes and centurions under her care; she paid honor to any esteemed and worthy noblemen who were then still alive, as if she were seeking out a leader and an opposing camp. When Nero found this out, he dismissed the military guard which she had once been given as the emperor's wife and had then kept as the emperor's mother, as well as the German watchmen who had been added to the same honor. And, so that she would not be thronged by a crowd of *salutatores*, he divided his house and transferred her to the part that had been Antonia's.

Tacitus has Nero punish Agrippina by attacking the very two forms of power that both the *Commentariolum petitionis* and Cicero identify as the basis of support for the powerful nobleman aiming for office in the late republic: the escort through the city and the *salutatores* at home.[42] In so doing, he exposes the fraud of imperial-grade republicanism, where the symbols of *dignitas* formerly reserved for Roman magistrates are now employed by women such as Agrippina. Moreover, the symbols themselves have also been transformed by the change in government, since the escort no longer consists of Roman *amici* and *clientes* in togas, but the military and German watchmen.

But for Tacitus the clearest sign that things have changed is the power invested in freedmen such as Pallas and Narcissus, and here too, predictably, the escort functions as a sign of that power. In fact, the most explicit act of "reading" the significance of an escort in the *Annals* occurs in Book 13, when Nero makes a pointed joke about the size of Pallas' entourage (*Ann.* 13.14):

et Nero infensus iis quibus superbia muliebris innitebatur, demovet Pallantem cura rerum quis a Claudio impositus velut arbitrium regni agebat; ferebaturque degrediente eo magna prosequentium multitudine non absurde dixisse, ire Pallantem ut eiuraret. sane pepigerat Pallas ne cuius facti in praeteritum interrogaretur paresque rationes cum re publica haberet.

Nero, furious at those who supported this arrogant woman [*sc.* Agrippina], stripped Pallas of his responsibilities, he who had been empowered by Claudius to act practically as commander of the kingdom. As Pallas was leaving with a great multitude of attendants, Nero is said to have remarked, not inappropriately, that Pallas was going off to his swearing-out ceremony. In fact, Pallas had arranged that there would be no interrogation of any deed in his past and that his account with the state would be squared.

Nero's joke that Pallas was heading off to leave office (that is, to perform his *eiuratio*, or swearing-out ceremony) is motivated by the fact that he was parading about with an escort more suited to a magistrate. The episode is in

---

[42] See e.g. *Comment. pet.* 34–8 and Cic. *Mur.* 70. On the continuing relevance of the *salutatio* in imperial Rome, see Leach 2004, 21.

many ways parallel to the Agrippina story we just encountered. In both cases, Tacitus draws attention to someone acting like a republican magistrate who has no traditional right to do so. In both cases, the escort is the visible proof of their status, and the emperor turns his attention to the size of that escort at precisely the moment when he strips them of their power. And in both cases, Tacitus draws attention to a time-honored republican institution that has been corrupted by the advent of the principate: in the case of Agrippina, it is not just that a woman parades around with an escort, but also that the escort itself has become militarized; in the case of Pallas, it is not just that an ex-slave acts like a magistrate, but also that by his influence he has managed to secure a pardon for all of his actions in advance, the exact inversion of the republican *eiuratio*, where the office-holder swore at the end of his term of office that he had broken no laws. In other words, for Tacitus, the institutions of the republic have been doubly perverted: when they survive, they do so in a debased way, and they are now performed by members of society who had no right to do so under the republic.

What, then, were good republican men supposed to do in this new climate? For this, we can turn to the *Agricola*, and here too we see Tacitus making reference to the phenomenon of the escort; after his successful term of service in Britain, Agricola returns to Rome, but is careful to avoid the normal welcoming spectacle as he enters the city (*Agr.* 40.3–4):

ac ne notabilis celebritate et frequentia occurrentium introitus esset, vitato amicorum officio noctu in urbem, noctu in Palatium, ita ut praeceptum erat, venit … ceterum uti militare nomen, grave inter otiosos, aliis virtutibus temperaret, tranquillitatem atque otium penitus hausit, cultu modicus, sermone facilis, uno aut altero amicorum comitatus, adeo ut plerique, quibus magnos viros per ambitionem aestimare mos est, viso aspectoque Agricola quaererent famam, pauci interpretarentur.

In order that his entrance into the city not be conspicuous, with a crowded multitude of men rushing to meet him, [Agricola] avoided the courteousness of his friends and came into Rome at night, and to the Palatine at night, just as he had been ordered … Moreover, in order that he might temper his military glory (which annoys men of leisure) with other virtues, he made the most of his retirement and leisure; he was modest in his appearance, relaxed in conversation; he was accompanied by only one or two friends. As a result, when they saw Agricola, very many people who are accustomed to judge great men by their ambition asked about his fame, but few understood it.

Tacitus' panegyric to Agricola at the expense of Domitian is revealing in its attitudes. Agricola is so eager to defuse the obvious threat of his military valor that he enters the city by night, going out of his way to avoid the *officia* of the numerous friends who presumably would have come out in great numbers to welcome him home in better times.[43] The inversion is clever: he moves through the city by night, usually a sign of devious intent, so eager is he to avoid any appearance of threatening popularity. Tacitus wants to suggest that Agricola practically flaunted his *lack* of ambition for power, and the characteristics that he fixes on are revealing: Agricola adopts a plainness in appearance, in speech, and in his very manner of walking, by eschewing the full retinue that was (as Tacitus so clearly implies) his right as a great Roman. Yet as much as Agricola tries to avoid the invidious attention of the emperor Domitian, his behavior connects him with another emperor: as Suetonius tells us, Augustus also secured a reputation for modesty by his avoidance of escorts when entering and leaving town.[44]

If Tacitus fixes on the republican nature of the escort to condemn the *princeps*, Pliny uses it as a source of praise in the *Panegyricus*. His memorable description of Trajan's first entry into the city as *princeps* emphasizes the fact that he walks rather than rides (thereby avoiding some of the connotations of the triumph), and makes himself accessible to the throngs who turn out to support him, and whose joy increases with each step of their new emperor.[45] Here is Pliny's fuller description of the scene (*Pan.* 23.1–3):

gratum erat cunctis … quod tantum <non> ultro clientibus salutatis quasdam familiaritatis notas adderes; gratius tamen, quod sensim et placide et quantum respectantium turba pateretur incederes, quod occursantium populus te quoque, te immo maxime artaret, quod primo statim die latus tuum crederes omnibus. neque enim stipatus satellitum manu sed circumfusus undique nunc senatus, nunc equestris ordinis flore, prout alterutrum frequentiae genus invaluisset, silentes quietosque lictores tuos subsequebare. nam milites nihil a plebe habitu tranquillitate modestia differebant.

Everyone was pleased … that you greeted your clients without prompting and then added some signs of camaraderie. And they were still more pleased that you walked slowly and calmly as far as the crowd of onlookers permitted; that the mob of people thronged around you too, indeed around you especially; that right away, on your very first day, you trusted everyone to be by your side. For you were not surrounded by a band of cronies; instead the finest men of the senate and of the equestrian order spread around you, to the extent that one or the other kind of crowd gained in number, and you followed behind your silent and quiet lictors. Moreover, the soldiers did not differ from the common people in dress, tranquility, or restraint.

---

[43] Cf. Sailor 2008, 96: "[Agricola's] homecoming is a humiliating inversion of the triumphal procession."

[44] For Augustus' leaving and returning to town at night, "lest he disturb anyone on account of their obligations" (*ne quem officii causa inquietaret*), see Suet. *Aug.* 53.2.

[45] Trajan enters the city for the first time as emperor on foot, not in a chariot: Plin. *Pan.* 22.1; the crowd's increasing joy as the princeps enters the city: *Pan.* 22.5. On the imperial escort, see Millar 1977, 61–9.

Although there is a slight dissonance in Pliny's description – the lictors and soldiers who accompany Trajan seem almost comically polite – the impression that Pliny wants to convey (and presumably Trajan before him) is a marked contrast to the militarism and secrecy of his imperial predecessors, and is a sign of the restoration of *libertas* that Trajan's reign promoted.[46] The new emperor continues this accessibility in his daily life by making himself available – again, on foot – for regular consultation (*Pan.* 24.2–3):

manet imperatori, quae prior oris humanitas, dexterae verecundia. incedebas pedibus; incedis. laetabaris labore; laetaris. eademque omnia illa circa te, nihil in ipso te fortuna mutavit. liberum est, ingrediente per publicum principe, subsistere, occurrere, comitari, praeterire: ambulas inter nos, non quasi contingas; et copiam tui, non ut imputes, facis. haeret lateri tuo, quisquis accessit, finemque sermoni suus cuique pudor, non tua superbia, facit.

You still have the same kind expression and restrained hand that you had before you were emperor. You used to walk on foot; you still do. You used to take pleasure in hard work; you still do. Everything is the same about you: your change in fortune hasn't changed you at all. Whenever the emperor goes out in public, anyone can stop, approach him, escort him, or pass him by. You walk among us, but not as if you were god's gift to us.[47] You make yourself available to us without any obligation on our part. Whoever approaches you stays by your side, and only his sense of decorum, rather than your arrogance, puts an end to the conversation.

The moralizing tone of Pliny's approval suggests that there was real political capital to be gained from walking through the city, even for the emperor; despite the change from republic to monarchy, the leading citizen still has much to gain by casting himself as a man of the people, and leaving himself available for walks with his citizens is the surest sign of affability and esteem. Furthermore, the acceptance of petitions from citizens was an important part of imperial ideology at all times, and traveling through the city by foot presumably flaunted the emperor's openness to this form of access.[48] Moreover, as Suetonius tells us (*Dom.* 19), Domitian tended to travel by litter through the city, so Trajan's walking is yet another way he can distinguish himself from his predecessor.

But Pliny's praise is not just meant to draw a contrast with Domitian. In fact, it seems that in advertising his availability for consultation by walking

---

[46] On Pliny's use of the *Panegyricus* "to express a definition of *libertas* within the confines of the unequal relationship of princeps and Senate," see Morford 1992 (quote at 590). On his rhetorical use of antithesis as a reflection of Trajan's own distancing from Domitian, see Bartsch 1994, 149–62. On the theme of *libertas reddita* ("liberty restored") in the work, see Gowing 2005, 121–2.

[47] For the translation of *ambulas inter nos, non quasi contingas*, cf. Mayor 1878 ad Juv. *Sat.* 8.28.

[48] On petitions to the emperor, see Millar 1977, 240–52 and Hauken 1998.

through the city, Trajan is continuing a tradition that was already old-fashioned by the first century BCE. In Cicero's *De oratore*, Crassus claims that leading citizens would promenade in the forum and wait for people to ask their advice on matters, in a kind of ancient, mobile version of office hours (*De or.* 3.133):

equidem saepe hoc audivi de patre et de socero meo, nostros quoque homines, qui excellere sapientiae gloria vellent, omnia, quae quidem tum haec civitas nosset, solitos esse complecti. meminerant illi Sex. Aelium; M'. vero Manilium nos etiam vidimus transverso ambulantem foro; quod erat insigne eum, qui id faceret, facere civibus suis omnibus consili sui copiam; ad quos olim et ita ambulantis et in solio sedentis domi sic adibatur, non solum ut de iure civili ad eos, verum etiam de filia conlocanda, de fundo emendo, de agro colendo, de omni denique aut officio aut negotio referretur.

Indeed I have often heard it said by my father and by my father-in-law that the same was true for us as well: that those who wanted to distinguish themselves by the glory of philosophy used to have a grasp of everything that the citizenry knew at the time. They remembered Sextus Aelius, just as we too have even seen Manius Manilius walking across the forum, and it was clear that by doing this he made his advice available to all his fellow citizens. And at one time everyone would approach such men, both when they were walking in this manner and when they were sitting at home in their chair, and defer to their judgment, not only on legal matters, but also on marrying off a daughter, on buying an estate, on agriculture, in fact on any agenda or business affair.

The dramatic date of the dialogue is 91 BCE, a generation before its publication in 55, so there is a double retrojection into the past here: Cicero imagines Crassus' generation, and Crassus looks back to the previous generation.[49] Cicero may be providing an idealized portrait of the *mos maiorum* rather than a historical reality, but that does not make it any less likely this ideal influenced Trajan's behavior. The symbolic power of Trajan's walks through the city is achieved not simply through the performed accessibility of the most powerful man in Rome: such an effect could be achieved by holding court in the palace, for example. The symbolism is also based in the equalizing power of walking: whatever the reality, Trajan gives his companions the impression of equal status as they move through the city at an equal height and pace.

---

[49] In Plaut. *Curc.* 470–84, "the longest and most striking Roman allusion in all of Plautus" (Moore 1998, 131), the title character gives a brief summary of the contemporary topography of Rome, with a brief comment on what kind of person frequents each space; "in the lower forum," he notes, "rich noblemen stroll" (*Curc.* 475: *in foro infumo boni homines atque dites ambulant*). Perhaps it is an allusion to the same practice?

In sum, both Tacitus and Pliny show that popularity in the early principate was still gauged by the size of a person's retinue, but that the meaning of that popularity depended very much on his or her relationship to the emperor; just as the popular spectacle of a triumphal parade became a privilege granted only to members of the imperial family, imperial control extended even to more quotidian forms of procession.[50] As they had in the past, the people could still signal their approval by turning out in droves to meet and consult with their leader; the various forms of escort so important to Roman political life in the republic did not disappear with the turn to the principate, but were now more tightly controlled and focused on the princeps and his family.[51]

LET YOUR SLAVES DO THE WALKING: LITTERS

Given the prevalence of street violence in ancient Rome, the elite habit of walking in groups had a practical dimension in addition to its more ostentatious one; it was surely not always apparent whether a group of escorters was offering political support or a security detail.[52] As we have seen, there was a tendency for authority figures in both the republic and the principate to emphasize the political or even democratic aspects of their entourage and to downplay the potential autocratic or regal associations. Such a move proved more difficult in the case of the litter, another common method of avoiding the masses while moving through the city.

Because of frequent negative jibes at those who travel by litter (there are four in Juvenal's first satire alone), it is often assumed that such travel was restricted to truly decadent members of society.[53] Such an assumption is reinforced by Suetonius' mention of a sumptuary law introduced by Julius Caesar that had apparently restricted the use of litters in the city of Rome to certain people, of a certain rank, and only on certain days (Suet. *Iul.* 43.1). Suetonius in fact mentions the edict in a general comment about Caesar's efforts to stem the tide of *luxuria*, and implies that it restricted the use of litters, scarlet clothing, and pearls, which gives a sense of the associative

---

[50] On the transformation of triumphal practice under Augustus, see Beard 2007, 295–305; Itgenshorst 2008.

[51] Cf. Wallace-Hadrill 1989b, 81: "[T]he network of patronage realigns [*sc.* in the principate], and all strands converge on the emperor at the centre." As the memory of republican institutions faded and imperial pageantry increased, later emperors relied more and more on travel by carriage; according to Ammianus (22.7.1), Julian's decision to go and greet his new consuls on foot was criticized by some as "affected and low-class" (*affectatum et vile*): see Adams 1993, 49 n. 26.

[52] On street violence in ancient Rome, see Lintott 1999; Africa 1971; Nippel 1988.

[53] For the associations of litter travel, see Brown 1983; McGinn 1998, 245–7; Laurence 1999, 138–9.

chain. And nearly a century before that, a fragment of a speech by C. Sempronius Gracchus betrays a similar ambivalence about the use of litters. According to Gracchus, who tells the story with severe disapproval, a degenerate Roman noble was being carried through the Italian countryside, when a peasant jokingly asked if the litter-bearers were carrying a corpse; at which point the aristocrat ordered the litter to halt, and had the peasant beaten to death on the spot, with the very leather straps that held the litter together.[54] The luxurious litter is not only corrosive of Roman moral standards but also quite literally harmful even to those who would not make use of it.

A few generations later, Cicero often refers to the use of a litter as damning circumstantial evidence, as in his attacks on Verres and Antony. He even makes the same funeral joke as the Venusine peasant in Gracchus' anecdote, about Antony, who was "carried through town in a covered litter, like a corpse" (*Phil.* 2.106: *operta lectica latus per oppidum est ut mortuus*). In the *Verrines*, the litter is just one of many attributes of Verres' over-the-top lifestyle that is meant to condemn him. One story among many involves his use of a litter to travel to his nocturnal trysts (*Verr.* 2.5.34):

cum paludatus exisset votaque pro imperio suo communique re publica nuncupasset, noctu stupri causa lectica in urbem introferri solitus est ad mulierem nuptam uni, propositam omnibus, contra fas, contra auspicia, contra omnis divinas atque humanas religiones!

When he had departed in his military uniform and offered solemn vows for his own command and for the republic as a whole, he was in the habit of being carried back to the city at night in a litter in the name of sex to the home of a woman who was married to one man, but offered up to all men. This was contrary to what was right, contrary to the auspices, contrary to all divine and human sanctity!

The ceremonies of departure and return for generals taking up foreign commands were a vital institution in Roman society, and there were certain expectations for how a successful commander should return home: once only, by day, (often) on foot, and back to his wife at home, with throngs of citizens cheering his way. Not, as here, every night, in a covered litter, to another woman's arms.[55] Almost every word in Cicero's accusation has either an inherently negative association or at the very least an unmilitary one: night (*noctu*), sexual disgrace (*stupri*), woman (*mulierem*), and of course, the litter itself.

---

[54] The fragment is preserved by Aulus Gellius (*NA* 10.3); see Malcovati 1976 48.49.
[55] On the development of the *adventus* ceremony, see Lehnen 1997; on the *adventus* ceremony in the later Roman empire, see MacCormack 1981, 17–89.

Yet other casual mentions of litter travel suggest that it was a viable form of transport for elites at all periods, and that accusations of luxury reflected an anxiety about public opinion, rather than a universal disdain. The elder Pliny famously reproaches his nephew for walking around the city, arguing that the time he spent on foot could be better spent in study (Plin. *Ep.* 3.5.16); clearly, travel by litter allowed a certain degree of refuge from the upheavals of the street. The younger Pliny's reference to his uncle's criticism manages to flatter both himself, for his old-fashioned insistence on getting around on foot, and his uncle, since his preference for a litter is motivated simply by his fanatical passion for study; the mention, then, also betrays the usual hint of disapproval for travel by litter.[56] Catullus 10, on the other hand, shows no such hint: when Varus' girlfriend knowingly asks to borrow Catullus' litter-bearers that he claims to have acquired in Bithynia, he is embarrassed because he has been caught in a lie, not by the fact of litter travel itself. Possession of a litter seems to have been a status symbol of sorts, and the usual benefits and envy accrued to its owner. In his public speeches, as we have seen, Cicero refers to travel by litter as a damning mark of luxury that does not require further comment.[57] Yet in a letter to his brother (*Q Fr.* 2.6) he mentions an evening visit to Pompey's *horti* in the Campus Martius; he took a litter there, and the casual and offhand way in which he mentions it, combined with the unguarded voice of one member of the elite writing privately to another, suggests that such travel may in fact have been more common than is generally believed (as the need for Caesar's edict would also imply).

Still the differences between the employment of an entourage and the employment of a litter were stark enough, particularly for the urban audience (not to mention the litter-bearers). The complexities of different types of processions and escorts rewarded the trained urban eye, and required the acquisition of a kind of grammar of urban walking; litters, by contrast, were a visible reminder not just of the small number of the elite but also of their literally elevated status, as they looked down on those below them.[58] Both entourages and litters involved a display of power, but the

---

[56] As does the elder Pliny's own grousing about the extent to which Romans relied on their slaves (referring to litter-bearers, lectors, name prompters, and doctors): "We walk with someone else's feet, we perceive with someone else's eyes, we greet with someone else's memory, and we live with someone else's care" (*HN* 29.19: *alienis pedibus ambulamus, alienis oculis agnoscimus, aliena memoria salutamus, aliena et vivimus opera*). See Fitzgerald 2000, 49–50.

[57] In addition to the examples above, see e.g. *Phil.* 2.58, 2.106.

[58] For the double meaning, see Juv. *Sat.* 1.158–9: "So the same man who poisoned three of his uncles is carried past on dangling mattresses and looks down on us from up there?" (*qui dedit ergo tribus patruis aconita, vehatur / pensilibus plumis atque illinc despiciat nos?*).

message was different in each case. And the record of elite attitudes to the litter clarifies for us what it meant when they eschewed its use.

CONCLUSION

In the famous parade of heroes in *Aeneid* 6, Virgil casts Aeneas in the role of a young boy asking his father to identify various bigwigs walking through the city, in a Roman version of Homer's *teichoscopia* (*Aen.* 6.860–5):[59]

> atque hic Aeneas (una namque ire videbat
> egregium forma iuvenem et fulgentibus armis,
> sed frons laeta parum et deiecto lumina vultu)
> 'quis, pater, ille, virum qui sic comitatur euntem?
> filius, anne aliquis magna de stirpe nepotum?
> qui strepitus circa comitum!'

Aeneas saw a young man walking beside him [*sc.* the older Marcellus], a young man conspicuous for his beauty and his shining weapons, but whose brow and eyes were hardly happy on his dejected face; at this point he asked, "Who is that, father, who in such a manner accompanies the other man as he passes? His son, or someone else in his magnificent family tree? What a din of companions around him!"

The parade of heroes has frequently been read as a metaphorical funeral procession, one of the ways Virgil has "Romanized" the Homeric model of Odysseus' *nekuia*.[60] In *Odyssey* 11, Odysseus waits for the shades to gather around him; here the shades file past showing little awareness of their audience, just as one might expect in a parade where both viewers and viewed accept their roles. Thus, Virgil evokes the didactic and communicative power of the Roman funeral procession. But I would argue that he also evokes the communicative power of other types of urban processions, such as the escort of high-status individuals, and therefore alludes to the communicative power of the escort that we have examined in this chapter. Just as the younger Marcellus escorts his ancestor (6.863: *comitatur*), he himself is accompanied by a throng of companions (6.865: *strepitus . . . comitum*), befitting his status in Augustan Rome. In fact, the Roman funeral procession itself evokes the institution of the escort: for what else is a funeral procession, in the Roman imagination, than an ideal *comitatus* for a dead man, passing through the city with an entourage no

---

[59] Norden 1957, 312 compares the parade of heroes to the *teichoscopia* in passing; Skard 1965, 56 rejects the comparison. Cf. Leach 1999, 126, who compares the scene to a son asking his father to explain the marble statues around the city.

[60] Skard 1965, 60–5 was the first to argue in detail that the parade of heroes was intended to evoke the elite Roman funeral; Bettini 1991, 145–7 develops the comparison further (and also provides a useful summary of other proposed models for the parade).

longer constrained by considerations of time or mortality? In this sense Virgil's parade of heroes represents yet another level of "improvement" over the traditional Roman funeral, for in Hades the young Marcellus can escort his famous ancestor, rather than the other way round. In a normal funeral procession, the dead nobleman is escorted by his ancestors, but in Virgil's idealized vision, the procession includes relatives from the past *and* future.[61]

The Virgilian parade of heroes differs from a funeral procession in another key respect: as Bettini points out (1991, 146), this parade is not an assembly of one *gens*, but of all the important men in Roman history.[62] So too the daily *deductio* is not an assembly of relatives, but of members of many different families; but the similarity ends there, for a procession escorting a great man is hierarchical to a greater degree than a funeral procession or even Virgil's parade of heroes. But that is not to say that Romans saw no connection between more ordinary forms of procession and family identity. Take for example Livy's account of the Fabii marching off to war against Veii in 477 BCE. The city was overextended with other wars, but the Veientines needed to be dealt with, so the Fabii volunteered to lead a private army on behalf of the state (Livy 2.49.3–5):

nunquam exercitus neque minor numero neque clarior fama et admiratione hominum per urbem incessit. sex et trecenti milites, omnes patricii, omnes unius gentis, quorum neminem ducem sperneres, egregius quibuslibet temporibus senatus, ibant, unius familiae viribus Veienti populo pestem minitantes. sequebatur turba propria alia cognatorum sodaliumque, nihil medium, nec spem nec curam, sed immensa omnia volventium animo, alia publica sollicitudine excitata, favore et admiratione stupens.

No army has ever processed through the city smaller in number or more illustrious in public opinion and admiration. Three hundred and six soldiers went by, all patricians, all from one family, none of whom you would reject as a leader at any time in history, no matter how distinguished the senate, and the strength of one family was threatening destruction for the Veientine nation. A crowd followed them, some of whom were their own friends and relations, thinking about nothing middling, neither hope nor anxiety, but only about the immensity of everything; others in the crowd were members of the public, animated with anxiety, dumb-struck with goodwill and admiration.

---

[61] Of course, as Polybius himself makes clear, the elite funeral alludes to the near future through its didactic influence on the younger relatives of the deceased. On the play of time in the parade of heroes, see Bettini 1991, 142–50.

[62] Leach 1999, 323 n. 31 compares it to the display of *summi viri* in the Forum of Augustus, and it is tempting to think that the Virgilian parade was an influence on that display. An influence, too, on Augustus' funeral (Cass. Dio 56.34): as a reader for the Press points out to me, a parade of great men from many families "is precisely the format adopted in Augustus' own funeral, which now looks 'anticipated' by Virgil."

Livy's description of the procession of the Fabii is a Roman aristocratic reverie. The Roman republic famously depended on the sharing of power by a very few families; the Fabian expedition is one of those special events used to justify that arrangement. The Roman republic is ruled by a handful of families because those families are themselves ideal versions of the state, and thus by metonymy represent the state itself. Hence the appeal of the elite funeral procession, where one family stands in for the entire state: the oligarchic ideal.

The connection between processions and family identity in the Roman republic explains why they became such a powerful tool of the emperors. The imperial family could lay claim to republican ideology by adopting the time-honored tradition of moving in groups through the city. The Ara Pacis, which depicts senators *and* family members walking with the new emperor, suggests that this process of adaptation started early. Of course, the transition to the principate is a transition to a time when one family really *does* become the state; the myth of the Fabii reassures Livy's Augustan readers that powerful families have always advertised their elite status by the very way they walk through the city. The rest of us, like Juvenal in his first satire, can only stand by and watch – or, if we are lucky, we can walk in their train, dumbstruck with goodwill and admiration.

CHAPTER 4

Cicero's legs

Cicero's *De oratore* imagines a conversation on eloquence among the leading Roman statesmen of the late second and early first century BCE, including L. Licinius Crassus and Q. Lutatius Catulus. As is typical in his early philosophical and rhetorical works, Cicero goes to great lengths to defend his choice of subject matter, and he transfers his anxieties to his characters, who frequently reflect in a rather self-conscious manner upon the form of the dialogue itself. On the morning of the second day of their discussion, for example, Crassus voices his concern that, with their Socratic style of question-and-response, they might pick up some of the bad habits of the Greeks, who are only too willing to debate any point, any time, anywhere, *ad nauseam* (Cic. *De or.* 2.18). At this point Catulus interjects, disputing the notion that all Greeks behave in this manner: the best Greeks – by which he means politically active Greeks – confined their philosophical disputation to their free time, their *otium*. To strengthen his case, and to allay Crassus' anxieties, he appeals to their surroundings; he draws particular attention to the portico of Crassus' Tusculan villa, in which they are walking, as an especially appropriate setting for philosophical conversation (*De or.* 2.20):

ac si tibi videntur qui temporis, qui loci, qui hominum rationem non habent, inepti, sicut debent videri, num tandem aut locus hic non idoneus videtur, in quo porticus haec ipsa, ubi nunc ambulamus, et palaestra et tot locis sessiones gymnasiorum et Graecorum disputationum memoriam quodam modo commovent? aut num importunum tempus in tanto otio, quod et raro datur et nunc peroptato nobis datum est? aut homines ab hoc genere disputationis alieni, qui omnes ei sumus, ut sine his studiis vitam nullam esse ducamus?

Yes, but even if you find those people rude who take no account of time or place or company – and so you should – surely you don't think that *this* is an inappropriate place [*sc.* for conversation]? Here, where this portico in which we now stroll, and this palaestra, and so many places to sit somehow set in motion the memory of the gymnasia and the philosophical disputes of the Greeks? Surely you don't think that this is the wrong time, in this generous period of leisure, which we are so rarely given and which has been given to us just when we wanted it so badly? Surely you don't think that people like us should be strangers to this type of discussion, we who think life is nothing without these pursuits?

Catulus' phrasing highlights the temporal, physical, and social boundaries of *otium*: for a respectable leisure, one must have the right time, the right place, and the right company (*temporis ... loci ... hominum*). The right place, of course, is the Roman villa. By the late republic it was somewhat more fashionable to advertise one's country home as a setting for relaxation and study than as a venue for agricultural production.[1] As Cicero shows us, certain architectural features in the Roman villa were consciously intended as settings for intellectual conversations, and were even designed to remind the visitor of the physical setting of Greek philosophy.

Catulus attempts to reassure Crassus by drawing attention not only to their physical setting but also to their physical activity: the act of walking itself contributes to the atmosphere of genteel intellectualism that Cicero evokes here. As Catulus' phrasing implies, the portico of Crassus' villa encourages movement of both body and mind; the architecture and decor literally sets their memories in motion (*memoriam ... commovent*), inspiring them to recall foreign places and activities while they stroll. This chapter explores the patterns of behavior and thought associated with the *ambulatio*: the contemplative walk that became a central practice of Roman leisure.[2] In the Roman imagination, taking a walk was an occasion for mental as well as physical exercise; the *ambulatio* was a setting for conversation with friends and even for philosophical inquiry in a Hellenized mode.

The Roman luxury villa was an appropriate setting for highbrow walking; indeed the villa and the *ambulatio* both participated in a culture of conspicuous consumption. The elite villa advertised the wealth of the owner by the devotion of (notionally) productive space to non-commercial leisure practices.[3] The leisurely walk, too, was decidedly uneconomical; like the processions we examined in the previous chapter, the *ambulatio* was not simply a way to get from one place to another. Indeed, the rise in popularity

---

[1] On the rise of the villa as an intellectual retreat, see e.g. Boëthius 1960, 95–103; André 1966, 477; D'Arms 1970, 12–17; Champlin 1982, 106–7; Mielsch 1987, 94–7; MacDonald and Pinto 1995, 3–6; Zanker 1998, 16–19 and 136–42.

[2] On the *ambulatio*, see especially Grimal 1984, 256–9; Weeber 1995, s.v. "Spaziergang"; MacDonald and Pinto 1995, 189; Scagliarini Corlàita 1997, 119–20; Dickmann 1997, 123; Kuttner 1999, 350–3; Bergmann 2001, 158 and 162–3.

[3] The tendency of the Roman elite to downplay the economic benefits of villa ownership does not mean that such benefits were non-existent; Purcell 1995 persuasively argues that productivity remained a fundamental concern, even for owners of luxurious villas. See also Marzano 2007 on the interplay of social and economic motives for villa ownership in central Italy.

of porticoes and enclosed peristyles, in which the aristocrat could pace back and forth within the confines of his own home, would have made the "impracticality" of the leisurely walk even clearer. Walking for leisure also advertised the economic independence of the walker, who could use his body for something other than generating profit. In this sense, the leisurely stroll was the ambulatory equivalent of a wasteful water display in an elite villa: the use of a basic natural "resource" (the legs) for pure enjoyment.

The anecdote about the cuckolded pauper from Apuleius' *Metamorphoses* hinges on just such an idea. When the laborer comes home early from work unexpectedly one morning, his adulterous wife hides her lover in a jar and prepares her best defense: a good offense (*Met.* 9.5):

patefactis aedibus adhuc introeuntem maritum aspero sermone accipit: "sicine vacuus et otiosus insinuatis manibus ambulabis mihi nec obito consueto labore vitae nostrae prospicies et aliquid cibatui parabis?"

She opened the door and greeted her husband with harsh words as he entered: "Oh! So you'll stroll about just like that, with your hands entwined, free and at leisure? By not accepting your usual job – is this how you'll provide for our livelihood and put food on our table?"

The implication is clear – even his wife expects this man to use his hands for something more than entwining behind his back. The leisurely walk shows the same disregard for the economic potential of his legs as his alleged pose does for his hands. The irony of course is that the *wife*, not the husband, is the wasteful one: she has "filled" the jar in the corner with her lover, rather than something of commercial value.

Lurking behind discussions of the *ambulatio* are considerations of class and privilege that may not always seem obvious at first glance: the *ambulatio* advertised an economy of the body that Roman elites viewed as the exclusive privilege of certain members of society. In this sense, the *ambulatio* was a performance of the elite attitudes to pace and social status that we examined in Chapter 1, as exemplified by the figure of the running slave. Centuries before Apuleius, Cato the Elder puts the point even more bluntly; he insists that the head slave in charge of the farm "shouldn't be a walker" (*Agr.* 5.2: *vilicus ne sit ambulator*). The incongruity of this chapter's title – Cicero's legs – serves to remind us of what Roman elites tended to ignore when they discussed walking for leisure.[4] In the case of Cicero's walks, and of the Roman *ambulatio* more generally, the emphasis was squarely on the mind, not the body.

---

[4] The chapter title is also a nod to works on Cicero's head (Richlin 1999) and hand (Butler 2002).

EXERCISING BODY AND MIND

Despite the emphasis on the intellectual benefits of walking for leisure, the benefits of walking for physical health were not altogether lost on the Romans. Even the leisure spaces connected to performance venues could be promoted for their contribution to public health, as Vitruvius does in his passage on the utility of *ambulationes* attached to theaters (*De arch.* 5.9.5):

media vero spatia, quae erunt subdiu inter porticus, adornanda viridibus videntur, quod hypaethroe ambulationes habent magnam salubritatem. et primum oculorum, quod ex viridibus subtilis et extenuatus aer propter motionem corporis influens perlimat speciem et ita auferens ex oculis umorem crassum, aciem tenuem et acutam speciem relinquit; praeterea, cum corpus motionibus in ambulatione calescat, umores ex membris aer exsugendo inminuit plenitates extenuatque dissipando quod plus inest quam corpus potest sustinere.

The spaces in the middle, between the porticoes and open to the sky, should be decorated with greenery, since walks in the open air possess great health benefits. First of all, because of the movement of the body, the fine and rarefied air from the greenery flows into the eyes and sharpens the sight; in so doing it removes the heavy moisture from the eyes and leaves behind clear vision and sharp sight. Moreover, since the body heats up with movement during a walk, the air reduces saturation by sucking moisture out of the limbs, and thins them out by dissipating whatever is more than the body can sustain.

We do not know how many of Vitruvius' contemporaries would have characterized the benefits of walking with such scientific precision, but we should not underestimate the importance in ancient thought of the proper modulation of dry and humid in the body. The male body could become feminized if it became too cool and humid; walking thus served as a potent preventive against emasculation.[5]

Medical writers also commend the health benefits of walking. Celsus extols its curative powers for a number of ailments, from epilepsy to post-nasal drip. It is also one of the many activities he recommends for the weak (*inbecilli*), "in whose number are a great portion of those who live in cities and almost all those who love literature" (*Med.* 1.2.1: *quo in numero magna pars urbanorum omnesque paene cupidi litterarum sunt*); in other words, anyone who would be reading Celsus' text.[6] He adds that great care should be taken by these weaklings not only to walk but to walk correctly (*Med.* 1.2.6):

[5] On the dry body as a masculine ideal, see Gleason 1995, 84–91; cf. 94: "Everybody in the second century knew that women's bodies were colder and damper than men's."
[6] On the physical dangers of a literary life, see von Staden 2000 and Nisbet 2003.

commode vero exercent clara lectio, arma, pila, cursus, ambulatio, atque haec non utique plana commodior est, siquidem melius ascensus quoque et descensus cum quadam varietate corpus moveat, nisi tamen id perquam inbecillum est: melior autem est sub divo quam in porticu; melior, si caput patitur, in sole quam in umbra, <melior in umbra> quam paries aut viridia efficiunt, quam quae tecto subest; melior recta quam flexuosa.

The following activities certainly provide good exercise: reading out loud, weapons training, playing ball, running, walking – but walking on a level surface is not especially good, since it is better that the body move with some variation in ascent and descent, unless, however, that body is extremely weak; moreover, walking under the open sky is better than walking in a portico; it is better, if the head can endure it, to walk in the sun than in the shade; better to walk in the shade made by a wall or by plants, than in the shade under a roof; and a straight walk is better than a meandering one.

Celsus' recommendations push back against the tendencies of his age: as he well knows, the majority of those who walk for exercise in cities will do so in covered colonnades and porticoes. But his exhortations to get out in the open air also have a more particular target. Just as the rhetoric of masculinity lies below the surface of Vitruvius' commendation of walking in the open air, Celsus' recommendations are aimed especially at potential deviants from the masculine norm.[7]

References elsewhere in literature confirm that the medical benefits of walking were not known only to the "scientists." In a well-known letter (*Ep.* 3.1), Pliny describes the retired life of the elderly Vestricius Spurinna, whose daily routine is as regular as the passage of the stars or the rotation of the earth.[8] Spurinna's rigor in maintaining a strict and formal schedule even in his old age is praised as an exemplum of how (and when) to retire; he reminds the reader of his rigorous service to the state through the rigor he maintains in his private retirement.[9] As Pliny emphasizes, his day is strictly punctuated by different exercises, but at the core of his routine are his walks. As part of his daily regimen, he walks three miles as soon as he rises, another

---

[7] As Nisbet 2003, 195–7 has shown, Celsus' scholarly weakling is a close relative of the effeminate "thin man" (λεπτός) who is a target of Greek sympotic literature.

[8] The passage of the stars: "Moreover, a well-ordered human life pleases me no less than the unerring motion of the stars" (*Ep.* 3.1.2: *me autem ut certus siderum cursus ita vita hominum disposita delectat*). The rotation of the earth: "Spurinna keeps to this pattern most faithfully; indeed he even cycles through these small things – small, that is, unless they are done every day – in a specific order and a kind of rotation (*Ep.* 3.1.3: *hanc regulam Spurinna constantissime servat; quin etiam parva haec – parva si non cotidie fiant – ordine quodam et velut orbe circumagit*).

[9] On the ways in which Pliny turns *otium* into a form of symbolic capital whose productive use is enabled by the peace and security of Trajanic Rome, see Leach 2003.

mile mid-morning, and another mile (in the nude!) mid-afternoon.[10]
Such activities are not just about keeping himself in shape; he is also
keeping his mind sharp (*Ep.* 3.1.4):

mane lectulo continetur, hora secunda calceos poscit, ambulat milia passuum tria
nec minus animum quam corpus exercet. si adsunt amici, honestissimi sermones
explicantur; si non, liber legitur, interdum etiam praesentibus amicis, si tamen illi
non gravantur.

When day breaks he stays in bed, and at the second hour he asks for his shoes and
walks three miles, exercising his mind no less than his body. If there are friends
present, the most worthwhile conversations unfold; if not, a book is read aloud,
sometimes even when his friends are present, provided that it does not burden
them.

For Pliny, this routine is an ideal retirement. Spurinna continues to com-
bine intellectual pursuits with walking and companionship, just as a Roman
aristocrat of any age should do. But the nature of his retirement now means
that instead of heading to the forum with clients to conduct his daily
business, he enjoys the back-and-forth movement of a stroll on the grounds
of his own private villa. Though his political life has been left behind, the
links between walking and thinking remain central to his vigor and to his
routine; Spurinna and his friends even make their way through a text as they
move through space.

The intellectual focus of Spurinna's walk recalls Pliny's own summertime
practice at his Tuscan villa; among the many daily activities of his life of
leisure is an after-dinner walk "with members of [his] household, among
whom there are men of learning" (Plin. *Ep.* 9.36.4: *mox cum meis ambulo,
quorum in numero sunt eruditi*).[11] The second part of that sentence is no
mere aside, but rather a way of advertising the intellectual content of the
ambling conversations of Pliny and his companions: his description presumes an awareness on the part of the reader that a walk with friends would
naturally include an erudite discussion. In this way Pliny's after-dinner
ambulatio is a natural complement to his solitary morning walk described
earlier in the letter, which is also as much an intellectual as a physical

---

[10] On Spurinna's regimen, and its mix of physical, intellectual, and social activities, see Johnson 2000,
      621–4; see also Henderson 2002 for the various ways in which Pliny's portraits of Spurinna and his
      uncle (*Ep.* 3.5) serve not only as models for behavior but also as contrasting paradigms of his own
      literary (and political) project. On the "daily round" motif in Roman culture, see Mielsch 1987,
      128–33; Laurence 1994, 124–32; Riggsby 2003, 179–86.
[11] According to Plutarch (*Cat. Min.* 68.1), Cato the Younger was also in the habit of enjoying an after-
      dinner walk with friends. For a comparison of the villa routines of Pliny and Spurinna, see Leach 2003,
      161–2. On the emphasis on time in Pliny's villa letters, see Riggsby 2003.

exercise: he tells us that he composes and dictates while he strolls.[12] Pliny is careful to emphasize the ways in which walking can exercise both body and mind; in the following section, we shall see that other authors besides Pliny frequently associated the *ambulatio* with friendly conversation. For Cicero in particular, the physical benefits of the *ambulatio* were eclipsed by its intellectual virtues.

WALKING AND TALKING

References to leisurely walks abound in Cicero's letters, and the activity is inevitably connected with conversation, consultation, joking, and other expressions of *amicitia*. These bonds could be tested, of course, by the author's distance from his friends. The epistolary genre often draws attention to the separation of writer and addressee that makes communication by letter necessary in the first place, and Cicero's letters are no different in this regard.[13] What stands out is the way in which Cicero so often expresses a wish not just to be reunited with the addressee but more specifically to take a walk with him, such as in Cicero's desperate plea to his friend Atticus, which we encountered in the introduction (*Att.* 1.18.1):

quare te exspectamus, te desideramus, te iam etiam arcessimus. multa sunt enim, quae me sollicitant anguntque; quae mihi videor aures nactus tuas unius ambulationis sermone exhaurire posse.

And so then I wait for you, I miss your company, I even demand your return. For there are many things that are worrying and distressing me, and if I only had your ear, I feel I could pour them all out in one walk's conversation.

The walk was such a standard setting for conversation, and such a standard part of the experience of friendship, that Cicero can easily refer to it as a unit of time (*unius ambulationis sermone*).[14] It can also function as a symbol of spatial proximity, as Cicero makes clear in a letter he wrote to his friend M. Caelius Rufus while serving as governor of Cilicia in 50 BCE; in the final section of the letter, Cicero bemoans his distance from his beloved friends and from his beloved city (*Fam.* 2.12.2–3):

---

[12] Plin. *Ep.* 9.36.3. Seneca (*Ep.* 15.6) also points out that exercise, and walking in particular, need not interfere with one's studies, and can even be an occasion for reading and dictating. Cicero dictated at least two of his letters while walking (*Att.* 2.23.1; *Q Fr.* 3.3.1), although he cites these instances as proof of how busy he is.

[13] On Cicero's references to the benefits and drawbacks of communication by letter, see Jenkins 2006, 37–50.

[14] Ovid (*Pont.* 4.5.38–9) also makes a connection between the measurement of time and the length of a walk with a friend, although in his case the walk lasts the entire day (see below).

urbem, urbem, mi Rufe, cole et in ista luce vive! omnis peregrinatio, quod ego ab adulescentia iudicavi, obscura et sordida est iis quorum industria Romae potest illustris esse. quod cum probe scirem, utinam in sententia permansissem! cum una mehercule ambulatiuncula atque uno sermone nostro omnis fructus provinciae non confero ... spem triumphi inicis: satis gloriose triumpharem; non essem quidem tam diu in desiderio rerum mihi carissimarum.

Rome, my dear Rufus, live in Rome and dwell in its light! I have been of the opinion ever since I was a boy that living abroad is a gloomy and dingy prospect for those whose ambition can shine at Rome. And since I well knew that, I wish I had stayed with my beliefs! By Hercules, all the benefits of provincial service do not compare to one little walk with you or one of our conversations ... You hint that I might hope for a triumph: my triumph would have been nice enough all right, but I shouldn't be apart from everything that is precious to me for so long.

The honor (and potential profit) of serving as governor of a remote province cannot compare to the brilliance of Rome, where every action has greater significance. Cicero longs for his walks and talks with Caelius not simply because walking is a nice way to spend one's free time – presumably he had free time in Cilicia as well – but because it is a way to stay in touch with one's friends and political allies. Cicero's walks are a way of reaffirming and maintaining his ties to a fellow senator and of staying in the political loop. Indeed the pleasure they hold far outweighs the benefits of provincial service; he would prefer, it seems, the private pleasures of a walk with a few friends to the public procession of a triumphal parade – the ultimate sign of a successful term in the provinces.

The private *ambulatio* was therefore clearly a privilege of close friend-ships, and was quite different (and felt to be so) from the public promenades of a Roman statesman and his throng of political allies, clients, and attend-ants. Cicero makes the contrast clear in the same letter to Atticus cited above, in a passage we encountered in the previous chapter (*Att.* 1.18.1):

nam illae ambitiosae nostrae fucosaeque amicitiae sunt in quodam splendore forensi, fructum domesticum non habent. itaque, cum bene completa domus est tempore matutino, cum ad forum stipati gregibus amicorum descendimus, reperire ex magna turba neminem possumus, quocum aut iocari libere aut suspirare familiariter possimus.

Those phony political friendships of mine have a certain shine in the forum, but they bring me no personal pleasure. Yes, my house is quite crowded in the morning, and I go down to the forum accompanied by herds of friends, but out of that entire crowd I can find no one with whom I can joke freely or sigh intimately.

Cicero draws a sharp divide between public and private, between business and leisure, between *clientes* and *amici*, between the crowds at home and the forum, and the singular lack of his best friend Atticus. Separation and absence are the generative force of the epistolary genre, which in turn strives to overcome them.[15] A letter, however, can only be a substitute for conversation, not for physical presence, and quite often the *ambulatio* in Cicero's letters becomes a symbol of the physical activity, and the physical proximity, that a letter cannot provide. Hence the constant emphasis on laughing, joking, dialogue – all the forms of conversation that depend on a give and take, an immediacy, a here-and-now element that a letter lacks. Pollio even ends a letter to Cicero by threatening to spend his retirement in a constant walk with him (*Fam.* 10.31.6):

quod familiarem meum tuorum numero habes, opinione tua mihi gratius est; invideo illi tamen, quod ambulat et iocatur tecum. quaeres, quanti id aestimem? si umquam licuerit vivere in otio, experieris; nullum enim vestigium abs te discessurus sum.

That you consider my friend one of your own is more pleasing to me than you can imagine. And yet I am jealous, because he is able to walk and joke around with you. How much do I think that privilege is worth, you ask? If we ever get to live a life of leisure, you'll find out: I won't be separated from you, not by a single step.

It is noteworthy that Pollio assumes that Cicero would signal his acceptance of this new friend by walking and joking with him; Pollio wistfully recalls the times that he and Cicero had spent together, and ends his letter in a way that emphasizes the separation and distance that their epistolary communication presupposes. For although he suggests hopefully that they might one day spend a life of perpetual leisure together, that eventuality would in fact mean the end of their epistolary relationship; he ends the letter, in other words, with an implicit desire to put an end to letter-writing, period.

This paradox of employing a genre to express a longing to make it obsolete is also conveyed by Ovid in his letters from Tomis, in which he takes full advantage of the creative possibilities of distance and exile, while also begging for those conditions to be lifted.[16] In one of his letters from exile, he writes to his friend Macer, reminiscing about the travels they had

---

[15] For this point, see Jenkins 2006, 9: "more than any other type of writing, letters emphasize the gap – whether temporal or spatial – between any sender and recipient: epistles are both emblematic of the gap and of human attempts to transcend it."

[16] The ways in which Ovid plays with motifs of exclusion and banishment in his exile poetry has clear literary affinity with aspects of his earlier work (e.g. the *exclusus amator*, the abandoned heroine); see Holzberg 1997, 181–3.

together, especially the way in which their conversations lightened their journey (*Pont.* 2.10.35–8):

> saepe brevis nobis vicibus via visa loquendi
>   pluraque, si numeres, verba fuere gradu.
> saepe dies sermone minor fuit inque loquendum
>   tarda per aestivos defuit hora dies.

The twists and turns of our talks often made our journey seem short; if you had counted them, our words surely outnumbered our steps. Often the day was shorter than our conversation, and the late hour of summer days did not suffice for our talking.

In his usual clever way, Ovid makes explicit the connection we have been exploring between walking and talking by suggesting a connection between the number of words and the number of steps: the irreducible parts, as it were, of their time together, and of their friendship. Later in the letter, Ovid tells Macer that he often recreates these conversations in his head, transporting his friend in his imagination to the harsh landscape of the Black Sea; Ovid asks him to return the favor and summon him in his mind to the more pleasant climes of Rome (*Pont.* 2.10.49–52). Ovid offers a remedy for separation and exile by emphasizing the powers of the imagination – and the power of the epistolary genre – to overcome the barriers of distance, and to reconstruct the physical experiences of friendship that require proximity, such as walking and talking together.[17] In this respect, Ovid may have influenced the philosopher Seneca, who makes a more explicit claim that the epistolary genre establishes a metaphorical space where friends can not only converse, but also dine and walk together (*Ep.* 55.11):

amicus animo possidendus est; hic autem numquam abest; quemcumque vult cotidie videt. itaque mecum stude, mecum cena, mecum ambula; in angusto vivebamus, si quicquam esset cogitationibus clusum. video te, mi Lucili; cum maxime audio; adeo tecum sum ut dubitem an incipiam non epistulas sed codicellos tibi scribere.

A friend must be kept in your mind, because the mind can never go away; it sees whomever it wants, every day. So then, study with me, dine with me, walk with me; we'd be in a tight spot indeed, if anything was closed off from our thoughts. I see you, my Lucilius; at this very moment I can even hear you. In fact I'm so close to you that I'm not sure whether I should begin to write you notes instead of letters.

Like Ovid, Seneca privileges the imaginary space of literature; the imagined act of walking (along with dining and studying) becomes a metaphor for *amicitia* itself. Seneca wants to privilege the mental experience of friendship,

---

[17] On the ways in which this poem emphasizes the power of poetry to transcend physical boundaries, and on the metaliterary implications of Ovid and Macer's journey, see Williams 1994, 42–8.

but to do so he can only resort to the familiar, daily experiences of time spent together, including the act of walking.[18]

The intimate connection between walking and talking in the Roman imagination made the *ambulatio* a common setting not only for time spent with friends but also for what we would call business meetings. We have already seen in the previous chapter Cicero's evocation of an archaic practice whereby important men would advertise their availability for consultation by strolling in the forum (*De or.* 3.133). The superior knowledge of the man offering advice to his fellow Romans suggests that the relative status of the men would be clear even before they started their walk. Yet surely part of the appeal of the *ambulatio* as a setting for dispensing advice was the illusion of equality as two or more men walked side by side. Part of the service that the great man performs is submitting himself to the equalizing power of walking with a man who might normally walk after or before him, as a client, or approach him seated during the morning salutation (the other setting for advice dispensation that Cicero mentions).[19] So too in the private home: Vitruvius tells us that the houses of noblemen should include "very large atria and peristyles, plantings and rather spacious walkways finished to a suitably splendid degree ... because in their homes they provide both consultations on public affairs and private decisions and opinions" (*De arch.* 6.5.2: *atria et peristylia amplissima, silvae ambulationesque laxiores ad decorem maiestatis perfectae ... quod in domibus eorum saepius et publica consilia et privata iudicia arbitriaque conficiuntur*).[20] The peristyle has commonly been described as the part of the elite house devoted to the *otium* of the home-owner, in contrast to the more public and *negotium*-focused atrium (on which more below); clearly, Vitruvius' description complicates that tidy picture. Yet at the same time the appeal of the peristyle for serious

---

[18] On the passage, see Ker 2002, 151–3; Saylor 2002. Cf. Sen. *Ep.* 75.1: "Just as I would talk if we were sitting or walking together – effortlessly and easily – that's how I want my letters to be" (*qualis sermo meus esset si una desideremus aut ambularemus, inlaboratus et facilis, tales esse epistulas meas volo*). Cicero also implies that a letter can unite the writer and recipient in a metaphorical walk; recounting for Atticus the state of affairs in Rome, he turns to an update on the electoral campaign by suggesting that he follow him into the Campus Martius (*Att.* 4.15.7). Also relevant are Pliny's well-known villa letters, in which he takes his addressee on a metaphorical tour of his Laurentine (*Ep.* 2.17) and Tuscan (*Ep.* 5.6) estates; see Bergmann 1995b. Riggsby 2003 complicates the usual reading of the letters as metaphorical tours, preferring the analogy of "a stack of (potentially resortable) snapshots" (175); his observation nicely accounts for the surprising *lack* of references to walking in the letters.

[19] Yet walking is not completely equalizing – there are privileged positions when walking in groups, as the parents of Cicero's friends angrily noted when they saw their children giving the young upstart from Arpinum the central position in their school-yard strolls (Plut. *Cic.* 2.2).

[20] MacDonald and Pinto 1995, 62 suggest that some of the ambulatory spaces at Hadrian's villa were likely used as places to conduct business while strolling.

discussion and consultation surely lay in the association of the *ambulatio* with conversation and *amicitia*.[21]

Holding a meeting while walking added a veneer of friendliness to a relationship that could be anything but friendly. Suetonius tells us that Tiberius would only give his political enemy (and potential assassin) Libo a private interview if his son Drusus were present: "and however long the conversation lasted, pretending he needed support, he kept a firm grip on Libo's right hand as he walked along" (Suet. *Tib*. 25: *secretum petenti* [sc. *Liboni*] *non nisi adhibito Druso filio dedit dextramque obambulantis veluti incumbens, quoad perageretur sermo, continuit*). Suetonius feels compelled to take note of Tiberius' special precautions during this walk, but the act of walking itself as a scene for political maneuvering, even with one's enemies, was *de rigueur*. Similarly, the younger Pliny describes a meeting with his friend Spurinna in the Portico of Livia, when Spurinna was pleading on behalf of M. Regulus to end their very public quarrel (*Ep*. 1.5.8–10). The Portico of Livia was a public space, and though it did not offer the privacy of a domestic peristyle, it still offered the covered colonnades and garden walkways that were conducive to walking and talking.[22] In short, the popularity of walking during business meetings depended in large measure upon the cultural practice of friends walking together at leisure, for it created the illusion that the meeting was more casual and friendly than it might actually have been.

There were, of course, occasional instances where Romans longed to be freed from the expectation of conversation during their walks. But the very way that such exceptions were made reveals the dominance of the norm. As we saw in the introduction to this book, Cicero points out that certain behaviors considered unacceptable in the easy setting of the *convivium* are entirely appropriate while walking or journeying with friends (*Off*. 1.144). He insists that we should not begrudge a fellow walker his silent reflection if he is thinking through a particularly intractable problem or working on a case; one suspects that Cicero is defending his own behavior in the course of making a point about manners. Walking with others is not *only* about conversation, in other words, though Cicero's insistence on special exceptions does suggest that friendly or studious conversation is the "default"

---

[21] Leach 2004, 34 suggests that the slight dissonance between the public and private associations of the peristyle arises from its use "as a transitional zone whose function is not so much exclusion as that of giving an elegant route of access to other privileged rooms situated on its corridors." For a discussion of Roman notions of privacy using the Roman house as a test case, see Riggsby 1997.

[22] On the significance of the portico setting in the encounter between Pliny and Spurinna, see Frakes 2009, 32–3. On the Portico of Livia, see Macaulay-Lewis 2009, 11–14.

mode of a walk with friends. Pliny makes a similar point in his description of Spurinna's morning walk (*Ep.* 3.1.4), which we encountered earlier in this chapter. When he has guests, Spurinna usually engages them in dignified conversation as they walk, but at times (provided it doesn't bother them) he subjects his guests to the activity he enjoys during his solitary walks: reading. Or rather, being read to: it was customary for elite Romans to employ a *lector*, so even Spurinna's "solitary" walks are most likely in the presence of a slave.[23] As a result, its verbal and performative quality makes this act of reading more akin to conversation than it is in our version of reading culture, as the master could ask his slave to pause and go back over a particular passage.[24] Nonetheless, the very way that Cicero and Pliny portray the act of avoiding conversation while walking as a special exception reveals the normative power of the association.

Ideally, however, the presence of good friends only enhanced the intellectual pretensions of the Roman *ambulatio*. As bodies moved, conversations advanced, and the discussion was free to follow the contours and sights of the surrounding space.[25] Then as now, the movement of the body might mimic the movement of the conversation. Those who have had the pleasure of walking with Italian friends, for example, can see the manipulation of movement forward as a kind of punctuation: the walker stops, for instance, when a particularly important point needs to be made, providing the physical equivalent of a boldface font or an exclamation point. Yet the connection between walking and talking can simultaneously serve to draw attention away from the body: the regular rhythm of a walk gives the mind freedom to wander as attention to the body recedes. This type of mental inquiry had particular associations in the Roman imagination; as we shall see in the next section, the intellectual associations of walking for leisure also have a historical explanation, since the Romans associated this activity with the Greeks in particular.

GREEK WALKING

During the Second Punic War, a senatorial debate arose in response to a delegation from the Sicilian town of Locri, where Pleminius, an officer under the command of Scipio Africanus, was abusing his position of power

---

[23] On *lectores*, see Starr 1991.

[24] On the performative and social nature of ancient reading culture, see Johnson 2000, 615–24.

[25] Hence the common use of walking in philosophical dialogue, whereby the participants encounter a certain object that then inspires the conversation; see e.g. Cic. *De or.* 1.28, *Leg.* 1.1, 2.3; Min. Fel. *Oct.* 2–3.

and treating the local allies as a conquered enemy. Scipio's political enemies blamed the lax behavior of the general as much as his officer (Livy 29.19.11–12):

praeter Plemini facinus Locrensiumque cladem ipsius etiam imperatoris non Romanus modo sed ne militaris quidem cultus iactabatur: cum pallio crepidisque inambulare in gymnasio; libellis eum palaestraeque operam dare; aeque [segniter] molliter cohortem totam Syracusarum amoenitate frui

In addition to the villainy of Pleminius and the devastation of the Locrians they openly discussed the very lifestyle of the general himself as not only un-Roman but even unmilitary: that he walked around in the gymnasium in a Greek cloak and sandals; that he was devoting his attention to little books and to the wrestling-ground; and that his entire cohort was enjoying the pleasures of Syracuse with equal effeminacy.

One is not quite sure which is worse: that Scipio dresses like a non-soldier, or like a non-Roman. However true the accusation, Scipio's Greek affectations carry the same ideological charge as the "villainy of Pleminius and the devastation of the Locrians." The accusations are clearly intended for a larger audience than the senate, and the attempt to discredit an opposing politician as unpatriotic, effete, and out of touch is still an effective technique today.[26] By sauntering around in Greek dress in the gymnasium, Scipio became an eternal symbol of the delicate balance a Roman leader had to strike when walking for leisure.[27] Tacitus even cites Scipio in his condemnation of Germanicus' walks in Egypt centuries later (*Ann.* 2.59):

M. Silano L. Norbano consulibus Germanicus Aegyptum proficiscitur cognoscendae antiquitatis. sed cura provinciae praetendebatur, levavitque apertis horreis pretia frugum multaque in vulgus grata usurpavit: sine milite incedere, pedibus intectis et pari cum Graecis amictu, P. Scipionis aemulatione, quem eadem factitavisse apud Siciliam, quamvis flagrante adhuc Poenorum bello, accepimus.

When Silanus and Norbanus were consuls [19 CE] Germanicus traveled to Egypt to become familiar with its antiquity. But concern for the province was a pretense: by throwing open the warehouses he lowered the price of grain and made use of many other things that pleased the masses. He walked around without soldiers, with his feet uncovered and in a cloak similar to the Greeks, in emulation of Scipio

---

[26] Cf. John Kerry's alleged Francophilia during the 2004 U.S. presidential race, which pegged him as both aristocratic and un-American; see Milligan 2004.

[27] Valerius Maximus, for instance, leads off his chapter "Illustrious Men Who Indulged Themselves in Dress or Other Refinements More Freely Than our National Custom Allowed" (3.6: *Qui ex illustribus viris in veste aut cetero cultu licentius sibi quam mos patrius permittebat indulserunt*) with Scipio's Sicilian exploits (3.6.1).

Africanus who, we understand, used to do the same things in Sicily, even though the Punic War was still raging.

Germanicus' strolls – in Greek slippers and Greek clothing – consciously evoke the behavior of Scipio in Sicily, according to the historian. Yet Tacitus is in somewhat of a bind here; presumably Germanicus' behavior in Egypt would not have pleased the Roman masses, yet elsewhere in the *Annals* he goes out of his way to depict Germanicus as a demagogue. The historian's clever solution is to mark his behavior as a concession to the provincial locals in Egypt. Germanicus thus becomes not only a demagogue, but also one whose behavior will change according to the character of the *demos* in question.

Scipio and Germanicus are blameworthy for adopting not only foreign dress but also foreign behavior; the implication is that their very manner of walking was patently non-Roman. The gulf of time that separates these two generals (and the century or so between Livy and Tacitus) testify to the persistent power of this idea in Roman culture. And the association of leisurely walking with Greek culture shows up in some of the earliest Latin literature, as a passage in Plautus' *Curculio* reveals. Here the title character complains about the thoughtless pedestrians who get in the way of the *servus currens*, giving us a fuller picture of what walking Greeks looked like in the Roman imagination (*Curc.* 288–91):

> tum isti Graeci palliati, capite operto qui ambulant,
> qui incedunt suffarcinati cum libris, cum sportulis,
> constant, conferunt sermones inter se<se> drapetae,
> obstant, obsistunt, incedunt cum suis sententiis.

And then there's those cloak-wearing Greeks who walk around with their heads covered, who stroll along stuffed with books and goody-bags. They stand around and talk things over like fugitives; they stop, they stand in your way, they saunter along with their aphorisms.

The stereotype that certain Greeks pay no heed to their surroundings is already familiar from Crassus' complaint in the *De oratore* with which this chapter began. The Greek walk does not pay enough attention to the walking itself: conversation, deep thought, and other mental activity take precedence over the steady movement forward of a more considerate walker.

The association of Greeks in particular with this style of careless walking has a history: Greek philosophers were notorious walkers.[28]

---

[28] Csapo 1989, 150–4 in fact reads the Plautus passage just cited as an adaptation of a Greek original, in which the joke was aimed specifically at philosophers. On the connection between wandering and Greek philosophy, see Montiglio 2005, 100–17 and 147–220.

The Peripatetics, after all, earned their nickname "because they used to discuss while walking in the Lyceum," an Athenian gymnasium (Cic. *Acad. post.* 1.17: *quia disputabant inambulantes in Lycio*); the Stoics, similarly, were associated with the Stoa Poikile in Athens, another ambulatory space.[29] According to Aulus Gellius (*NA* 20.5.5), *peripatos* – a word that, like Latin *ambulatio*, can refer either to the act of walking or to a space for it – was used by Aristotle as a metaphor for "discussion" or "lecture." At one point, Aristophanes even uses the word to mean "topic of discussion," which suggests that the metaphorical application of the word may precede Aristotle.[30] Certainly before Aristotle's union of walking and philosophical discussion comes Plato, whose ambulatory tendencies are the subject of ridicule in one of Alexis' fragments (fr. 151 *PCG*):[31]

εἰς καιρὸν ἥκεις· ὡς ἔγωγ' ἀπορουμένη
ἄνω κάτω τε περιπατοῦσ' ὥσπερ Πλάτων
σοφὸν οὐδὲν εὕρηκ', ἀλλὰ κοπιῶ τὰ σκέλη.

You've arrived just in time: in my confusion, I've been walking back and forth like Plato, but I haven't been able to come up with anything clever: I have, however, worn out my legs.

Plato's dialogues indeed give us many examples of philosophers on the move, strolling while they argue, perhaps most memorably in the beginning of the *Protagoras*, when Socrates and Hippocrates arrive at the house of Callias only to see Protagoras and his acolytes pacing in flight-formation back and forth in the courtyard (*Prt.* 314e–315b). Montiglio (2005, 171–9) has argued that walking in the Socratic dialogues typically serves only as an intellectual warm-up, and that the serious conversations are held while everyone is seated. This is generally true: in the *Protagoras*, for instance, Socrates and Hippocrates converse a little while pacing in the courtyard of Socrates' house, and then while en route to see Protagoras; after watching with some amusement the choreography of Protagoras and his followers, they initiate serious dialogue while everyone is seated.[32] Moreover, Plato

---

[29] On the connection between the Stoics and the Stoa Poikile, see Camp 1986, 72. The connection between Stoic philosophers and walking persisted; centuries later, Seneca will reminisce about engaging his teacher Attalus in philosophical debates while he walked (*Ep.* 108.3).

[30] Ar. *Ran.* 953, a reference I owe to Jud Herrman.

[31] Cited by Montiglio 2005, 173.

[32] There are, however, exceptions, as Montiglio notes: the *Laws* take place while the characters are walking (*Leg.* 625a–b), as does the outer narrative of the *Symposium* (though not, of course, the actual dialogue; *Symp.* 173b). The *Theages* takes place in the stoa of Zeus Eleutherios (121a), though it is not clear whether the participants are sitting or walking.

also represents the act of concentrated thought as a *pause* in walking: in the *Symposium*, Socrates arrives late to the party after standing for some time lost in thought (175a–c), while during the symposium itself Alcibiades recalls the time that the philosopher spent a full day and night standing in place, even attracting an audience, while puzzling over a particular problem (220c–d).[33] "His immobility as a thinker," as Montiglio (2005, 173) neatly puts it, "reflects his unshakeable commitment to philosophy."

But whatever the reality of the situation – that is, whether Socrates and company "really" walked and talked even as much as Plato depicts – it is undeniable that Greek philosophers had a reputation for ambulatory conversation, and that the connection between walking and philosophical dialogue was exploited by Roman authors as well. Although many of his philosophical dialogues also take place while the characters are seated, Cicero in fact uses the motif of the strolling conversation more often than Plato does. In addition to the second book of the *De oratore*, the first book of the *De legibus* recounts a walk on Cicero's property in Arpinum. Books 1–4 of the *Tusculan Disputations* take place while the characters stroll in the "Academy" of Cicero's Tusculan villa; the first book of the *De divinatione* takes place in the same villa, as the characters walk in Cicero's "Lyceum." The trend continues in the first two books of the *De finibus*, set in the *ambulatio* of Cicero's villa at Cumae, as well as in the fifth book, which recounts an afternoon walk in Plato's Academy in Athens.[34] Cicero's slight departure from the Platonic model in the relative frequency of walking dialogues may reflect his eclectic independence from strict allegiance to any philosophical school.[35] The ambulatory setting of the second book of the *De oratore* has in fact been read in a similarly metaliterary way by Leeman *et al.* (1985, 183), who suggest that the pose of the participant speakers reflects the character of the discussion: the Platonic first book is set beneath a plane tree that explicitly evokes the setting of the *Phaedrus* (*De or.* 1.28), while the fact that the second book takes place while the characters walk in Crassus' portico (*De or.* 2.12, 2.20) may evoke the Aristotelian *peripatos*.[36]

---

[33] The anecdote is part of a speech by Alcibiades on Socrates' amazing physical endurance, which became part of his popular image; the chorus in Aristophanes' *Clouds*, alluding to Socrates, suggests that you too can be a philosopher "if you don't get tired out standing or walking" (*Nub.* 415: καὶ μὴ κάμνεις μήθ' ἑστὼς μήτε βαδίζων).

[34] For the references to walking in each of these dialogues, see *Leg.* 1.15, 2.1; *Tusc.* 1.7, 2.10, 3.7, and 4.7; *Div.* 1.8; *Fin.* 2.119, 5.1.

[35] Cicero's philosophical allegiances are somewhat controversial; see Glucker 1988.

[36] On the literary staging of the dialogue and the correspondences with Plato's *Phaedrus*, see Görler 1988. On the evidence for the use of plane trees in Roman landscaping, see Jashemski 1979, 51–3 and 331.

For Cicero, then, the appeal of walking as a dramatic backdrop for philosophy was twofold. On the one hand, the pose of the participants explicitly recalls the popular image (both literary and cultural) of strolling Greek philosophers. On the other hand, walking for leisure was also a regular habit of the Roman aristocracy, as we have seen; by situating these dialogues in the leisure practices of Roman villa culture, Cicero recreates an environment that was recognizably familiar to a certain segment of his readership. By casting his Roman aristocrat-philosophers as strolling and talking, Cicero dramatizes, in the very poses and movements of his characters, his entire philosophical project: the importation and adaptation of Greek philosophical ideas to a uniquely Roman setting.[37]

There may, therefore, be another reason why Cicero eclipses Plato in the frequency of his ambulatory dialogues: the discrepancy may be further evidence for the Roman attempt to "out-Greek" the Greeks in the privacy of their own increasingly Hellenized villas in the late republic, as parodied by Varro in his *De re rustica* (2 pr. 2). It is no accident that the majority of Cicero's philosophical works are set in the Roman villa, where the boundary between Greek and Roman was under constant negotiation.[38] The abundance of colonnaded walkways and garden paths in Roman villa design served to remind the visitor not simply of Greek architectural forms, but of activities, patterns of movement, styles and topics of conversation that were all marked as Hellenized. Recall Catulus' words in the *De oratore* with which the chapter began, where he explicitly compares the portico of Crassus' Tusculan villa in which they are walking to similarly appointed Greek gymnasia and palaestrae.[39] We may be tempted to dismiss such comparisons as part of the literary staging, since the dialogue self-consciously sets itself up in emulation and rivalry with Plato's *Phaedrus*. Yet Cicero's private correspondence also testifies to the Roman fashion for equipping villas with Hellenized spaces. He shows great concern in a number of letters to Atticus that his new Tusculan peristyle be decorated in a fashion appropriate to a palaestra and gymnasium, notoriously going so far as to refer to it quite regularly as his "Academy" (his "Lyceum" would be added later). In doing so, he was following the lead of his contemporaries, who strove to recreate in the

---

[37] See Zetzel 2003 for a more general study of Cicero's attitudes to Greek culture, using the *De oratore* as a frame.

[38] Bergmann 2001, 155–63; for the combination of Greek and Roman elements in the domestic sphere more generally, see Beltrán Fortes 1995; Zanker 1998, 16–19 and 33–43; Wallace-Hadrill 1998, 88–91.

[39] On the history and social function of the Greek *gymnasion*, see Delorme 1960 and Fisher 1998.

seclusion of their country estates various natural and man-made land-marks from the Greek east.[40]

The aim of evoking the world of the gymnasium in the private home was clear: these were spaces intended to advertise the intellectual refinement of the homeowner, spaces for conversation and reflection with friends. The Greek civic spaces that offered a setting for the intellectual gymnastics of philosophers had been transplanted to private retreats in the Roman countryside, where not only the architecture and decor (statues, paintings) but even the poses of the gentlemen (sitting on benches, strolling in porticoes) recreated Hellenized repose. Particularly essential to this recreation were ambulatory spaces: not only porticoes, but also garden paths, cryptoporticoes, and *xysti*.[41] Walking for leisure was thus not only a privilege of the cultured Roman elite, but also a scene for the Roman negotiation of Greek culture. The intellectual discussion that often accompanied such walks, the spaces in which these walks occurred, even the notion of leisure as a goal to be pursued – all were marked as Greek in the Roman imagination, and were attributed to the Hellenization of Roman aristocratic culture that was a feature of Rome's history from the very beginning but was especially associated with the second century BCE.[42]

It is surely not a coincidence that during this period the Pompeian house began to incorporate the peristyle, a garden area surrounded by porticoes on one or more sides.[43] The Pompeian town house of the late second century BCE (the so-called atrium house) expands to accommodate a peristyle at the back, an open court or garden surrounded by covered colonnades (hence Vitruvius' use of the term *peristylium*).[44] The use of a Greek word to

---

[40] Cicero mentions his Academy (either by name or by indirect reference) in a number of early letters to Atticus (see *Att.* 1.4, 1.6, 1.8, 1.9, 1.10, and 1.11); on his "Lyceum," see *Div.* 1.8. For the villa decoration of Cicero and his contemporaries, see Neudecker 1988, 8–30. On the phenomenon of naming parts of the villa for other places, see Görler 1990, 169–74.

[41] The use of the term *xystus* (or *xystum*) by the Romans for a space different from the one that the Greeks termed a ξυστός (according to Vitruvius, *De arch.* 5.11.4 and 6.7.5, the latter was covered, and the Roman *xystus* was not) highlights the fact that the effect of these borrowings was felt to be more important than their accuracy. See Leach 2004, 38.

[42] See esp. Gruen 1992.

[43] On the Roman domestic peristyle, see Maiuri 1946, 316–22; Grimal 1984, 206–16; Wallace-Hadrill 1994, 17–23; Dickmann 1997; Ellis 2000, 31–5; Leach 2004, 34–40. Mielsch 1987, 97 sees the rise of peristyles in town houses and palaestrae in villas as completely independent, which seems unlikely. The inconsistent nomenclature of Roman ambulatory spaces defies such easy categorization; see Dickmann 1999, 35–7 for an overview of the terms and their uses. A more likely explanation is offered by Leach 2004, who treats the rise of such spaces in town houses, villas, and even in public buildings (such as the Portico of Pompey) as aspects of the same phenomenon: the "concept of the peristyle as a seat of intellectual self-representation" (40).

[44] Despite the almost universal adoption of the term "peristyle" in modern literature, the use of *peristyl(i)um* to describe this part of the house is extremely rare outside of Vitruvius' work; see Maiuri 1946, 306–16 and Leach 1997, 59.

describe this new space is telling, and the shift from atrium house to peristyle house is usually understood as a reflex of the increased Hellenization of Roman culture.[45] In particular, the peristyle offered a space for privileged access at the rear of the *domus*, as opposed to the more public atrium at the front of the house.[46] Larger peristyles (such as those in the House of the Faun at Pompeii) would allow the homeowner to offer his privileged guests a private space for ambling conversation, a space that advertised not only the wealth but also the culture of the *dominus*.[47] Smaller peristyles may or may not have provided enough space for a relaxed stroll, but in either case conveyed the homeowner's commitment to a Hellenized leisure.

But, as we shall see in the next chapter, the fascination with walking among the Roman aristocracy was more than a simple tribute to the lifestyle of Greek philosophers. Rather, it was a manifestation of a deep-seated cultural metaphor, also inherited from Greece, that connected the movement of the body and the movement of the mind. The physical setting of elite walks may have been the colonnades and porticoes of Roman houses and villas, but the mental journeys inspired by such walks aimed for far greater destinations.

---

[45] For a critique of the traditional evolutionary model, see Wallace-Hadrill 1997.
[46] Wallace-Hadrill 1994, 38–60 is the most useful treatment of the different levels of access in the *domus*; see also Grahame 1997; Dickmann 1999, esp. 41–8; and Hales 2003, 97–134.
[47] On the peristyles of the House of the Faun, see Dickmann 1997.

CHAPTER 5

Theoretical travels

In the opening scene of Varro's *De re rustica*, the author arrives at the temple of Tellus on the Carinae in Rome only to find some acquaintances already there, contemplating a picture of Italy on the wall.[1] After some brief pleas-antries, one of these acquaintances, Agrasius, initiates the dialogue proper with a question: "Tell me, since you've all walked through many lands, have you ever seen a place more cultivated than Italy?" (*Rust.* 1.2.3: *vos, qui multas perambulastis terras, ecquam cultiorem Italia vidistis?*). Agrasius' use of *peram-bulare* ("walk through") to refer to extensive travels is particularly suggestive.[2] As the opening question reveals, the painting of Italy is not only the inspiration for their conversation, but also a visual metaphor for the entire book, which invites the reader to contemplate Varro's representation of the fertile Italian countryside.[3] The reference to travel thus anticipates the dis-cussion that follows: although the participants sit on benches in the middle of Rome, their conversation will stroll through Italian farms and fields.

As we shall see in this chapter, walking is an apt metaphor for the travels that Varro and his friends have undertaken throughout the Mediterranean, and are about to embark on in their dialogue. This intersection of literal and metaphorical journeys encapsulates a cultural metaphor that exerted great influence on Greek philosophical thought and Roman leisure practices: the

---

[1] The painting is often referred to as a map, although the Latin is not so specific; Varro finds his friends "looking at Italy painted on the wall" (*Rust.* 1.2.1: *spectantes in pariete pictam Italiam*). Heurgon 1978, 102 argues that Varro here alludes to a map that happens to be unattested elsewhere; Dilke 1998, 39 has a similar interpretation. On the other hand, Kubitschek 1919, col. 2042 points out that the painting may just be a personification of Italy.

[2] *Perambulare* is used, e.g., of the travels of Hadrian, "who had a love of not only ruling the world but also traveling it" (Fronto *Ep.* 229.16–17 van den Hout: *orbis terrarum non regendi tantum, sed etiam perambulandi diligentem*); see *TLL* x.1.1185.64ff., 1186.37ff. (Schmitz). *Ambulare* can also refer to the act of traveling: see Shackleton Bailey's (1968) note ad Cic. *Att.* 7.1.1 and *TLL* 1.1873.68ff. (Gudeman).

[3] See Reay 1998, 88. The use of a map as an icon of a literary project is strikingly parallel to Cicero's assessment of the impact of another of Varro's works, his *Antiquitates*: Romans were wandering lost in their own city, when Varro's greatest work came along and showed them the way home (*Acad. post.* 1.9). See Edwards 1996, 16–17.

connection between the movement of the body and the accumulation of knowledge. The principal example of this association is, of course, travel. As the traveler encounters new people and places, his or her understanding of the world broadens; there is knowledge that can only be gained by being away from home. The ancient Mediterranean and Near East abounded in stories of lessons learned abroad. As Silvia Montiglio has shown, in sixth- and fifth-century Greece, wandering transformed from an activity with ambivalent associations at best to a mode of existence actively pursued by sages and authors.[4] Indeed travel became so associated with wisdom that philosophers actively sought out travel metaphors to describe the operations of the mind, even in the absence of literal journeys. Plato and Aristotle, for example, appealed to the institution of *theoria*, a form of travel that was a cross between tourism and pilgrimage, as an analogy for philosophy itself; philosophers could travel in their minds and contemplate greater truths through mental inquiry, even without taking a single step.[5]

As we shall see, the metaphorical appropriation of *theoria* by fourth-century Greek philosophers persists in the Roman imagination, and philosophers such as Seneca frequently employ walking imagery as a metaphor for the operations of the mind. This chapter examines some of the intellectual history that lies behind the popularity of the *ambulatio* in Roman culture and reveals how elite Romans acted out the connection between the movement of the body and the accumulation of knowledge in the comfort and safety of the private villa. The villa setting encouraged owners and their guests to participate in a form of metaphorical travel within their own private environs. Walking in the upper-class home put both body and mind in motion, transporting the aristocrat beyond the physical confines of his villa; for upper-class Romans, the very act of walking was often just as allusive, just as constructed, as their literature and architecture.

GREEK AND ROMAN *THEORIA*

The connection between the movement of the body, the traveler's gaze, and the acquisition of knowledge – already present in the third line of the *Odyssey* – was a cornerstone of Greek thought long before the practice of

---

[4] Montiglio 2005. For other explorations of the history of intellectual travel in ancient Greece, see Redfield 1985; Sassi 1991; Hartog 2001; Nightingale 2004. On the figure of the wandering poet in ancient Greece, see Hunter and Rutherford 2009.

[5] On the metaphorical appropriation of *theoria* by Greek philosophy, see Rausch 1982; Nightingale 2004. The legacy of this phenomenon, as is well known, is that a word with very concrete associations turns into our word "theory" – the very antithesis of real-world experience.

theoria arose.[6] In its specialized meaning, *theoria* referred to the act of sending ambassadors, or going as ambassadors, to witness a festival or other ceremonies in a *polis* that was not one's own.[7] The word comes to be used more generally for traveling to see and learn about other places and people; famous *theoroi* include Solon and Herodotus, whose inquisitive journeys are both the cause and the result of their wisdom: they travel to learn, but they also travel because they are wise.[8] The most famous episode in the tradition surrounding Solon's travels is recounted in the first book of Herodotus (1.30.2), where the Lydian king Croesus takes advantage of the wisdom Solon has acquired in his *theoria* around the Mediterranean, and asks him who he thinks is the most blessed man on earth. Indeed, the Herodotean narrative is a likely influence on the Varro passage just mentioned: when asking his friends whether they have ever seen a more cultivated land than their own Italy, Agrasius evokes not only Croesus' self-satisfied pride, but also his implication that travel results in the accumulation of wisdom.[9]

The conversation that follows Agrasius' question includes a discussion of places, such as the Arctic, where the interlocutors could only have traveled in their readings (*Rust.* 1.2.4). Such a metaphorical application of travel and the experience of travel is not inconsistent with the notion of *theoria*. The civic activity of traveling ambassadors is appropriated by the philosophers of the fourth century BCE – by Plato and Aristotle in particular – as a metaphor for the activity of the philosopher who, in the words of Nightingale (2004, 6), "gazes with the 'eye of reason' upon divine and eternal verities."[10] It is the *mind* of the philosopher, rather than the philosopher himself, that

---

[6] On the influence of the opening lines of the *Odyssey* on subsequent interpretations of Odysseus, see Hartog 2001, 36.

[7] On *theoria*, see Rausch 1982, 12–37; Redfield 1985; Dillon 1997, 1–26; Rutherford 1998, 131–5 and 2000; Nightingale 2004, 40–71; Montiglio 2005, 118–46; Elsner and Rutherford 2005, 1–32.

[8] See Montiglio 2005, 118–46. The intellectual nature of Solon's *theoria* is especially emphasized by Herodotus; other ancient accounts provide additional motives for his time away from Athens, such as business (Arist. *Ath. Pol.* 11.1) or politics (Plut. *Sol.* 25.5): see Rutherford 2000, 135 n. 15. On the temporal paradox presented by the voyages of the wise (the model for which is Odysseus, who is wise before his travels, but also because of them), see Hartog 2001, 90–1.

[9] Furthermore, the visual emphasis of Agrasius' question (*ecquam cultiorem Italia vidistis*) may remind the reader of the visual nature of Solon's travels (*theoria* literally means a "seeing"), and the visual emphasis of these sorts of travels in general in archaic and classical Greece; see Rutherford 2000, 134–8. It may be just a happy coincidence that the setting of the dialogue, the temple of Tellus, recalls the name of Solon's most blessed man, the Athenian Tellos, although Varro does show a similar love of linguistic (and onomastic) play elsewhere in the text, especially in the names of the characters (e.g. *Rust.* 3.2.2).

[10] The metaphor was apparently first used by Pythagoras; when asked for a definition of philosopher, he offered as an analogy those who attend a festival not to compete or to make money but to watch (Iambl. *VP* 58–9; Cic. *Tusc.* 5.8–9). See Sassi 1991, 17.

travels through time and space to arrive at truth; Plato recasts the philo-sophical mission as a "*theoria* of all time and existence" (*Resp.* 486a: θεωρία παντὸς μὲν χρόνου, πάσης δὲ οὐσίας).[11] The result is a withdrawal into the life of the mind, and a distance between the philosopher and the physical world around him, with occasionally humorous results: Socrates takes as the model of the contemplative man the philosopher Thales, who fell into a pit while studying the stars.[12] The Hellenistic philosopher Pyrrho was similarly oblivious to the physical world around him (Diog. Laert. 9.62):

ἀκόλουθος δ' ἦν καὶ τῷ βίῳ, μηδὲν ἐκτρεπόμενος μηδὲ φυλαττόμενος, ἅπαντα ὑφιστάμενος, ἁμάξας, εἰ τύχοι, καὶ κρημνοὺς καὶ κύνας καὶ ὅλως μηδὲν ταῖς αἰσθήσεσιν ἐπιτρέπων. σώζεσθαι μέντοι, καθά φασιν οἱ περὶ τὸν Καρύστιον Ἀντίγονον, ὑπὸ τῶν γνωρίμων παρακολουθούντων.

His life was consistent with his philosophy; he never avoided or paid attention to anything, accepting whatever he might encounter – carts, cliffs, dogs – and on the whole entrusting nothing to his senses. Yet he was protected, according to Antigonus of Carystus and his followers, by his friends, who tracked him closely.

The walk of the philosopher, absorbed in the wanderings of his mind, was fraught with peril. This may explain the appeal of pacing back and forth in stoas and other well-defined walkways: there was little chance of getting lost or hurt.

Such a disavowal of the real world was, of course, anathema to a level-headed Roman aristocrat. Yet there is ample evidence that the notion of a "theoretical" life of the sort surveyed here still held some appeal in a Roman context, albeit in altered guise. In particular, the notion persisted that the intellectual or creative thought process involved metaphorically traveling in the mind to the object of inquiry. Indeed the most famous formulation of this philosophical commonplace is Lucretius' memorable passage on Epicurus' heroic shattering of boundaries with his thoughts: "The lively power of his mind overcame and proceeded far beyond the flaming walls of the universe and he rambled through the infinite whole with his thoughts and his mind" (1.72–4: *ergo vivida vis animi pervicit, et extra | processit longe flammantia moenia mundi | atque omne immensum peragravit mente*

---

[11] Cf. Nightingale 2004, 102 n. 12. See also Monoson 2000, 206–37 for Plato's metaphorical use of the *theates* (theater-goer) and the *theoros* as models of philosophical inquiry in the *Republic* and *Laws*.

[12] Pl. *Tht.* 174a. Cf. Nightingale 2004, 23–4. Socrates himself is famously lampooned in similar terms by Aristophanes: in his first appearance in the *Clouds* the philosopher descends from above in a basket, announcing that he is "airwalking and pondering around the sun" (*Nub.* 225: ἀεροβατῶ καὶ περιφρονῶ τὸν ἥλιον).

animoque).[13] We have already seen Varro's use of *perambulare* to evoke literal and metaphorical journeys at the beginning of the *De re rustica*; in the remainder of this section, I would like to focus on a more elaborate development of the motif by the younger Seneca.[14]

The philosopher Seneca spent eight years in forced exile on the island of Corsica during the first part of the emperor Claudius' reign, and among the works he wrote there was a short essay consoling his mother Helvia for her son's fate. The work essentially consists of a series of reasons why exile is supposed to be so unpleasant, and Seneca's point-by-point philosophical refutation of these arguments.[15] One selling point of exile, which Seneca returns to on more than one occasion, is the complete freedom it affords for intellectual pursuits, particularly the contemplation of the physical world; as long as he lives Seneca cannot be deprived of his mental powers, nor of the universe itself (*Helv.* 8.4–5):

mundus hic, quo nihil neque maius neque ornatius rerum natura genuit, <et> animus contemplator admiratorque mundi, pars eius magnificentissima, propria nobis et perpetua et tam diu nobiscum mansura sunt quam diu ipsi manebimus. alacres itaque et erecti quocumque res tulerit intrepido gradu properemus, emetiamur quascumque terras.

Nature has created nothing greater or more magnificent than the universe, and the human mind, which contemplates and gazes in wonder at it, is its most extraordinary part. Both the universe and the human mind are our eternal property and will remain with us as long as we ourselves remain on this earth. And so wherever life takes us, briskly and with heads held high we should hurry on with fearless steps, whatever lands we may traverse.

We have already seen in Chapter 2 Seneca's love of walking metaphors for human existence.[16] Here he casts the human mind in particular as *contemplator mundi* ("a contemplator of the universe"): *contemplatio*, with its

---

[13] Cf. Cic. *Fin.* 2.102. For other ancient uses of the philosophical commonplace of the mind soaring through the universe, see Jones 1926, 97–100 and Russell 1964, 165–6. On "the view from above" as a philosophical topos, see Hadot 1995, 238–50. For the wanderings of the mind, Lucretius and Cicero both use *peragrare*, another word that, like *perambulare*, can refer both to walking (esp. rambling over country fields) and traveling; see *TLL* x.1.1182.61ff., 1183.64ff. (Schwind). Cf. Sen. *Ben.* 5.12.2, where Seneca uses the experience of walking through varied terrain as a metaphor for the efforts of the mind to untangle problems of differing levels of complexity.

[14] For an analysis of Seneca's use of travel metaphors, see Lavery 1980, 151–5; on the theme of travel in Seneca's writings, see Garbarino 1996; Montiglio 2006.

[15] On the broader implications of Seneca's treatment of exile (literal and metaphorical) in the essay, see Williams 2006.

[16] Here we see a further elaboration of Seneca's views on "walking the right way": some speed is acceptable, so long as the path is true. As he notes elsewhere (*Vit. beat.* 1.1), if the path is off even by a little bit, then haste will only increase the distance to the goal. Cf. *Vit. beat.* 17.4, where Seneca notes that, though still not perfect, he is a "runner" (*cursor*) compared to his lame critics.

combination of visual and mental purview, is virtually a Latin translation of *theoria*.[17] Seneca continues by enumerating the sorts of celestial phenomena he delights in, and although the metaphor for his intellectual investigation of the stars and planets is to this point purely visual, he hints at space travel in his concluding remark (*Helv.* 8.6):

dum cum his sim et caelestibus, qua homini fas est, inmiscear, dum animum ad cognatarum rerum conspectum tendentem in sublimi semper habeam, quantum refert mea quid calcem?

And so long as I am among these phenomena and – so far as it is humanly possible – mingle with heavenly things, and so long as I always keep my mind up above, aiming for the contemplation of related things, what difference does it make what ground I tread?

Seneca's statement can be read as a defense of the philosophical pose lampooned by comedians (head in the stars, with no account taken of the immediate world around him): one man's absent-mindedness is another man's studied indifference to his physical environment.[18] The notion that studying the stars involves figuratively traveling to them is only hinted at here, and qualified by the phrase *qua homini fas est* ("so far as it is humanly possible"). Seneca saves his most explicit development of the motif for the final paragraph of the work, which beautifully combines the philosophical precursors of a metaphorical *theoria* with his specific situation as an exile on a remote island. Seneca explains to his mother why, despite his life in exile, he is content (*Helv.* 20):

qualem me cogites accipe: laetum et alacrem velut optimis rebus. sunt enim optimae, quoniam animus omnis occupationis expers operibus suis vacat et modo se levioribus studiis oblectat, modo ad considerandam suam universique naturam veri avidus insurgit. terras primum situmque earum quaerit, deinde condicionem circumfusi maris cursusque eius alternos et recursus; tunc quidquid inter caelum terrasque plenum formidinis interiacet perspicit et hoc tonitribus fulminibus ventorum flatibus ac nimborum nivisque et grandinis iactu tumultuo-sum spatium; tum peragratis humilioribus ad summa perrumpit et pulcherrimo

---

[17] In his version of the famous story of Pythagoras' definition of philosophy, Cicero uses the word *contemplatio* (*Tusc.* 5.9) where Iamblichus uses θεωρία (*VP* 58); see Sassi 1991, 17.

[18] It hardly needs saying that this is a convenient stance for an exile, who has been forced into such a situation precisely *because* of his involvement in the political world. Cf. Ferrill 1966, who reads Seneca's embrace of philosophical thought in the work as an attempt to secure a return to Rome by publicly renouncing his political ambitions. Williams 2006, 173, on the other hand, sees Seneca's essay as an "aggressive response to the Roman power that exiled him," since the ability of the *sapiens* to adopt a cosmic point of view trivializes the more mundane power of the Roman imperial apparatus.

divinorum spectaculo fruitur, aeternitatis suae memor in omne quod fuit futur-
umque est vadit omnibus saeculis.

Let me tell you how you should think of me: as happy and as upbeat as in the best of
times. In fact, these *are* the best of times, because my mind is totally free from every
concern and is left alone to its work. At times, it takes pleasure in less serious
studies, and at other times, eager for truth, it stands up to contemplate its own
nature and the nature of the universe. First it investigates the lands and their
physical setting, then the state of the surrounding ocean, and its alternating ebb and
flow. Then it takes a look at all the terror that lies between heaven and earth, and
this expanse of sky that seethes with thunder and lightning and blasts of wind and
rain and the attack of snow and hail. Then, once it has rambled over these lower
areas, it breaks through to the heights and enjoys the most beautiful spectacle of all
divine things, and, conscious of its own immortality, it moves through everything
that was and will be through all the ages.

Seneca concludes his essay in full crescendo, with a powerful defense of
the life of the mind. For, in Seneca's formulation, the landscape of the
mind is limitless; notice his effortless collocation of the human mind
and the universe (*ad considerandam suam universique naturam*). Seneca
is content, despite his exile, because his studies offer his mind a freedom
of movement that is physically impossible for anybody (or any *body*),
exiled or free; his mind is free to survey the entire known world, and,
having traveled there, it leaps into the sky, the heavens, and even back
and forward in time.

Seneca's enthusiastic adaptation of Greek philosophical models for
thought may seem completely ordinary, until we remember that his situation is entirely contingent on the political realities of exile and punishment that Seneca is trying so hard to play down. His insistence on the
boundary-defying powers of the mind *almost*, but not quite, makes us forget
about the very real limitations on his exiled body, confined to the outskirts
of the Roman empire. This lingering presence of the political behind
Seneca's defense of intellectual activity is very Roman; it reminds us of
the similarly ambiguous status of *otium* in the aristocratic imagination,
which depended upon political engagement for respectability.[19] Seneca in
fact directly addresses this ambiguity in the *De otio*, where he defends the
vita contemplativa by appealing to the Stoic notion that the cosmos con-
stitutes a "second republic" of which we are all citizens; by retiring to a life of
contemplative leisure, we turn from active participation in our local

---

[19] The notion of an honorable leisure was an obsession for Cicero in particular, as we have already seen
in the *De oratore* passage in Chapter 4; see André 1966, 281–90. On Seneca's views about *otium* and
political engagement, see Griffin 1976, 315–66.

republic and opt for a universal citizenship.[20] The contemplative life is therefore not a rejection of the active life, but rather the embrace of an active life of a different sort: the curiosity to see and learn may call us to literal action (e.g. travel across the seas), or to metaphorical action, such as the "unraveling of antiquities" by reading or the journey of our mind through the cosmos (*Ot.* 5). Seneca's defense of the contemplative life therefore brings together the two strands of *theoria* – the physical and the mental – that we encountered earlier in this chapter: according to Seneca, nature has not only made us curious to explore her hidden mysteries with our minds, but she has also constructed our bodies so that we may more easily gaze upon her beauty, standing upright, necks craned to the skies.[21]

Seneca's reverie is one paradigm for the continued relevance of *theoria* in a Roman context; like the absent-minded Pyrrho, Seneca hopes to convince us that the pleasures of mental inquiry can overcome the mundane reality of physical experience. It is not, however, the only possible paradigm. In the next part of this chapter, I would like to argue that the practice of walking for leisure in the Roman villa builds upon the notion of intellectual activity as mental travel and reunites it with the bodily movement and experience of space central to the original definition of *theoria*. The aristocratic *ambulatio*, with its combination of physical and mental activity, brings together the two competing meanings of *theoria* to create something uniquely Roman.

"WALKING IN HISTORY"

The fifth book of Cicero's *De finibus* takes place in Athens, as the interlocutors stroll in Plato's Academy. As the characters begin to reflect on the satisfaction gained from seeing the actual places once traversed by their cultural heroes, it becomes clear that the inspiration for and pleasure derived from their travel is intellectual. Lucius Cicero, a young cousin of the author's, and apparently a fan of Athenian oratory, caps the conversation with the following observation (*Fin.* 5.5):

quamquam id quidem infinitum est in hac urbe; quacumque enim ingredimur, in aliqua historia vestigium ponimus.

In any case that sort of experience is endless in this city; for wherever we walk, we place our footprint in some history.

---

[20] Sen. *Ot.* 4. On the development of the Stoic idea of two republics, see Schofield 1991, 64–74; Williams 2003, 5–6, 11, and 79–80.

[21] Sen. *Ot.* 5.4. The idea that our bodies were specifically constructed for contemplation is not original to Seneca; see Williams 2003 ad loc.

Cicero and his friends are not only retreading ancient ground (walking *on* some history), but also walking *in* it, adding themselves to some old story, reliving the past. These latter-day *theoroi* are quite self-consciously modeling their travels after the intellectual journeys of past philosophers, but with added benefit: they not only acquire the sort of knowledge that naturally accrues when traveling away from home, but they also are able to retrace the steps of previous philosophical walks. Cicero and friends add their own footprints to those of their departed heroes, and by walking the same ground they connect with them on both a metaphorical and a metonymic level.[22]

Although the previous four books of the *De finibus* (and indeed virtually every one of Cicero's philosophical dialogues) take place in the confines of Italian villas, the move from Italy to Athens at the beginning of Book 5 is not as dramatic a change in scenery as it might first appear.[23] We have already examined in Chapter 4 the propensity of Roman elites to configure their villas as evocations of Greece. At times this impulse to evoke Greece even led to an attempt at simulation. The somewhat more secluded confines of the country estate encouraged the homeowner to engage in flights of fancy that he might then pretend to denigrate among friends. Or at least that is what Cicero seems to do: in the beginning of Book 2 of the *De legibus*, he does not disagree as Atticus pokes fun at villa owners for the habit of calling a water channel a "Euripus" (after the strait between Euboea and Boeotia) or a "Nile" (*Leg.* 2.2):

magnificasque villas et pavimenta marmorea et laqueata tecta contemno. ductus vero aquarum quos isti Nilos et Euripos vocant, quis non, cum haec videat, inriserit?

I disapprove of luxurious villas and marble floors and paneled ceilings. Really, the water channels that they call "Niles" and "Euripuses" – who wouldn't laugh when they saw them?

Yet Cicero is himself a shining example of the Roman elite practice of simulating foreign spaces within the private confines of the villa; as we have already seen, he even went so far as to design replicas of both the Lyceum and the Academy on his Tusculan grounds.[24] Elsewhere in his letters we get

[22] Cf. *Orat.* 12, where the walks of the Academy are referred to as the places where Plato left his first footprints; or *Leg.* 2.4, where Atticus reflects on the fact that visits to the actual grounds of one's heroes are all the more moving because of the presence of their *vestigia*. On the power of place in Cicero's philosophical and rhetorical works, see Vasaly 1993, 26–33.
[23] *Fin.* 1 and 2 are set in Cicero's villa at Cumae, while 3 and 4 are set in the library of Lucullus' Tusculan villa.
[24] On Cicero's Academy, see *Att.* 1.4, 1.6, 1.8, 1.9, 1.10, and 1.11; he even notes that he wrote *Att.* 1.10 while sitting there (*Att.* 1.10.3). On Cicero's Tusculan villa, see Schmidt 1899, 466–72; Neudecker 1988, 11–14.

the impression that in building such spaces he may have been simply keeping up with his contemporaries. According to a letter to Atticus (15.9.1), Caesar's assassin Brutus had an estate at Lanuvium that included a Persike Porticus and a Eurotas, named respectively for Sparta's famous stoa and its principal river. Another letter seems to suggest that another property of Brutus' boasted of a Parthenon, prompting Shackleton Bailey to remark that "presumably he had an 'Athens' as well as a 'Lacedaemon.'"[25] The most notorious example of such an impulse is of course Hadrian's villa, where the *Historia Augusta* tells us that the emperor tried to emulate various famous natural and man-made landmarks from Greece and elswhere around the Roman empire (SHA *Hadr.* 26.5):

Tiburtinam villam mire exaedificavit, ita ut in ea et provinciarum et locorum celeberrima nomina inscriberet, velut Lyceum, Academian, Prytaneum, Canopum, Poicilen, Tempe vocaret. et, ut nihil praetermitteret, etiam inferos finxit.

His villa at Tivoli was a marvel of construction, such that he inscribed upon it the names of the most famous provinces and locales; for instance, he called one part the Lyceum, another the Academy, the Prytaneum, the Canopus, the Stoa Poikile, and [the vale of] Tempe. And, so that he wouldn't leave anything out, he even fashioned an underworld.

Even though we have no assurance of the veracity of this claim – it could well be, for example, a parody of the emperor's penchant for travel – modern scholarship on Hadrian's villa has been dominated by this one little passage, testifying that the fascination with the evocation of famous monuments and topography holds as much power over our imagination as it did over that of wealthy Roman aristocrats.[26] And the cultural metaphor of *theoria* and the connection it offered between walking in the real world and traveling in the mind was the intellectual foundation of these attempts to evoke faraway places and times.[27]

But before we imagine that these aristocrats were building exact replicas of famous monuments from around the world, in an ancient version of Disney World's Epcot Center, we must remember that the connection that

---

[25] Shackleton Bailey 1966, 388. On Brutus' "Lacedaemon," see Cic. *Att.* 15.9.1; on Brutus' "Parthenon," see *Att.* 13.40.1.

[26] MacDonald and Pinto 1995, 189 connect the "time-honored villa activity" of strolling conversation with the fashion for naming villa buildings for foreign spaces as both an advertisement of culture and as a stimulus for conversation.

[27] Cf. Bergmann 2001, 155: "Just as the *theoria* of pilgrimage combined vision with mental inquiry to reach a path of reasoning and eventually revelation, Romans at home cultivated their minds by creating, and then inhabiting, zones of learning."

these spaces strove for was as much intellectual as physical.[28] Cicero's Academy and Lyceum need not *look* like the real ones, but they should *feel* like them; the point, in other words, is not imitation but evocation, or what Bettina Bergmann (2001, 155) terms a "landscape of allusion." Hence the importance of the act of walking itself, for the connection between villa design and the places it evokes is above all experiential: it is the *experience* of the place that is meant to be analogous, how a villa owner's Academy looks and feels as he strolls through it with friends.[29] Cicero's literary representation of Plato's Academy in the *De finibus* and his architectural evocation of it at his Tusculan villa work in very much the same way, transporting the visitor or reader to distant lands in order to stimulate conversation or reflection.

Nor need we imagine that this impulse was necessarily about an exotic experience, focusing on the landscapes of Greece or Egypt. The villa, and the countryside in general, could also be configured as a moral landscape, reminding visitors of an idealized *Roman* past. The walk through a villa therefore afforded the visitor the opportunity to travel in his mind not only to other spaces, but to other *times*. This metaphorical time travel is akin to the Roman perception of domestic space as a repository of memory. I refer to the well-known ancient mnemonic device whereby the art of memorization is imagined as the placement of images in various parts of the house, and the art of remembering is the act of walking through this imaginary house, and retrieving the images as one passes.[30] We might also think of the display of ancestor masks in the atrium as further evidence of the relationship of the home to memory.[31] Similarly, the connection between the villa and the memory of a particular individual has been explored in an article by John Bodel; there was a tendency for a villa or house to keep the name of its original owner even after he had died and it no longer remained in his family.[32] The villa of Scipio Africanus still attracted visitors centuries after his death, and the younger Seneca in a well-known letter (*Ep.* 86) relates for us just such a visit. While examining the modest baths of the villa, he

---

[28] On the intellectual connection made by naming parts of the villa for famous topographical features, see Görler 1990, 170–1.

[29] For the idea that exact fidelity to original sites was not the principal concern for these villa owners, see Zanker 1998, 139; Bergmann 2001, 157–8. Cf. Riggsby 2003, who emphasizes the need for Roman cultural historians to pay more attention to "qualitative" as opposed to "quantitative" space, with particular reference to Pliny's villa letters.

[30] The classic study is Yates 1966; for its relation to domestic design, see Bergmann 1994 and Baroin 1998.

[31] Flower 1996, 185–222.

[32] See Bodel 1997. On memory and the Roman town house, see Hales 2003, 46–50.

engages in the sort of mental *theoria* that we saw him espouse earlier in response to his exile, shuttling back and forth between Scipio's time and his own. Unlike in the *Consolatio ad Helviam*, however, the object of his *contemplatio* is human behavior, not the natural world: he takes pleasure in "contemplating Scipio's customs and our own" (*Ep.* 86.5: *magna ergo me voluptas subiit contemplantem mores Scipionis ac nostros*).[33] The modest remains of Scipio's villa transport Seneca (and his readers) to simpler times; but in another letter (*Ep.* 12), the decrepit state of Seneca's own suburban villa forces the philosopher to deal with the present, and with his own advancing years. The deteriorating condition of the estate (including the buildings, grounds, and slaves) mirrors the aging of Seneca's own body, and inspires his contemplation of the nature of old age, and of time in general.[34]

For a more explicit development of the idea that a stroll through a country estate could inspire philosophical reflection about other times and places, we come back to Cicero. In the prologue to the second book of the *De legibus*, he walks with his brother Quintus and his friend Atticus near his villa at Arpinum.[35] The setting for this walk is somewhat different than many of the others we have encountered so far: Cicero and his companions walk not in the built environment of a portico or peristyle, but in the natural setting of the Italian countryside, along the river Fibrenus. The passage is frequently cited as one of the rare instances in Latin literature where there is a clear appreciation for the beauty of a natural landscape; but as Cicero explains to Atticus, he cherishes the spot for more than just its natural beauty, for they are walking on the very grounds where he was born and raised (*Leg.* 2.3):

si verum dicimus, haec est mea et huius fratris mei germana patria. hinc enim orti stirpe antiquissima sumus, hic sacra, hic genus, hic maiorum multa vestigia. quid plura? hanc vides villam, ut nunc quidem est lautius aedificatam patris nostri studio, qui cum esset infirma valetudine, hic fere aetatem egit in litteris. sed hoc ipso in loco, cum avus viveret et antiquo more parva esset villa, ut illa Curiana in Sabinis, me scito esse natum. quare inest nescio quid et latet in animo ac sensu meo,

---

[33] On *Ep.* 86, see Henderson 2004, 93–157 and Ker 2009, 346–53. Seneca's *contemplatio* may also evoke the idea of *theoria* in its original meaning, since the visit is cast as a religious pilgrimage of sorts (see Ker 2002, 157–60); Seneca composes the letter "after having venerated the shade and the altar [of Scipio]" (*Ep.* 86.1: *adoratis manibus eius et ara*). Cf. Henderson 2004, 94–5, who adduces the tale of the pirates who treat Scipio's villa (and Scipio himself) as objects worthy of veneration (Val. Max. 2.10.2).

[34] The metaphor of the mirror is from Ker 2009, 335. On *Ep.* 12, see also Henderson 2004, 24–7.

[35] The preposition "near" is deliberately vague; it is unclear whether or not the countryside they walk through is part of Cicero's estate.

quo me plus <aequo> hic locus fortasse delectet, <nec sine causa> si quidem etiam
ille sapientissimus vir, Ithacam ut videret, immortalitatem scribitur repudiasse.

To tell the truth, this [*sc.* Arpinum] is my and my brother's real homeland. We
grew up here, from very ancient roots, our sacred rites are here, our family is here,
many traces of our ancestors are here. What more need I say? You see that villa – as
it stands now, it has been built up in a more lavish fashion by the efforts of my
father, who, since he was of ill health, practically spent his life here, in his books.
But you should know that I was born on that very spot, when my grandfather was
alive and when the villa was small in the ancient fashion, like the villa of Manius
Curius in Sabine country. So there remains for me an indescribable feeling deep in
my mind and in my heart, and this place pleases me perhaps more than it should,
though not without reason, since even that wisest of men is said to have rejected
immortality so that he might see Ithaca again.

In spite of the beauty of the natural setting, it is the presence of human
culture and in particular of his own family that makes this place so appealing
to Cicero.[36] This human presence is conveyed not only by the metaphorical
footprints of ancestors who are long dead but also by the villa itself, which
serves as their memorial. As with Seneca's villa, the state of their homestead
mirrors the state of Cicero and his *gens*, but in this case, the villa has
improved with age, having expanded and acquired decorations while its
famous son has risen through the ranks of Roman society. When Cicero
asks Atticus to look beyond the present villa and to imagine the villa as it
once was, he takes him back in time as they walk through this ancient
ground and retrace the steps of his ancestors.[37] But we should not forget the
fact that this walk evokes other *places* as well as other times. After all, the
model for this dialogue, Plato's *Laws*, takes place as the speakers walk to see
the cave of Zeus on Mount Ida in Crete, while the stroll along the river
Fibrenus recalls the walk by the banks of the Ilissus outside the walls of
Athens in the beginning of the *Phaedrus*.[38] Despite the natural setting, in

---

[36] See Vasaly 1993, 30–3; Farrell 2001, 18–27.

[37] Compare Pliny's claim that a visit to his Tuscan villa is like a visit to an earlier age: "The summers are
amazingly mild: there is always a breeze that keeps the air moving, more often a breeze than a full
wind. For this reason there are many elderly people in the area: you might see grandparents and great-
grandparents of those who are no longer children; you might hear old stories and tales of those who
have passed away, and when you arrive there, you might think that you were born in another age"
(*Ep.* 5.6.5–6: *aestatis mira clementia: semper aer spiritu aliquo movetur, frequentius tamen auras quam
ventos habet. hinc senes multi: videas avos proavosque iam iuvenum, audias fabulas veteres sermonesque
maiorum, cumque veneris illo putes alio te saeculo natum*). On the intersection of time and space in this
letter, see Riggsby 2003.

[38] Atticus will explicitly evoke the *Phaedrus* later in this scene (2.6), when he is reluctant to dip his toe in
the Fibrenus as Socrates had in the Ilissus. On the correspondences between the *De legibus* and the
Phaedrus, see Görler 1988, 218–20 and Dyck 2004, 20–2. The idyllic setting of the *Phaedrus* has a long
literary afterlife; for a selection of ancient citations and allusions, see Hardie 1998, 238–9.

other words, their environment is no less constructed than Crassus'
Tusculan portico in the *De oratore*, and despite the careful focus on
Roman (and Italian) identity, the Greek precedents for both their walk
and their conversation form a constant subtext.[39]

Cicero provides a clue to unraveling this nexus of associations by his
allusion to Odysseus, who is the symbol for everything that is at stake in this
scene: travel, including *theoria*, intellectual curiosity, homecoming, philosophy, and even Greek identity itself.[40] Cicero's love for Arpinum recalls
Odysseus' love for Ithaca, and the intensity of their affection is directed not
only at their fatherlands but also at their *fathers*: the lingering image of
Cicero's father reading in his refurbished villa is a sign that we too should
read this scene more closely. For in the famous epilogue to the Homeric
Odyssey, Laertes also lives his life removed from politics; when father and
son reunite, Odysseus finds him digging in his garden.[41] Once again, the
natural spaces of the Greek world are transformed into the constructed,
intellectual space of the Roman villa: we find Cicero's father not in his
garden, like Laertes, but in his study.[42] And the same holds true for their
sons: unlike Odysseus, the original *theoros* (*ille sapientissimus vir*: that wisest,
or perhaps most *philosophical* man), Cicero and his companions do not
travel around the Mediterranean, but rather walk in a leisurely manner
through a space that is at once Greek and Roman, at once natural and man-
made, at once real and imagined.

WALKING WITH PHILOSOPHERS

soli omnium otiosi sunt qui sapientiae vacant, soli vivunt; nec enim suam tantum
aetatem bene tuentur: omne aevum suo adiciunt; quidquid annorum ante illos
actum est, illis adquisitum est. nisi ingratissimi sumus, illi clarissimi sacrarum
opinionum conditores nobis nati sunt, nobis vitam praeparaverunt. ad res pulcherrimas ex tenebris ad lucem erutas alieno labore deducimur; nullo nobis saeculo
interdictum est, in omnia admittimur, et si magnitudine animi egredi humanae

---

The dramatic setting of Plato's *Laws* is mentioned by Cicero at *Leg.* 1.15; it is perhaps relevant that
Atticus' estate at Buthrotum was nicknamed the Amaltheum (cf. *Leg.* 2.7), because of a reconstruction
of the cave where Amalthea suckled baby Zeus: see Bergmann 2001, 155.

[39] Moreover, in the passage that immediately follows the one cited above, Atticus compares Cicero's
love for his ancestral estate to his own love for his adopted *patria*, Athens: there too he is moved by the
vestigia of his adopted ancestors (Greek philosophers), at whose graves he performs a *contemplatio*
(*Leg.* 2.4).

[40] Cf. Hartog 2001, 25: "The *Odyssey*, with its poetic anthropology, provides the basis for the Greeks'
vision of themselves and of others."

[41] *Od.* 24.226–42. On the function of the garden setting in the Homeric passage, see Henderson 1997.

[42] Cf. Seamus Heaney's early poem "Digging," in which the son's literary activity picks up where the
father's farming leaves off: "Between my finger and my thumb | The squat pen rests. | I'll dig with it."

inbecillitatis angustias libet, multum per quod spatiemur temporis est. disputare cum Socrate licet, dubitare cum Carneade, cum Epicuro quiescere, hominis naturam cum Stoicis vincere, cum Cynicis excedere. cum rerum natura in consortium omnis aevi patiatur incedere, quidni ab hoc exiguo et caduco temporis transitu in illa toto nos demus animo quae inmensa, quae aeterna sunt, quae cum melioribus communia?

They alone are at leisure who leave time for philosophy; they alone are alive. For they clearly view not only their own lifetime: they add all time to their own. Whatever time has passed before their lives has been added to their lives. If we are not too ungrateful [*sc.* to appreciate it], those most illustrious founders of the revered schools of thought were born for us, they provided ahead of time a model of living for us. We are escorted to the most beautiful things, which have been rescued from the shadows into the light by someone else's labor. No age is forbidden to us. We are given access to everything, and if there is a desire to use the vastness of the mind to step out of the narrow passageways of human weakness, then there is a vast span of time through which we may stroll. One can argue with Socrates, hesitate with Carneades, rest with Epicurus, conquer human nature with the Stoics, leave it behind with the Cynics. Since the universe allows us to walk in the fellowship of every age, why don't we give ourselves over with all our mind from this narrow and fleeting passage of time to those things which are immense, which are eternal, which are shared with our betters?[43] (Seneca, *Brev. Vit.* 14.1–2)

The pursuit of philosophy allows its practitioners to walk through all time, alongside long-dead heroes. Seneca unites the two strands of the culture of the *ambulatio* that we have examined in this and the previous chapter. On the one hand, walking is a metaphor for the operations of the philosophically informed mind, which can be led to a contemplation of the most beautiful things as it strolls through all space and time. On the other hand, walking is also the physical pose to adopt when communing with philosophers who practiced their craft while walking. That the culture of the *ambulatio* is in the background here is further emphasized by the section immediately following, in which Seneca draws a contrast between the type of mental walking he promotes and the hustle-bustle of clients running through the city (*Brev. vit.* 14.3–4):

isti qui per officia discursant, qui se aliosque inquietant, cum bene insanierint, cum omnium limina cotidie perambulaverint nec ullas apertas fores praeterierint, cum per diversissimas domos meritoriam salutationem circumtulerint, quotum quemque ex tam inmensa et variis cupiditatibus districta urbe poterunt videre?

The sort of people who run around from one obligation to another, who disturb themselves and others around them – once they have finished acting like madmen,

---

[43] This translation relies on Williams' commentary on the passage (2003, 211–13).

once they have walked every day across everyone's threshold, bypassing no open doors, once they have circulated their money-grubbing "good mornings" through houses far and wide – how few people out of a city so immense and so distracted by different desires will they be able to see?

As Williams 2003 has shown, the excursus on the daily folly of clients who run throughout the city clarifies the imagery of the preceding section. The freedom of the philosopher is a freedom of movement: unlike the clients who feel compelled to run from one house to another, begging for access to their patrons, the philosopher "*always* has open access to all of *his* patrons, whether Socrates or Carneades, Epicurus or Zeno."[44] The language of *clientela* highlights the contrast: we philosophers "are escorted to the most beautiful things" (*ad res pulcherrimas . . . deducimur*), unlike clients who themselves escort their patrons around town. Conversely, the word used to describe the clients' motion through the houses of their patrons (*perambulaverint*) is a negative foil to the metaphorical travel that is the privilege of the philosopher and his friends; *perambulare*, as we saw at the beginning of the chapter, can also refer to the act of traveling. We have already examined a similar condemnation of the futility of such daily routines in Seneca's essay *De tranquillitate animi* (see above, Chapter 2), in which he suggests that a client's helter-skelter movement through the city reflects a similar disruption in his state of mind. But now we can fully appreciate the specific sense of place behind Seneca's condemnation: why do people run through every type of house all over the city when they could walk at leisure in just one? Why do they try to see every sort of person when they could visit a select few in their minds through the magic of philosophy? Even the implicit economic relationship between clients and their patrons could be rendered irrelevant if they only reclaimed ownership of themselves.[45]

As we have seen throughout this chapter, Roman domestic decor allowed the visitor to spend his time exactly as Seneca recommends: his mind could travel wherever it wanted, with any and all intellectual heroes from other ages, even as his body passed through spaces filled with representations of those heroes. We saw in Chapter 2 that it was beneficial even to walk like the *sapiens*; in the privacy of his own home, the Roman aristocrat could not only walk *like* the sage, but he could also walk *with* whichever one he chose. The owner of a well-appointed Roman villa walked amidst the statues and

---

[44] Williams 2003, 23 (his italics). Cf. 213, where he points out that Seneca "emphasize[s] the philosopher's freedom of movement in contrast . . . to the suffocating routine endured by Roman clients."

[45] On the significance of Seneca's economic language in his philosophical writings, see Ker 2006, 35–41.

busts of many potential exemplars for his behavior; indeed so did the many
Romans who walked in public porticoes decorated in much the same way.[46]
It is as if these Romans are already practicing an amateur Stoicism; Seneca
only has to convince them to adopt a more introspective form of walking
amidst these same figures.

But of course there were other philosophical schools of thought popular
among the Roman elite; Seneca's is only one version of how the *ambulatio*
might mesh with philosophical doctrine. In a well-known poem (*Silv.* 2.2),
Statius recounts a visit to the villa of Pollius Felix on the cape of
Surrentum.[47] As Statius describes the villa, he suggests that his patron's
decorative scheme fosters his Epicurean repose (*Silv.* 2.2.63, 69–72):

> quid referam veteres ceraeque aerisque figuras?
> . . . ora ducum ac vatum sapientumque ora priorum,
> quos tibi cura sequi, quos toto pectore sentis
> expers curarum atque animum virtute quieta
> compositus semperque tuus?

What can I say about the ancient figures of wax and bronze? [What can I say
about] . . . the faces of leaders and poets, and the faces of previous philosophers,
whom it is your concern to follow, whom you know with all your heart – you who
are free of cares, whose mind is calm with quiet virtue, and you who are ever your
own man?

Statius clearly situates his patron's sculptural display in the context of his
philosophical allegiance; like a good Epicurean, Pollius lives a life free of
cares (*expers curarum*), save for the one care of "following" (*sequi*) the
philosophers whose busts adorn his villa.[48] Pollius' villa – and all Roman
villas decorated in such a fashion – rendered concrete and visible the sort of
philosophical reverie endorsed by Seneca. In this sense, it is especially
suggestive that both verbs Statius uses to describe Pollius' philosophical
practice – *sequi* ("follow") and *sentire* ("perceive") – have a literal and a
figurative connotation. Pollius both perceives his Epicurean forebears in
bronze form and is intimately familiar with them "in his heart," in precisely
the sort of interior communion that Seneca encourages. And the

---

[46] Kuttner's 1999 article on the Portico of Pompey is an exemplary study of the cultural metaphor of
walking as travel extended beyond the setting of the Roman villa. Cf. Vespasian's Templum Pacis,
which Josephus tells us was filled with so many works of art that a visit could take the place of a
sightseeing trip around the world (*BJ* 7.5.7 [158–60]). On the use of public porticoes as art galleries,
see also Macaulay-Lewis 2009.
[47] On the poem, see Bergmann 1991; Myers 2000; Newlands 2002, 154–98; Zeiner 2005, 178–90.
[48] On Statius' construction of Pollio's villa as an "Epicurean citadel of the mind," see Leach 2003, 154.

ambulatory nature of that communion allows Pollius to "follow" his predecessors in more senses than one.[49]

We may also look to contemporary Roman domestic ensembles to find a version of the experience alluded to by Seneca and Statius. The Villa of the Papyri at Herculaneum is a frequently cited example.[50] The chance find of a library dominated by Epicurean authors has encouraged a number of scholars to see the peristyle of the villa as the physical manifestation of *ataraxia* or even as an evocation of Epicurus' garden.[51] While there have been attempts to secure a specific didactic message in the statuary, more recent scholars have emphasized the eclecticism of the collection, acknowledging the likelihood that the collection developed over the course of a century under the direction of more than one owner.[52] The latter approach often results in a greater emphasis on the hypothetical viewer's reception of the collection – for where one viewer might see an overriding logic to the entire display, another might prefer to see different patterns, or no pattern at all. The key, of course, is that the walk of the viewer determines the order and arrangement of the collection.[53] Art historians in recent decades have begun to study a number of ensembles from the perspective of the viewer rather than the patron or artist, imagining patterns of movement through a collection, suggesting where the ancient visitor may have moved, looked, and lingered.[54] But, as I hope to have shown, even if the viewer is compelled to walk for practical reasons – how else could he or she take in a collection as vast as that of the Villa of the Papyri, for example? – the *ambulatio* itself has a highly developed cultural context, prompting associations of movement and the acquisition of knowledge, and priming the viewer to travel in mind

[49] On the *ambulatio* imagery in the poem as a whole, see esp. lines 42–4: "My eyes were barely sufficient for the long line of sights; my steps were barely sufficient, as I was led through everything one by one" (*vix ordine longo | suffecere oculi, vix, dum per singula ducor, | suffecere gradus*). On the ways in which Statius constructs the poem as a tour, see Bergmann 1991.

[50] For a comparison of *Silv.* 2.2 and the Villa of the Papyri, see e.g. Myers 2000, 110.

[51] On the villa and its collection, see Pandermalis 1971; Sauron 1980; Wojcik 1986; Neudecker 1988, 105–14; Warden and Romano 1994; Dillon 2000, 22–30 and 36–9; Mattusch 2005.

[52] For this view, see Mattusch 2005, xiv, 15, and 332–3. On the preference for eclecticism in Roman sculptural collections, see Bartman 1991, 73–5.

[53] As recognized by Warden and Romano 1994, 232: "different contrasts were presented as a visitor moved from place to place. The climax came in the larger peristyle, at the very point when a visitor reached its western end – the end of the presentation, so to speak – and began to retrace his steps back out of the villa. The visitor was manipulated visually and spatially and the tour de force was to be found in the splendid large peristyle to the west."

[54] Drerup 1959 is the standard treatment of the phenomenon of "framed views" in Roman domestic architecture; other treatments of domestic design that pay special attention to the role of the viewer or visitor include Scagliarini Corlàita 1974–6; Bek 1980, 164–203; Clarke 1991, 1–29 (and *passim*); the essays in Moormann 1993; Bergmann 1994 and 1999; Wallace-Hadrill 1994, 38–61; Elsner 1995, 49–87; Dickmann 1999, esp. 347–74; Dillon 2000, 36–9; Platt 2002; Kuttner 2003; Hales 2003, 97–134.

as well as body. If we cannot know, in other words, how the average visitor *did* experience a collection such as the one in the Villa of the Papyri, we can nevertheless imagine how someone like Seneca might have described it.

Imagining Seneca at the Villa of the Papyri raises a final point: while he could certainly enjoy his reverie of walking among these long-dead philosophers in bronze and marble, it would, in this case, involve a kind of tunnel vision, as he sauntered past statues of Hellenistic dynasts, athletes, and Pan having sex with a goat. Judging from the collection practices of those villa owners for whom we have evidence, elite Romans preferred an expansive itinerary for their metaphorical travels.[55] They wanted to travel past their own replicas of famous artworks, past the kinds of statues that would decorate actual Greek gymnasia or Hellenistic palaces, past the heroes and heroines of myth and history. In the next and final chapter, we shall take a longer look at how one Roman homeowner orchestrated for his guests an *ambulatio* through a Homeric landscape.

---

[55] On the collection practices of Roman villa owners, see especially Neudecker 1988.

CHAPTER 6

Walking with Odysseus

The elite Romans living in the elaborately decorated villas and town houses of the late republic and early empire were constantly confronted with an optical illusion. The walls of their houses were typically covered with paintings that consistently challenged the viewer to look both *at* the wall and *through* it, whether onto an imaginary garden, or at a famous scene from Greek mythology, or into a receding abyss of architectural forms. Nor was the illusion restricted to the decoration only: just as painted architectural features could frame artificial views, real architectural elements could frame real views, whether out onto the surrounding countryside – if one was lucky enough to be in a country villa – or onto other areas within the house itself. Lines of sight might be carefully arranged so as to call into question the very distinction between real and artificial views; this constant interplay of views both fictive and real in the Roman house is a reflection of what Bettina Bergmann has called the "desire to blur the line between vision and representation."[1]

The subject of this chapter is a well-known example of just this sort of visual play: the Roman fresco known as the Odyssey Landscapes (Figs. 1–5).[2] Unlike contemporary paintings of the mid first century BCE, in which either figural or architectural subjects dominate, the fresco is famous for its emphasis on *natural* forms: rocks, cliffs, crags, bays, caves, trees, islands, and ocean all compete for the viewer's attention.[3] In the midst

---

[1] Bergmann 1992, 39; see also Bergmann 2002 on the interplay of art and nature at the villa at Oplontis. On "framed views" in Roman domestic architecture, see Drerup 1959.

[2] The painting is currently housed in the Sala delle Nozze Aldobrandine at the Vatican, save for a fragmentary panel (Fig. 5) in the Palazzo Massimo alle Terme in Rome. The bibliography on the painting is vast. Biering 1995 is the most complete treatment; von Blanckenhagen 1963 is still a useful overview, although his central thesis – that the painting is a copy of a Hellenistic original – is not universally accepted (further discussion below). Coarelli 1998 has more recently provided a thorough reassessment of the painting's original setting.

[3] The mid first-century date has been called into question by Biering 1995, 181–90; he argues on stylistic grounds that the fresco is a product of the last decade of the first century BCE. At least two scholars have already rejected the new date, however: see Coarelli 1998, 26–30 and Tybout 2001, 35–6. Coarelli's argument is largely based on the fact that fragments of a pre-Julian calendar were discovered at the site, though it is not clear why the landscapes and the calendar were necessarily painted at the same time.

Figure 1 Odyssey Landscapes, panels 2 and 3. Vatican Museums.

Figure 2 Odyssey Landscapes, panels 4 and 5. Vatican Museums.

Figure 3 Odyssey Landscapes, panels 6 and 7. Vatican Museums.

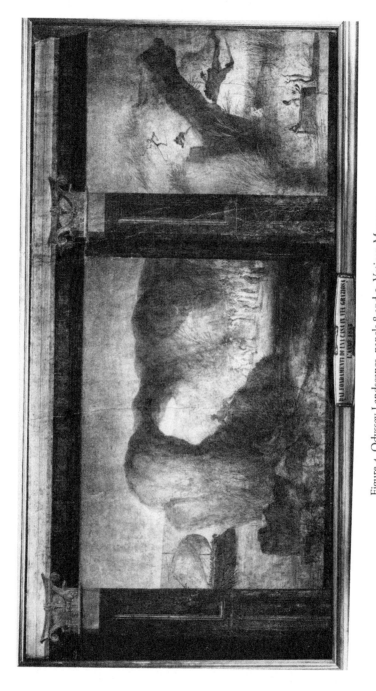

Figure 4 Odyssey Landscapes, panels 8 and 9. Vatican Museums.

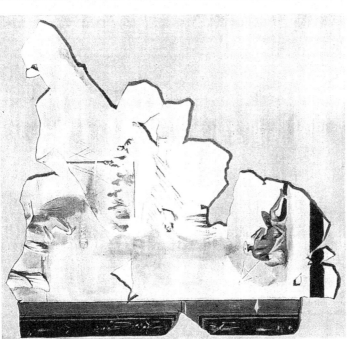

Figure 5 Odyssey Landscapes, fragmentary panel. Left: black and white sketch reproduced with permission from Licia Vlad Borrelli, "Un nuovo frammento dei 'paesaggi dell'Odissea'," *Bollettino d'Arte* 41 (1956) 289–300: Fig. 1, p. 290. Right: photograph of original courtesy of the Museo Nazionale Romano.

of this dramatic natural setting are miniature figures enacting scenes from the Homeric *Odyssey*: specifically, from the part of the *Odyssey* narrated by Odysseus himself, including his encounter with the Laestrygonians and with Circe, the *nekuia*, and the voyage past the Sirens.

The mural's modern designation as the "Odyssey Landscapes" perfectly captures the interplay of myth and nature that is its most famous feature; in addition to the human figures and the natural setting, however, the wall decoration has a third element, a fact that is sometimes overlooked both in scholarship and in reproductions of the work. Framing the landscape is a series of painted red pillars, evenly spaced, creating the illusion that the viewer must look through a colonnade in order to see the mythical landscape "beyond" it (Fig. 6).[4] These pillars serve to divide the frieze into individual units more conducive for viewing. By its very compositional technique the mural encourages the viewer to look past this architectural frame; yet to do so is to ignore the fact that these pillars are as much a representation as the landscape "behind" them, and are therefore as worthy of interpretation as the rest of the painting.

In what follows, I will argue that the portico frame of the Odyssey Landscapes is no mere narrative device, but a reference to the experience of the *ambulatio*, the act of walking for leisure and contemplation which, as we have seen in the previous two chapters, was an essential feature of Roman leisure. The painted portico invites the strolling viewers to contemplate the philosophical associations of the Odyssey Landscapes, and even to reenact, in the comfort of a private home, the journey of Odysseus himself.

THE ODYSSEY LANDSCAPES: AN OVERVIEW

The Odyssey Landscapes were hailed as a landmark of Greco-Roman art immediately upon their discovery in Rome in 1848.[5] The construction of low-income housing along the Via Graziosa on the Esquiline came to a standstill when workers discovered a segment of *opus reticulatum*; subsequent exploration revealed panels 2 and 3 of the Odyssey Landscapes (Fig. 1).[6] Excavation of the rest of the fresco was then interrupted by

---

[4] Throughout this chapter I will use the term "pillar" for the painted architectural supports, since they are rectangular in cross-section. In so doing, I follow the terminology suggested by Ginouvès 1992, 63, who reserves "pillar" for independent supports which are square or rectangular in cross-section, and "pier" for massive or irregular supports; in practice, however, the two terms are often reversed, as he himself notes.

[5] See, for example, Braun 1849, 27: "Zwischen [den Pilastern] aber entfalten sich landschaftliche Scenen von einer Großartigkeit und Originalität des Vortrags, wie er kaum sonst wo vorkommt."

[6] Although technically inaccurate, "panel" is still a useful way to refer to the individual scenes that appear between the pillars of the painted portico. The first panel was already destroyed when the

Figure 6 Reconstruction (by author) of the Odyssey Landscapes as originally arranged. Watercolors of the individual panels are reproduced with permission from Ralf Biering, *Die Odysseefresken vom Esquilin* (Munich 1995).

disputes both large and small: that year, the city was paralyzed by civil unrest that led to the short-lived *repubblica romana* (1848–9), while on the Via Graziosa Sig. Filippo Bennicelli, who owned the house under which the remaining panels of the Odyssey Landscapes continued, managed to hold up excavations by demanding more money from the state.[7] Emil Braun, secretary of the Deutsches Archäologisches Institut in Rome, lamented the fact that a painting of such importance was left to languish in the elements for almost a year, but further damage was inflicted by the archaeologists themselves, who ordered restorations of the painting during and after its excavation.[8]

A summary of the original circumstances of the excavation is important, since the findspot was buried, along with the Via Graziosa itself, by the construction of the Via Cavour in the 1880s. Moreover, any original excavation reports have also been lost, and we are left with the rather unsystematic account of Pietro Matranga, a Hellenist at the Vatican library who wrote the first monograph on the painting.[9] Our knowledge of the original context of the work is therefore frustratingly limited. We cannot be sure, for example, what type of room the fresco decorated (atrium, peristyle, and cryptoporticus have all been suggested), nor do we know for certain whether or not the excavated building was a *domus* at all, though this is usually assumed. Matranga (1852, 103–37) actually argued that the structure was the Portico of Livia, but the location of the portico on the marble plan does not support his thesis.[10] More recently Kuttner (2003, 112) has pointed out that the paintings were discovered in an area that boasted numerous suburban *horti*, while Coarelli 1998 insists that the paintings decorated a grand *domus*, part of which (though not the part that held the Odyssey Landscapes) can be identified on a fragment of the marble plan.[11] Similarly, there is some confusion in the scholarship

---

painting was discovered, and left *in situ*, so by convention the first extant panel (the initial encounter between Odysseus' men and the Laestrygonian princess; Fig. 1) is referred to as the second (as in von Blanckenhagen 1963 and Biering 1995, among others).

[7] See Henzen 1850, 167. For an overview of the available evidence for the discovery and excavation of the Odyssey Landscapes, see Biering 1995, 167–80 and 195–6.

[8] The most damaging restoration was the application of a fixative that altered the original colors; a second round of restorations in 1952–6 removed the fixative, but also some of the original painting in panels 4 and 5. See Biering 1995, 14–19.

[9] Matranga 1852. The bulk of the monograph is only tangentially related to the painting: the first chapter (1–53) uses the landscape paintings to argue that the Laestrygonians inhabited the area around modern Terracina, *c.* 90 km SE of Rome, while the second chapter (55–100) proposes that *Od.* 7.104 refers to the carding of wool, and not the grinding of grain. The two appendices (pp. 103–48) focus more specifically on the painting and the details of its discovery and excavation.

[10] On the Severan marble plan of Rome, see the Stanford Digital Forma Urbis Romae Project (available at: http://formaurbis.stanford.edu/).

[11] The *domus* in question is not on the same axis as the Odyssey Landscapes wall, so Coarelli's identification is hardly conclusive. Moreover, there is still no reason to rule out the possibility that the painting decorated a public building. In this chapter I follow the scholarly consensus by assuming

about the placement of the frieze on the wall itself; most accounts claim that the frieze was situated high up, although, as Biering (1995, 169–70) has convincingly argued, the notion that we have an exact measurement is based on a misreading.[12] Still, the open vista on the upper part of the wall is a relatively common feature of the Second Style, and it is reasonable to assume that the frieze was somewhere above eye level.[13]

The incomplete state of our knowledge has even been exaggerated by scholars: there has been some debate, for example, over whether or not the frieze would have continued on more than the one excavated wall, even though Matranga explicitly states that there were panels on the adjacent wall that were left unexcavated because they were in such a state of disrepair.[14] Nonetheless, we still do not know what percentage of the original frieze we possess, nor what the wall looked like beneath the landscapes. Yet the central scholarly controversy surrounding the work centers not on any of these unknowns but on the one aspect of the painting that would seem to be beyond dispute: despite the fact that the Odyssey Landscapes are one of the relatively few examples of ancient wall painting unearthed in the city of Rome itself, scholars have questioned whether the work is really "Roman." Peter von Blanckenhagen argued at great length in an article of 1963 that the fresco was a copy of a now lost Hellenistic original, and the painting has long enjoyed a kind of dual citizenship, serving as a dependable highlight in handbooks on both Roman and Hellenistic art.[15] The temptation to see in

that the painting was part of a domestic ensemble, but my argument that the painted portico evokes the *idea* of walking, and its many intellectual associations in late republican Rome, could apply just as easily to public or private decoration.

[12] Matranga 1852, 112 n. 12 gives a measurement from the floor to the beginning of a vault (5.5 meters), which some have used (see e.g. Coarelli 1998, 31) to place the bottom of the frieze about 4 meters high. But, as Biering points out, there is no suggestion in Vespignani's drawings that the ancient floor was excavated, nor is there any indication of a vaulted ceiling; Biering argues that Matranga has misidentified as a vault the beginning of an arch much higher on the wall, and that the measurement reflects the depth of the excavation, not the height of the paintings.

[13] For the open upper part as a feature of the Second Style, see Engemann 1967, 39–57.

[14] Matranga 1852, 109. One of Vespignani's drawings (Matranga 1852, Plate 10; reprinted in O'Sullivan 2007, Fig. 5) clearly shows the outline of the portico frame on the wall at right angles to the wall with the Odyssey Landscapes. Andreae has argued in a number of publications (e.g. Andreae 1962, 108 and 1988, 282) that the first panel must have depicted the Polyphemus episode, on the grounds that it could not have been omitted; since, however, there was another frieze preceding the destroyed panel, the argument does not hold. Biering 1995, 172–4 has tentatively suggested that the fragmentary Sirens panel (Fig. 5) was originally on a third wall, at right angles to the extant frieze.

[15] Von Blanckenhagen 1963 was not the first to make this general point, though his is the most complete development of the argument. His article, in addition to being an excellent overview of the painting and its problems, also has a thorough summary of the scholarship on the disputed origin of the painting. For its prominent placement of the painting in a work on Hellenistic art, see Pollitt 1986, 185–209, esp. 185–6 and 208–9, though his treatment of its origin is quite balanced; he notes that the Odyssey Landscapes "brought Hellenistic technique into a world increasingly dominated by Roman

the mural evidence for an elaborate (but almost entirely lost) tradition of Hellenistic landscape painting has been too much for scholars to resist. For one thing, much of Roman wall painting, particularly that of the First and Second Style, has direct or indirect antecedents in Greek painting.[16] Furthermore, the development of the bucolic genre by Hellenistic poets such as Theocritus and Moschus cries out for the visual analog that a tradition of Hellenistic landscape painting would provide.[17] The discovery of the frieze of the hunt on the so-called tomb of Philip at Vergina in 1977 has done little to settle the debate: the natural setting of the hunt suggests that Macedonian painters were interested in landscape as more than a mere backdrop to human action, yet the frieze could hardly prevent us from continuing to call the Odyssey Landscapes the first extant example of full-fledged landscape painting in the Western tradition.[18] Suffice it to say for now that, whatever the antecedents of our fresco may have been, its setting requires us to consider the painting in its Roman context, and how it would have been viewed by Roman viewers – however Hellenized.[19]

THE PORTICO FRAME

Despite the scholarly controversy surrounding the painting's sources, critics have always readily agreed that the painted frame of red pillars was a Roman idea. Yet for the most part, and particularly for those scholars who argue that the Odyssey Landscapes are a copy of a Hellenistic original, the identification of the frame as a Roman contribution to the painting has acted as a sort of

---

taste and are a product of the fusion of the two cultures" (208). Cf. Leach 1988, 41: "[I]n the study of Roman painting one must accept the proposition that originality does not preclude a blending of Roman and Greek."

[16] The First Style is essentially a Hellenistic style: Bruno 1969; Mielsch 2001, 21–5; Baldassarre *et al.* 2002, 67–70. Tybout 1989, 109–86 argues that what we consider the Second Style is simply the Romano-Campanian instantiation of a broader Hellenistic *koine*.

[17] Zanker 2004 argues for parallels between the Odyssey Landscapes and Moschus' *Europa* (pp. 50–1) and (pseudo-?)Theocritus 25 (pp. 89–91), although he does not claim that the paintings are a copy of a Hellenistic original. Further complicating the question of the origin of the Odyssey Landscapes is that many of the characters in the painting are labeled in Greek; rather than proving the existence of a Greek original, however, the labels are simply another way in which the painting advertises its "Greekness," as Beard and Henderson 2001, 54 aptly note. On the use of Greek labels in Roman wall painting, see Thomas 1995.

[18] On the tomb and its frieze (with numerous photographs and line drawings), see Andronicos 1984, 97–119. For a similar assessment of the relationship between the landscape of the Vergina frieze and the Odyssey Landscapes, see Small 1999, 568.

[19] As Wallace-Hadrill 1998, 91 puts it in a different context, "To be Roman, go Greek." For other analyses of aristocratic Romans playing Greek in the privacy of their own homes, see Neudecker 1988, 8–30; Zanker 1998, 16–9 and 33–43; Bergmann 2001. The problem of Greek originals and Roman recreations has always plagued Roman art, and is becoming a focal point again, as an instance of Roman reception of Greek culture; see Bergmann 1995a; Kuttner 1995; Gazda 1995 and 2002; Perry 2005; Marvin 2008.

back-handed compliment, so that the addition of the pillars becomes one of the Roman innovations that has done a disservice to the Greek "original."[20] Numerous reproductions of the mural do away with the pillars altogether, as though by doing so we might have more direct access to a lost masterpiece of Hellenistic art.[21] Indeed the very fact that we commonly refer to the painting with the plural "landscapes" (and the individual scenes as "panels" or "pictures") subordinates the portico frame to the "real" subject of the fresco.

Yet no matter how we understand the origin of the painting, the red pillars deserve consideration in and of themselves, if only because they are a fundamental part of the painting's organization. A hypothetical reconstruction of the frieze as originally arranged makes it clear that the colonnade would have made an immediate impression on the viewer – if not as striking as the landscapes themselves, nonetheless difficult to ignore (Fig. 6). Although the pillars at first glance appear to constitute a single row, closer inspection reveals a second row of pillars in the shadows, partially occluded by the first row, and that both rows support an architrave and a roof (Fig. 7).[22] The form, then, is that of a portico (Greek *stoa*, Latin *porticus*): a covered colonnade that was ubiquitous in Greek and Roman architecture both as a framing device for other spaces (gardens, temple precincts, streets) and as an independent structure.[23] In the first four panels (Figs. 1–2), the back pillar can be seen to the right of the front pillar; starting with the second pillar of panel 6 (Fig. 3; cf. Fig. 6), however, the back pillar appears to the left of the front pillar. The effect, then, is a trick of perspective: the imagined viewing position of the extant frieze is in front of the sixth panel (that is, at the palace of Circe), which is marked as central by the placement of the rear pillars.[24] As we shall see further on, this centrality is reinforced by

[20] Von Blanckenhagen's reaction (1963, 106) is typical of the critical assessment: "The peculiar and certainly exaggerated fashion of having frames cutting off parts of figures and objects must be explained, all the more because, to my knowledge, this form of 'illusionism' is unique in ancient painting."

[21] Lydakis 2004, 200–1 goes so far as to reconstruct a Hellenistic "original" by putting panels 3–5 side by side, without the framing pillars.

[22] It is not clear whether we are supposed to imagine the second row as free-standing pillars or engaged pilasters along a back wall; in the case of the latter, some of the observations below about figures intentionally "disappearing" behind the pillars would not correspond to the portico as "really" painted, but I would argue that we should not press the realism of the architectural reconstruction too far.

[23] Coulton 1976 offers a history of the Greek *stoa*, although he is primarily interested in free-standing *stoai*, not the four-sided peristyles that develop in the Hellenistic period to frame open spaces; on the *porticus*, see MacDonald 1986, 33–66; Anderson 1997, 247–50; Frakes 2009; Macaulay-Lewis 2009.

[24] Roman wall painting ensembles of the Second Style usually establish a viewing point (sometimes reflected in the floor decoration) from which the wall is meant to be seen; see Scagliarini Corlàita 1974–6, 9–10 and Clarke 1991, 41–5. The differing perspectives of the portico frame (to be viewed

Figure 7   Close-up of the top left corner of Panel 2 of the Odyssey Landscapes, showing the
two pillars and connecting architrave. Sketch by author.

the special status of the sixth panel itself, which is distinguished from its
adjacent panels both in composition and in narrative technique.

It seems clear then that the painted frame represents a portico, but what
kind of portico is this? Would the ancient viewer recognize the form? The
question is not an idle one. Vitruvius famously criticized contemporary
trends in Roman wall painting for a lack of realism, lamenting the
depiction of fantastical architectural features that could not have existed
in the real world.[25] Did a portico such as this, with thin red pillars and
golden capitals, exist in the ancient world? It is not immediately apparent

from below) and the landscape itself (to be viewed from above) have vexed interpreters of the
painting, and fuel von Blanckenhagen's hypothesis (1963, 111–12) that the landscape was not originally
designed for this setting. As Biering 1995, 160 points out, however, the landscape itself shows little
internal consistency of perspective (he compares the size of Odysseus' ships [Fig. 2] and Circe's palace
[Fig. 3]), so the expectation of a consistent perspective shared by the landscapes and the portico
frame should not be assumed. Moreover, there is the possibility that the intended illusion was not that we
are looking out at a "real" landscape, but that we are looking at a representation of a portico decorated
with a landscape painting: a representation of a representation. If this is the case, we would not expect
a consistency of perspective between frame and landscape.

[25] Vitr. *De arch.* 7.5.3–8; on the passage, and its relationship to Third Style ensembles, see Ehrhardt 1987,
152–62; Clarke 1991, 49–53.

Figure 8 Pompeii: Portico of the Praedia of Julia Felix. Photo by author.

what material these red pillars are supposed to represent: are they painted wood, painted stucco, or some sort of fantastically colored marble, like the surreal colors boasted by the panels of the late First Style of Pompeian wall painting?[26] Although it is true that porticoes typically employed cylindrical columns and not pillars for support, there are exceptions. The so-called Hall of the Doric Pillars at Hadrian's villa has monumental marble pillars for supports.[27] On a somewhat humbler scale, the Praedia Iuliae Felicis at Pompeii boasts a two-sided colonnade with slender pillars that are very similar in impression and scale to the narrow pillars of the Odyssey painting (Fig. 8).[28] Similarly, although the Greek stoa almost always featured columns, marble pillars were used on occasion; considering the possibility that

[26] The gilded capitals might suggest marble, but the garish red seems a bit too bright for *rosso antico*, which is how Biering 1995, 21 identifies the material. If this is meant to simulate marble, perhaps we are meant to imagine that the marble is painted?

[27] MacDonald and Pinto 1995, 80 interpret the space as a basilica, renaming it the "Ceremonial Precinct," "a spacious building for state business and occasions."

[28] On the portico, see Parslow 1989, 267–9, esp. n. 153 for analogs in wall painting (including the Odyssey Landscapes) and in Italian archaeological remains.

the Odyssey Landscapes portico was displayed at some height, the use of rectangular pillars on the upper level of two-story stoas at Delos is particularly noteworthy.[29] In addition to these examples, we can only assume that wooden pillars were a common support for simpler porticoes, and would obviously not survive today.

A more useful point of comparison for our portico is offered by Roman wall painting itself, and this is the usual point of reference in scholarly discussions of the portico frame. One of the hallmarks of the Second Style of Roman wall painting is the opening of the wall in a trompe l'oeil effect, onto a seemingly endless receding architectural vista.[30] Supporting columns are an essential feature of this decoration, giving the sense of monumental civic or religious space; the Second Style paintings from the Villa at Oplontis are a well-known example. Occasionally this sort of decoration includes porticoes supported by slender pillars very much like the ones that front the Odyssey Landscapes, such as the fresco from room 23 of the Villa at Oplontis, or the west wall of room 5 (the Room of the Masks) in the House of Augustus on the Palatine (Fig. 9).[31] Similarly, we may look to contemporary wall painting for examples of painted porticoes being used as a frame for the rest of the painted wall. Room 6 (the Room of the Garlands) in the House of Augustus has a series of thin red and yellow pillars painted on three of its sides (Fig. 10); the upper part of the wall is thereby divided into "panels" quite similar to the Odyssey Landscapes, though the framed view opens onto another colonnaded courtyard instead of a mythological landscape.[32] Scholars have seen numerous points of reference for the profusion of colonnades and porticoes in the Second Style, including public sacred architecture, theatrical design, and palatial grandeur.[33] Eleanor Winsor Leach has argued that what she terms the "porticus" style reflects above all the architectural features of contemporary *domestic* space, where colonnades and porticoes were an essential feature; as we shall see, this too is

[29] On the use of rectangular pillars instead of columns in Greek architecture, including their use as "the characteristic feature of the Delian upper order," see Coulton 1976, 129–30.

[30] On the historical development of the Second Style, see especially Beyen 1960, 13–33.

[31] Cf. also the Second Style decoration in room 20 of the House of the Cryptoporticus at Pompeii (1.6.2–4); see Pugliese Carratelli 1990–2003, vol. I, 231 (Figs. 65–6). Most scholars have seen in these porticoes the influence of *scaenae frons* architectural design (see e.g. Leach 2004, 93–100), though it is worth pointing out that the stage fronts are themselves trying to evoke the grandeur of palatial porticoes.

[32] Room 12 (The Ramp Entrance) in the House of Augustus also has an upper zone framed by pillars, though at a much greater height; see Carettoni 1983, Table 98 (and color table 2 for the north wall of the Room of the Garlands). Cf. also room y of the House of the Silver Wedding at Pompeii (5.2.1); see Pugliese Carratelli 1990–2003, vol. III, 747–9 (Figs. 153–7).

[33] For a useful discussion of the various points of reference, real and imaginary, of the Second Style, see Barbet 1985, 44–52; see also Ehrhardt 1991.

Figure 9 Rome: House of Augustus, Room of the Masks. Photo by Koppermann, DAI-Rom 1966.0024.

Figure 10 Rome: House of Augustus, Room of the Garlands. Photo by Koppermann, DAI-Rom 1966.0031.

where I think we should look to understand the full reference of the frame of the Odyssey Landscapes.[34]

A final point of comparison for the function of the Odyssey Landscapes frame is the common ancient practice of displaying art in stoas and porticoes. Colonnades were often used as art galleries; most famously, the Stoa Poikile in Athens earned its name from the paintings displayed there, depicting various highlights in Athenian military history, including the battle of Marathon and even the Trojan War.[35] That the stoa was an ambulatory space no doubt contributed to its use as a venue for the display of art, and the tradition continues in the public porticoes that appear around Rome in the late republic, most notably in the Portico of Pompey.[36] We know from Pliny the Elder for example (*HN* 35.144) that panel paintings of the Trojan War decorated the late republican Porticus Philippi in Rome.[37] The appeal of placing artworks in a space explicitly designed for leisurely strolls was in no small part due to the fact that the movement of the viewer contributed to the creation of a narrative flow. In a few cases, most notably the Telephos frieze at Pergamon, in which a narrative sculptural frieze is positioned in a three-sided portico, the connection between the movement of the viewer and the movement of the story is explicit.[38] Furthermore, the proximity of the columns and the frieze demands that the viewer step outside the portico to take in any significant stretch of narrative; the Telephos frieze thereby becomes a real-life analog for the Odyssey Landscapes, by its use of architectural supports to divide and frame a continuous narrative. In fact, von Blanckenhagen argues that the hypothetical original landscape may have decorated the wall of a portico, so that the Roman addition of the painted frame is trying to evoke the original viewing experience.[39]

---

[34] On the "porticus style," see (most recently) Leach 2004, 85–92. On the use of columns as framing elements in Roman domestic architecture, see Wallace-Hadrill 1994, 35–6; on framed views more generally as a characteristically Roman phenomenon, see Drerup 1959 (though I would qualify somewhat his claim at 149 that such views are not intended to be enjoyed while walking).

[35] See Pausanias 1.15.1–4.

[36] On the portico of Pompey, see Gleason 1990; Kuttner 1999. On the Roman use of public porticoes for the display of art, see Macaulay-Lewis 2009.

[37] The portico, with its double colonnade and Homeric paintings, is a possible influence on the Odyssey Landscapes; on the portico, see Richardson 1977, 359–61.

[38] The connection between the Telephos frieze and the Odyssey Landscapes is made by von Blanckenhagen 1957, 80. On the narrative art of the Telephos frieze, see Stewart 1996.

[39] Von Blanckenhagen 1957, 80; see also Vlad Borrelli 1956, 299. Cf. von Blanckenhagen 1963, 126: "[W]e may call the original Odyssey frieze a painted counterpart to [the Telephos frieze.]" While such a specific source for the portico frame seems to be a bit too neat, the general use of the portico as a frame in the Second Style has been traced to the Hellenistic practice of using real porticoes

As it happens, a passage in Vitruvius offers corroborating evidence that landscape painting was especially common as a display in porticoes. He offers an aetiology of sorts for the Second Style, and in the process reveals that the Odyssey Landscapes as we know them may in fact be the only surviving example of a subgenre (*De arch.* 7.5.2.):

postea ingressi sunt ut etiam aedificiorum figuras, columnarum et fastigiorum eminentes proiecturas imitarentur, patentibus autem locis uti exedris propter amplitudines parietum scaenarum frontes tragico more aut comico seu satyrico designarent, ambulationes vero propter spatia longitudinis varietatibus topiorum ornarent a certis locorum proprietatibus imagines exprimentes – pinguntur enim portus, promunturia, litora, flumina, fontes, euripi, fana, luci, montes, pecora, pastores – nonnulli locis item signorum megalographiam habentes deorum simulacra seu fabularum dispositas explicationes, non minus Troianas pugnas seu Ulixis errationes per topia, ceteraque, quae sunt eorum similibus rationibus ab rerum natura procreata.

Later, they also began to imitate the forms of buildings, and the projecting grandeur of columns and pediments. Moreover, in open spaces such as exedrae, because of the size of the walls, they began to draw stage settings in the tragic, or comic, or satyric mode. At the same time, they began to decorate ambulatory spaces, on account of their great length, with varieties of landscape, modeling their pictures on the true characteristics of places (for there are paintings of harbors, promontories, shores, rivers, springs, straits, shrines, groves, mountains, livestock, shepherds), with some in places even including paintings of statues, likenesses of the gods or the organized unfolding of stories, and even the battles of Troy, or the wanderings of Odysseus through landscape, and other things which, in ways similar to these, were begotten by nature.[40]

As many commentators have noted, the natural features that Vitruvius identifies as constitutive of the genre of landscape painting – harbors, headlands, shores, rivers, and so on – can all be found in the Odyssey Landscapes; even without the explicit reference to "the wanderings of Odysseus through landscape" we would surely be reminded of our painting.[41] Vitruvius' tone in this passage is a positive version of the

---

as frames (see Robertson 1955, 59). As Osborne 1987 has shown, however, the manipulation of views through a colonnade and the forced participation of the viewer's movement in the creation of the meaning of an artwork are at least as old as the Parthenon frieze.

[40] On the passage, Tybout 1989, 55–107 is essential; he however prefers the reading *nonullis locis* (attested in a few manuscripts), making the final part of the passage refer to "some spaces" (in general), and not just *ambulationes* (see 76–7). As is clear from my translation (and from what follows), I prefer the majority manuscript reading (and *lectio difficilior*) *nonnulli locis*; in any case I see the connection between Homeric myth and ambulatory space that Vitruvius seems to be making here as circumstantial evidence, and not as essential to my argument.

[41] Cf. Pliny's famous description (*HN* 35.116–17) of the landscapes of the Augustan-era painter Studius, though Ling 1977, 3 argues that Pliny's description does not correspond well to the Odyssey Landscapes.

moralizing aesthetic reaction to the Third Style that we witnessed above: he approves of the Second Style for its commitment to depicting things drawn from the real world, whether natural or man-made. Similarly, he posits a "natural" relationship between the subject of wall painting and its architectural setting (and, by extension, its viewing context): spaces that are enclosed and offer the viewer a chance for stationary contemplation are more suited to architectural displays, while longer spaces invite the strolling viewer to appreciate the subtle variations of landscape along a longer wall.[42] The painted portico draws attention to the participation of its viewers in the unraveling of the story that is depicted before them; it is a visible reminder, a metaphor for the viewers' act of walking, which is integral to both the act of viewing and the act of interpreting the frieze. In the section that follows, I will look at some of the ways in which the painted portico of the Odyssey Landscapes achieves a similar narrative effect, as the viewer is led through this imaginary *ambulatio*.

THE NARRATIVE WALK

In his study of the Odyssey Landscapes, Ralf Biering has shown through ultraviolet photography that the framing pillars were sketched before the rest of the painting, proving that they formed an integral part of its genesis.[43] Those who posit a Hellenistic original could argue that the underdrawing of the architectural frame hardly discredits their theory; its most vocal proponent, von Blanckenhagen, in fact insisted that this must have been the case, claiming that "the place of the pillars must have been fixed before the painting of the frieze started."[44] Von Blanckenhagen interprets as a sign of careful planning the fact that the pillars do not occlude any important scenes; yet, at the same time, the fact that a few less significant figures are cut off by the portico he interprets as a sign that the painting was originally conceived as a continuous landscape without an architectural frame, and that these small characters would not have been covered in the original. One could, however, draw precisely the opposite

---

[42] As it happens, the correspondence is not as common as Vitruvius would suggest, or at least not in our extant remains; for the evidence, see Tybout 1989, 97–107, who concludes that Vitruvius has the general picture right (i.e., that the size of rooms was an important influence on Second Style wall ensembles) even if the specific details do not withstand scrutiny. Scagliarini Corlàita 1997 draws a similar conclusion about Vitruvius' description of ambulatory spaces.

[43] Biering 1995, 23–5.

[44] Von Blanckenhagen 1963, 111.

conclusion. Having some events partially concealed by the pillars only heightens the illusion that there is an actual portico through which the viewer sees the landscape. Given how many figures there are in the third panel (some sixteen, not including animals: Fig. 1), it would look somewhat contrived if all the action managed to keep itself *within* the frame of the two pillars; to maintain the illusion, the painter must give the impression that the action takes place without awareness of the painted frame.[45] The disappearance of none but insignificant figures behind the pillars thus argues all the more compellingly that this painting was conceived for its original location, pillars included.

A closer examination of how each panel relates to the portico frame will show how integral it is to both the narrative progression of the frieze and the kinetic experience of the viewer. In all of the sections but one, the portico clearly serves to frame one particular episode of the Homeric narrative, so that each panel is in some sense describing one action.[46] Yet at the same time there are elements in each scene that serve to bridge the gap from one side of the pillar to the next. In panel 2, for example (Fig. 11), in which Odysseus' men are greeted by the Laestrygonian princess, the overall mood is one of deceptive tranquility. Such a mood is reinforced by the peaceful characters who frame the main action of that scene, such as the reclining figure just to the left, watching the scene with no apparent malice.[47] Another figure lies on the rock above the Laestrygonian princess, suggesting that the place from which she has just come is a peaceful one. Most important for our purposes is the pastoral scene to the right of Odysseus' men, which extends into the first third of the next panel. The cowherds, the shepherd reclining on a rock, the goats drinking from the spring – all lull the viewer into the same dangerous complacency which will be the doom of Odysseus' men, whose backs are literally turned to the oncoming violence in panel 3.[48] The

[45] Cf. Biering 1995, 164, who points out that the pillars are not merely frames for the action, but rather create an additional level of illusion. Ling 1991, 111 makes a similar point, though he still treats the frieze as a copy, albeit "freely adapted."

[46] The exception, panel 6 (Fig. 3), is famous for its simultaneous depiction of two distinct moments in the Circe story; see below.

[47] She is usually identified as a personification of the spring at which the princess is drawing water when she is met by Odysseus' men; according to Biering 1995, 125 only the last two letters of her label [KPH]NH are still legible.

[48] As Lowenstam 1995, 197–8 points out, the presence of the pastoral scene is most likely a reference to Odysseus' description of the Laestrygonian land as a place where the night is so short that "in that place a man who did not sleep could have earned two paychecks, one for driving cattle, and the other for herding white sheep; for close together are the paths of night and day" (Hom. *Od.* 10.84–6).

Figure 11 Odyssey Landscapes (in nineteenth-century reproduction by H. C. Krohn), Panel 2. From Woermann, *Die antiken Odyssee-Landschaften* (Munich 1876), Plate 1.

peaceful mood is in fact transported into the next scene by the cowherd, who disappears behind the red pillar (thereby echoing the movement of the viewer), and by the spring, which runs from one section to the next. The portico therefore plays an important part in the narrative strategy: as the pastoral scene progresses before, behind, and after the pillar, the viewer is fooled into thinking that the pillar is in fact not serving as a frame at all, since it is not a transitional marker here and does not seem to separate scene from scene. This reinforces the (false) sense of security evoked by the scene itself, and renders the violence of the Laestrygonian attack all the more sudden and unsettling.[49]

The third panel continues the forward progression of the narrative by maintaining the overall left-to-right movement of the first scene: the violence is introduced as the first Laestrygonian bends a tree to the right and thereby points us to the focal point of the panel (Fig. 12). Yet there is also a Laestrygonian pulling a Greek from the swamp in the lower right

[49] The antithesis of tranquility and violence also mirrors the Homeric episode, which "begins as if it were going to be another *Phaiakis*, but transforms itself unexpectedly and horrifically into another *Cyclopeia*" (Cook 1995, 71).

Figure 12 Odyssey Landscapes (in nineteenth-century reproduction by H. C. Krohn),
Panel 3. From Woermann, *Die antiken Odyssee-Landschaften* (Munich 1876), Plate 2.

corner; his movement, in the opposite direction, adds to the energy and
confusion. The counterpart to this vignette is the one immediately to its
right, a little further in the background, where the violence enacted on the
dying Greek is similarly reinforced by the truncated representation of his
body, although here the body is covered not by marshy water, but by the
familiar red support of the portico. The effect, however, is no less disturb-
ing; despite the fact that we cannot see Odysseus' man, we have no doubt
about his violent end. The portico therefore has a similarly narratological
function as before; although the section ends with the opposite mood from
the first, the effect is achieved in much the same way. As the Laestrygonian
pushes the helpless Greek both underwater and "offstage," we realize that
the violence will spill over into the next frame. As in the first instance, the
pillar not only serves to define the third section, allowing us to give the
picture one coherent reading, but it also propels the story (and the viewer)
forward, making it apparent that the violence cannot be contained by the
visual frame.

The organization of the fourth panel is quite different from the previous
two; there is a certain symmetry enforced by the embracing arms of the bay,
but the effect is to emphasize the dwindling prospects for Odysseus' men

Figure 13 Odyssey Landscapes (in nineteenth-century reproduction by H. C. Krohn), Panel 4. From Woermann, *Die antiken Odyssee-Landschaften* (Munich 1876), Plate 3.

(Fig. 13). Instead of the left-to-right movement of the first two panels, here our eyes are drawn to the middle, just as the Laestrygonians in the foreground focus their attention on the bay, intent on the destruction of the Greeks and their ships. Unlike the previous two transitions, there is no occluded figure to encourage movement to the next scene, and the viewer is just as trapped between those two pillars as the Greeks are in that narrow bay. Yet the violence does spill over somewhat onto the next frame: on the bottom left corner of panel 5 there is a Laestrygonian about to crush a tiny Greek victim with a rock (Fig. 14). While the previous sections had figures which propelled the narrative forward, here we have a little scene which looks back to the previous one. It is the analog of the death at the right edge of panel 3, in which the Greek is being pushed underwater, and the symmetrical arrangement of the two murders, on either side of the pillars of panel 4, punctuates the narrative pause of the fourth scene.

But one ship does escape, and in the fifth panel we follow Odysseus' ship as it appears from behind a huge rock (Fig. 14).[50] The viewer will now

[50] The name tag inscribed above the ship confirms that Odysseus is on board, but we do not actually see him in the extant narrative until his dramatic entrance in panel 6.

Figure 14 Odyssey Landscapes (in nineteenth-century reproduction by H. C. Krohn), Panel 5. From Woermann, *Die antiken Odyssee-Landschaften* (Munich 1876), Plate 4.

remember from the Homeric story that Odysseus had the foresight which his companions lacked, leaving his ship outside that narrow harbor (*Od.* 10.95–6). The section is in some sense similar to the previous one, with land on either side, and water in the middle. But this is a strait, whereas the other was a bay, and the effect of the scene is one of transition, in contrast to the confining danger of panel 4. The transition is emphasized by the contrast between the violent scene on the left side of the panel and the peaceful one on the right, the reclining personifications of the shoreline, the *aktai*. The figure on the right of panel 5 in particular recalls the *krene* personification from panel 2, and the attentive viewer should recall that the tranquility which that figure introduced was in fact an illusion. And while the violent scene on the lower left looks back to the previous panel, the figures on the right look forward to the next scene, pointing the narrative past the pillar and into the house of Circe.

As noted earlier, panel 6 is marked as the central panel by the architectural perspective of the columns (Fig. 15). Aside from this, there are other features that distinguish it from the rest of the extant frieze. Here for the first time the action takes place not in a landscape but in an architectural setting, namely, the palace of Circe. Yet it is clear that the painter has

Figure 15 Odyssey Landscapes (in nineteenth-century reproduction by H. C. Krohn), Panel 6. From Woermann, *Die antiken Odyssee-Landschaften* (Munich 1876), Plate 5.

partially collapsed the boundaries between outside and inside: not only are we situated in a courtyard with a tree, but the courtyard itself is also not clearly demarcated by architecture, and despite Odysseus' entry through the front door, it appears to be open to the surrounding landscape. Furthermore, the house itself, with its yellow-brown stucco, plainly recalls the cliffs depicted earlier in the frieze, and blends quite naturally into the existing landscape.

The Circe panel is also distinguished from the rest of the frieze by its narrative experimentation: the painter has juxtaposed two different moments in time in the same frame, almost side by side. On the left, Circe greets Odysseus at the door, and on the right, Odysseus draws his sword on the sorceress. The panel is therefore a particularly dramatic example of continuous narrative, in which two or more different episodes involving the same characters appear against the same backdrop.[51] Strictly speaking, the entire Odyssey frieze is a continuous

---

[51] Cf. Stansbury-O'Donnell 1999, 146 (emphasis his): "*Continuous* narration is one in which the agents reappear against a common background in an integrated pictorial field, with time shifting from one scene to the next and space either changing or remaining the same." For a useful introduction to the scholarship on ancient visual narrative, see Stansbury-O'Donnell 1999, 1–8.

narrative, since Odysseus appears more than once along the length of the painting. In this sense, the Odyssey Landscapes employ a narrative technique familiar from Hellenistic art, such as the Telephos frieze at Pergamon.[52] The Odysseus and Circe panel, however, is an instance of what von Blanckenhagen (1957, 81) called "strict" continuous narrative, in which the same character(s) are depicted in the same visual field at two distinct moments of the story.[53]

It is not a coincidence, I would argue, that this narrative play comes at the center of the frieze.[54] The sixth panel confirms the connection between the narrative movement of the painting and the walk of the viewer, for both acts of movement are halted in the same frame: the viewer is encouraged to linger on this scene by the perspective imposed by the portico, which marks the place where the ideal viewer might stand and contemplate the entire wall. Moreover, the narrative paradox of the Circe panel occurs at precisely the moment where the portico frame offers the viewer a similarly ambiguous narrative message. Just as the narrative strategy of the painting expects the viewer both to follow a narrative progression over time in the first few panels and to take in two different moments in time in the sixth panel, the portico frame conveys to the viewer two contradictory suggestions: to walk the length of the wall through this fictive ambulatory space and at the same time to view the entire wall while standing in front of the central panel. In fact, we might say that the viewer, like Odysseus in this scene, is asked to be in two places at once.[55]

The similarity between the viewer and Odysseus established by the sixth panel brings us to another meaning of the portico frame. For the walk of the

---

[52] Carl Robert, the first scholar to develop a history of ancient visual narrative, was also the first to identify continuous narrative as a characteristic of Hellenistic art (earlier examples notwithstanding); see Robert 1881, 46–50.

[53] Von Blanckenhagen argues that this type of continuous narrative was a Roman development, and there are indeed many examples in Pompeian wall painting (see, for example, Leach 1981 and 1986); since he believes that the Odyssey Landscapes are a copy of a Hellenistic original, this forces him to argue that the addition of a second set of Odysseus, Circe, and servant is (along with the portico frame) the only Roman contribution to the painting. For the suggestion that continuous narrative is a legacy of Roman triumphal painting, see Holliday 2002, 89. On Roman visual narrative techniques, see Brilliant 1984.

[54] Of course, since we do not know the length of the original wall, we do not know if the Circe panel was the exact physical center of the frieze, but the portico perspective makes it clear that it was the notional center.

[55] For a similarly playful use of continuous narrative, see Leach's reading (1981, 315–16 and 9–20) of the Diana and Actaeon panel from the Casa del Frutetto in Pompeii; in that painting, the painter depicts Actaeon at three different stages of his encounter with Diana, and the manipulation of the viewer's shifting gaze evokes both the metamorphosis of the hunter and the act of viewing central to the myth itself.

viewer does not just evoke the narrative "movement" of the fresco (or, for that matter, of the *Odyssey*); it also evokes the movement of Odysseus himself. As we have seen in earlier chapters, the act of walking for leisure would evoke in the viewer an array of associations, including the cultural metaphor that connected physical movement and intellectual inquiry, travel and the acquisition of knowledge and wisdom: precisely, in other words, what the hero depicted on the other side of the fictive portico was famous for. The portico frame thus mediates between the walk of the viewer and the travels of Odysseus himself. In the final section of this chapter we will see what philosophical lessons the viewer, put into the right frame of mind by the intellectual associations of the *ambulatio*, might acquire by walking with Odysseus.[56]

PHILOSOPHICAL WANDERINGS

By the first century BCE, it was a commonplace that Homer could be considered the father of philosophy, with various schools competing for the right to claim him.[57] The mining of Homeric poetry for philosophical lessons is especially associated with the Stoics, but they did not, as Philodemus makes clear, claim exclusive rights to the activity: "so we hear that Homer is said to be the inventor of philosophy by not merely the critics but the philosophers themselves, and not those from one school only but from all" (*Rhet.* Sudhaus vol. II, p. III = *PHerc* 425 fr. 21, 8–14: ὥστ[ε] φιλοσοφίας μὲ[ν] αὐτὸν εὑρέτην λεγόμενον ἀκούειν οὐχ [ὑπὸ] τῶν κριτικῶν μό[νον ἀλ]λὰ καὶ τῶν φιλοσόφων <αὐ>τῶν, οὐδὲ μιᾶς μό[νον αἱ]ρέσεως ἀλλὰ πασ[ῶν]).[58] Treating Homer as the "inventor" of

---

[56] Bergmann 2001, 158 also draws a parallel between the travels of Odysseus as represented in the Odyssey Landscapes and the *ambulatio* of the Roman aristocrat (though without explicit reference to the portico frame): "The Odyssey Frieze is one of many integrative landscapes in which a story could evolve in stages or a figure enact his life in a kind of cinematic flow. That movement through a constructed realm was physically experienced by visitors to a well-outfitted park or villa garden, who could 'travel' the world, from present to past and back again, by passing through provocative zones filled with the appropriate regional vegetation and figures from a myth or historical event." On the impact of travel and tourism on Hellenistic and Roman art, see Cohen 2001. On the influence of ancient cartography on Roman landscape painting, including the Odyssey Landscapes, see Doherty 2010.

[57] The bibliography on this topic, both ancient and modern, is enormous. The best single resource is Buffière 1956, a survey of philosophical readings of the *Iliad* and the *Odyssey*, with an emphasis on allegorical interpretation; also useful are Lamberton 1986, 1–43 and the essays in Lamberton and Keaney 1992. On philosophical readings of the *Odyssey* and Odysseus in particular, see Buffière 1956, 365–91, and *passim*; Stanford 1963; Kaiser 1964; and Rutherford 1986.

[58] For the Greek, see Janko 2000, 126, from whom I have also taken the translation. For the sentiment, cf. Sen. *Ep.* 88.5. On Stoic readings of Homer, see Long 1992.

philosophy is in part a reflex of a more general tendency to treat the *Iliad* and the *Odyssey* as the foundational texts of Greek culture, and to refer to Homer as an authority that all Greeks could share.[59] Yet the practice of Homeric exegesis by ancient philosophers was also inspired by specific philosophical questions that the texts raised; for example, allegorical readings of Homeric characters and episodes were popular in part because they excused Homer for his "immoral" representations of the gods, who could now be read as allegories of the physical world.[60]

In addition to opportunities for allegorical interpretation, the poetry of Homer offered numerous "starting points" (ἀφορμαί) for philosophical inquiry, particularly as a source of ethical recommendations for human behavior.[61] It is the latter for which Odysseus was a useful model, and not only because he is arguably the most developed and complex character in the Homeric corpus. The journey of a hero who sees the towns and comes to know the minds of many people was, and remains, an irresistible metaphor for the human condition and our journey through life, and, as Richard Rutherford in particular has shown, we should not allow the later history of sometimes fanciful moralizing readings of the *Odyssey* to obscure the fact that the poem itself encourages such readings.[62] Predictably, different schools were attracted to different aspects of Odysseus' journey. Stoic readers chose to emphasize his long sufferings and his steadfast pursuit of his homecoming, even in the face of powerful temptations.[63] Cynics also promoted Heracles and Odysseus as models of self-sufficiency and prototypes for proper behavior in difficult circumstances.[64] Perhaps most surprisingly, there were also prominent Epicurean interpretations of Odysseus' behavior, despite the school's legendary reputation for

---

[59] See Buffière 1956, 10–13; Nagy 1979, 6–11.

[60] According to the scholiasts, the Presocratic philosopher Theagenes of Rhegium was the first to employ allegorical interpretation in defense of Homer; see Theagenes DK 8 A2. On Theagenes and the origins of allegoresis, see Ford 1999. On allegorical readings of Homer, see Buffière 1956, 45–65; Lamberton 1986; Hardie 1986, 22–9; Long 1992.

[61] See Asmis 1991, 20–1 for Philodemus' use of the term with reference to Homer in *On the Good King according to Homer* (*PHerc* 1507) col. 43.16–20.

[62] Rutherford 1986. Cf. Hartog 2001, 15–39, who reads the *Odyssey* as "poetic anthropology" (25), and explores the ways in which both the poem and the figure of Odysseus participate in the construction of Greek identity. On the allure of Odysseus' wanderings as a model for intellectual inquiry in the fifth century BCE, see Montiglio 2005, 123–9.

[63] On the Stoic Odysseus, see Sen. *Constant.* 2.1 (cited above, Ch. 2); Buffière 1956, 374–7; Stanford 1963, 121–7.

[64] On Diogenes' legendary self-sufficiency (αὐτάρκεια), see Diog. Laert. 6.78, cited by Dudley 1937, 17 (cf. 36–7). On the Cynic attraction to Odysseus, see Buffière 1956, 372–4. Höistad 1948, 94–101 reads the *Odysseus* by the proto-Cynic Antisthenes as a work of philosophy; Antisthenes also wrote a lost work *On Circe* (see Decleva Caizzi 1966, 84–5).

hostility to poetry.[65] Odysseus' words in praise of the pleasures of the banquet in the palace of Alkinoos (the so-called Golden Verses) may have been cited with approval by Epicurus (who was later dubbed the "Phaeacian philosopher" by the hostile Heraclitus).[66] Philodemus elsewhere suggests that philosophy's ability to enchant the mind was greater than that of the Sirens, and this too may have been in reference to Epicurus, who seems to have compared the seductive lure of *paideia* to a Siren song.[67]

As a Greek philosopher prominent in Roman aristocratic circles of the first century BCE, Philodemus brings us closer to both the time and the culture of the Odyssey Landscapes. His reliance on Homer to impart lessons to Roman aristocrats shows that Homeric poetry not only continued to play a central role in philosophical conversation but also functioned as a shared repository of culture and knowledge among Hellenized Romans.[68] This is not the place to go into an extended account of the role that Homeric poetry played in late republican Rome, but there are a few examples directly relevant to the scenes depicted in the Odyssey Landscapes. Roughly contemporaneous with the painting is an often cited passage of Lucretius, who allegorizes the torments of Hades as the torments of the human soul in this life. Tellingly, three of the four underworld myths depicted in the painting (Fig. 4) are mentioned by Lucretius, including that of the Danaids, who do not make an appearance in the Homeric *Odyssey*.[69] Seneca's dismissal of this type of allegory of Hades as "Epicurean poppycock" (*Ep.* 24.18: *Epicuream cantilenam*) suggests that it may have been an Epicurean topos used by authors besides Lucretius; if so, we might expect an educated viewer of the painting to be familiar with the allegory.

---

[65] "Legendary" is perhaps the key word, since recent work on Epicurus disputes the extent to which he condemned poetry. For a useful survey, with bibliography, see Janko 2000, 9–10.

[66] Asmis 1995, 16–17. Whether or not Epicurus cited Odysseus' words, the connection between the Golden Verses and Epicurean philosophy seems to have attracted some notoriety, which may lie behind Philodemus' promise to Piso that the conversation at his humble celebration of Epicurus' birthday will be "much sweeter than the land of the Phaeacians" (*Anth. Pal.* 11.44.6 [= Phld. *Ep.* 27.6 Sider]: Φαιήκων γαίης πουλὺ μελιχρότερα). There is a long history of philosophical reaction to the Golden Verses, most famously Socrates' critical summary in the *Republic* (390a–b); see Kaiser 1964, 213–23.

[67] On Philodemus' reference to the Sirens, see *PHerc* 222 (Gargiulo 1981); on Epicurus' possible evocation of the Sirens, see fr. 163 Usener (with Clay 2004). Philosophers (and others) frequently used the Sirens as a metaphor; see Kaiser 1964, 111–36.

[68] On the place of Homer in Roman culture, see Farrell 2004.

[69] Lucr. 3.978–1023 (Tityus: 984–94; Sisyphus: 995–1002; "Danaids": 1003–10). The Danaids are not in fact mentioned by name by Lucretius, and Lowenstam 1995, 208–18 points out that their appearance in the painting marks the first extant (explicit) conflation of the Danaid myth with the Pythagorean myth of the water carriers in Hades. On the history of the water-carrier myth, see Keuls 1974.

A generation or two later Horace – another Roman poet with Epicurean allegiances – offers one of the more famous personal readings of the *Iliad* and the *Odyssey*. While his friend Lollius Maximus is busy in Rome, the poet is at leisure in Praeneste, culling philosophical lessons from Homer, for Homer tells us "more plainly and eloquently than Chrysippus and Crantor what is honorable and what is shameful, what is expedient and what is not" (*Epist.* 1.2.3–4: *qui, quid sit pulcrum, quid turpe, quid utile, quid non, | planius ac melius Chrysippo et Crantore dicit*).[70] He goes on to list possible things we might learn from the *Iliad*, stressing the bad behavior of men in wartime, motivated by "sedition, treachery, crime, passion, and rage" (1.2.15: *seditione, dolis, scelere atque libidine et ira*). By contrast, the *Odyssey* displays the usefulness of ethical behavior and philosophical wisdom in the face of personal challenges (*Epist.* 1.2.17–26):

> rursus, quid virtus et quid sapientia possit,
> utile proposuit nobis exemplar Ulixen,
> qui domitor Troiae multorum providus urbes
> et mores hominum inspexit latumque per aequor,
> dum sibi, dum sociis reditum parat, aspera multa
> pertulit, adversis rerum immersabilis undis.
> Sirenum voces et Circae pocula nosti;
> quae si cum sociis stultus cupidusque bibisset,
> sub domina meretrice fuisset turpis et excors;
> vixisset canis immundus vel amica luto sus.

Or again, as a useful example of what virtue and wisdom can achieve, [Homer] has given us Odysseus, that tamer of Troy, a man of foresight, who examined the cities and behavior of many people; while arranging a homecoming for himself and his companions, he endured many hardships all over the broad sea, but he never sank in the challenging waves of life. You're familiar with the songs of the Sirens and the potions of Circe. If he had been so stupid and greedy as to drink them along with his companions, he would have been the loathsome and unfeeling property of that whore mistress; he would have lived out his life as a dirty dog or as a muck-loving sow.

Horace replicates the metaphorical utility of Odysseus' actions to his contemporary readers by translating directly from his source: lines 19–22 recreate the first five lines of the *Odyssey*. Moreover, there is a second adaptation at play here, as Marcello Gigante has shown: despite the apparent Stoic flavor of Odysseus' *virtus et sapientia*, Horace depends upon Philodemus' *On the Good King according to Homer* for much of his

---

[70] On Horace's varied philosophical allegiances in his *Epistulae*, see Mayer 1986.

argument here.[71] The Epicurean intertext undercuts Horace's rejection of the philosophers, Chrysippus and Crantor, and renders his "everyman's" reading of Homer as highly ironic, in typical Horatian fashion.

Yet in this way too Horace's exegesis provides a useful parallel for the Odyssey Landscapes. Just as the reader can appreciate Horace's poem with or without the nuance of the reference to Philodemus, the viewer of the Odyssey Landscapes can approach a "philosophical" reading of the painting from multiple angles. As in Horace's poem, a basic knowledge of the stories of Circe and the Sirens is presumed by the painting (*Sirenum voces et pocula Circae nosti* . . .), and conversation about the relevance of such myths to the daily lives of contemporary viewers can proceed whether or not they are familiar with specific philosophical allegories of these figures.[72] In many ways, this would be true whether or not the portico frame were present; the ninth panel (Fig. 4), for example, would surely make recent readers of Lucretius think of his allegory of the torments of Hades, with or without the framing pillars. But what the portico frame suggests is that the walk of the viewer and the "walk" of Odysseus are somehow parallel, and that both journeys will lead to the accumulation of knowledge. By depicting Odysseus traveling through landscape, in a continuous narrative, the painter invites the viewer to travel along with the hero, in this imaginary portico, thereby learning what he learned on his own travels.

Although we do not possess all of the painting, what we do have encourages a developmental reading of Odysseus' character as he passes along the wall of this late republican house.[73] If we take the Circe panel as the halfway point of our narrative, as the perspective of the columns demands that we do, we may notice a clear difference between the Odysseus of the first half and the Odysseus of the second half. The first half of the narrative is given over to the slaughter of the Greeks by the superhuman Laestrygonians. What is noticeable about this part of the

---

[71] Gigante 1984, 296–8. For an extended study of the Philodemean influence on Horace's *Epistulae*, see Armstrong 2004 (and 276–81 on *Epist.* 1.2 in particular).

[72] By way of comparison, the Odyssean sculptural program at Sperlonga has inspired a similar range of responses, with Odysseus either embodying Stoic virtues (Andreae 1974, 105) or demonstrating an adaptability that resists simple philosophical allegiances (Stewart 1977, 78). On the Sperlonga grotto, see Conticello and Andreae 1974; Kuttner 2003; Squire 2003.

[73] For a defense of the view that the notion of character development existed in ancient thought, see Gill 1983, and for the development of the Homeric Odysseus in particular, Rutherford 1986. More relevant to our discussion is Jeffrey Fish's reconstruction of column 36 of *On the Good King according to Homer*, in which Philodemus seems to argue that Odysseus underwent a philosophical "correction" in the *Odyssey*; see Fish 2004, 112–14.

story is that our hero is completely absent from the picture; as we observed earlier, Odysseus does not appear in the extant pictures until his ship escapes the monsters in the fifth section (Fig. 14), and he does not do so in his actual person, but rather in an inscription. The first we see of the hero is his entrance into Circe's palace in the central panel (Fig. 15). His absence from the Laestrygonian episode in many ways parallels the Homeric model, in which Odysseus sends his men in to reconnoiter (*Od.* 10.100–2). And while we could say that the narrative emphasizes his ingenuity, since he remembered to leave his ship outside the harbor whereas his men did not, we could not assess the Laestrygonian adventure as a successful episode for our hero, given the loss of men and ships it entailed. Similarly, if the first panel did in fact depict his men setting free the winds while Odysseus slept,[74] the artist will have chosen another difficult episode in the travels of Odysseus; while it may not reflect badly on the hero, since he is not personally responsible for the disasters, the release of the winds is nevertheless not a shining example of his ability to overcome danger through *virtus* and *sapientia*. The overall pattern of the first half of the frieze, we might say, is Odysseus being controlled by his circumstances, and not the other way around.

This is precisely what makes the choice of the central panel so interesting (Fig. 15). We have already seen that this panel is one of the more daring examples of continuous narrative, depicting as it does two successive scenes at the same moment, in the same frame, indeed virtually side by side. The contrast is of course heightened by the framing colonnade, which has given every other scene its own internal coherence, as successive scenes in an ongoing narrative. But here the device is broken in dramatic fashion, and we are forced by the narratological switch to linger here. Moreover, the perspective of the framing portico places the ideal viewer directly before this scene, suggesting not only its centrality but also the subordination of the other panels, in some sense, to it. As we have seen, the central panel is doubly jarring: the portico frame enforces a metaphor of ambulatory contemplation, yet its perspective *also* demands a stationary pose in front of this central panel. What is interesting for our study is that this breakdown occurs precisely at the point in the painting where Odysseus breaks the pattern developed in the first half of the narrative; here we see Odysseus transformed from the controlled to the controller. When Odysseus is welcomed into Circe's palace, his men have already

---

[74] A possibility suggested by the personified winds in the upper left corner of the second panel (Fig. 11); see von Blanckenhagen 1963, 104.

been turned into animals; again, it may reflect worse on the susceptibility of his men than on his own qualities as a leader, but the overall pattern of bad luck is maintained. In the narrative gap, however, Odysseus has drunk the cup, but it has no effect on him, protected as he is by Hermes' moly. As he draws his sword, he reasserts his control over the narrative, a control which will remain to the end of our extant fragments. Indeed, in our last (fragmentary) panel (Fig. 5), we can barely make out Odysseus, tied to the mast, so that he may hear the Sirens without succumbing to their deadly charm. The episode is duly famous, and easily moralized by later readers as the proper way to enjoy things without enjoying them too much.[75] Horace, master of the *aurea mediocritas*, clearly reads it as such, and it is fitting for our analysis that the two scenes he singles out in *Epist.* 1.2 (*Sirenum voces et Circae pocula*, 23) are both to be found in the Odyssey Landscapes.

The ethical reading suggested above is just one possible philosophical reading of the episodes depicted, and need not exclude other readings.[76] This is the point of the portico frame: the metaphor of ambulatory philosophical contemplation that it imposes allows for individual reactions and personal interpretations, and is thus meant to spur discussion among the strolling viewers.[77] The portico frame of the Odyssey Landscapes played an essential role in the interpretation of the painting by acting as a mediating device, an interpretive lens through which the Roman viewer was encouraged to see connections between the wanderings of Odysseus and the *ambulatio* of the Roman aristocrat. The painted portico refers not only to an architectural form, but also to an entire culture that would have been intimately familiar to a viewer of that painting in the mid first century BCE, bringing together associations of movement of the body, acquisition of knowledge, philosophical contemplation, mythology as exemplum, and travel. By combining an allusion to this culture with the fantasy world of mythological landscape, the artist has taken an aspect of the viewer's *Lebenswelt* and elevated it to the level of

---

[75] See Buffière 1956, 380–6, and Kaiser 1964, 121–31.

[76] Lowenstam 1995, 213–14, for example, briefly entertains (and rejects) a Pythagorean reading of the Odyssey Landscapes.

[77] Bettina Bergmann has shown in a number of articles the various ways in which the arrangement of wall paintings at Pompeii evokes the Roman rhetorical practices endemic to Roman aristocratic thought and behavior; see Bergmann 1994 and 1999, esp. p. 101: "It was in rethinking and arguing fundamental social issues of myths that Romans could articulate their own current problems. The strategies of that self-reflection, I believe, are comparable to the arrangements of myths in Roman rooms, where the abilities learned at school – to speak, listen, envision – became recreational pleasure."

myth.[78] Like Philodemus in his letter to Piso, this Roman homeowner promises his guests a strolling conversation as sweet as (or sweeter than) Odysseus' conversation with the Phaeacians.

---

[78] Kuttner 2003, 112 makes the intriguing suggestion that the palace of Circe in panel 6 (Fig. 15) evokes the aristocratic *villa maritima*.

Conclusion

E la Roma di oggi? Che effetto fa a chi arriva per la prima volta?

And the Rome of today? What effect does it have on someone arriving for the first time?

Fellini's Roma (1972)

The culture of Roman walking is as old as Rome itself – at least according to Virgil, whose *Aeneid* includes the "primeval" story of a Roman *ambulatio*. The poet decides to introduce his readers to the site of Rome by having Aeneas walk through it, as the Arcadian king Evander and his Trojan guest wend their way through groves and hills destined for greatness (*Aen.* 8.306–12):

> exim se cuncti divinis rebus ad urbem
> perfectis referunt. ibat rex obsitus aevo,
> et comitem Aenean iuxta natumque tenebat
> ingrediens varioque viam sermone levabat.
> miratur facilisque oculos fert omnia circum
> Aeneas, capiturque locis et singula laetus
> exquiritque auditque virum monimenta priorum.

Then, having fulfilled the divine rites, they all make their way to the city. The aged king went along, and he had beside him as he walked his companion Aeneas and his own son, and he lightened their way with different stories. Amazed, Aeneas throws his ready glance all around; he is taken by the places and, delighted by each one, he asks and learns about the monuments of heroes past.

Aeneas' amazement may strike the modern reader as an overreaction, since Virgil goes out of his way to emphasize the primitive state of the proto-*urbs*: no marble here, nor even much brick, just cows grazing on the future site of the Forum Romanum and on the ridge that would become one of Rome's most upscale neighborhoods, the *Carinae* (*Aen.* 8.360–1). Instead, Aeneas' amazement may be read primarily as a vehicle for the reaction of the contemporary audience, for whom there was not only the antiquarian and aetiological appeal of Rome in a primitive state, but also the reflected grandeur of the Augustan city – the inevitable lens through which the reader sees Evander's "Rome."[1] As many scholars have shown, Virgil plays with the multiplicity of viewers and audiences by refusing to adopt a single chronological frame for the topography.[2] Some sites, like the Argiletum (8.345–6), still existed in a different form in Augustan Rome, and are revealed to be as old as the city itself – indeed, older, since the settlement predates Rome. Others are referred to by names that can only be known to a later audience, such as the Tarpeian Rock (8.347) and the Roman Forum. The most dramatic juxtaposition of chronological viewpoints comes in the famous parenthetical comment on the Capitoline Hill, "now golden, but once upon a time bristling with wild brambles" (8.348: *aurea nunc, olim silvestribus horrida dumis*). The inclusion of the temporal adverb *nunc* in the midst of such a vivid story about a previous age is jarring, and intentionally so, for it dramatizes the reader's participation in this guided tour.

This temporal play is not only typically Virgilian but also typically Roman. Virgil's proto-Rome reflects the temporal fluidity of his contemporary urban landscape, where a space like the Roman Forum was filled with commemorations of vastly disparate moments in history. As Catharine Edwards (1996, 10–11) puts it so well in her analysis of this scene, "Rome was always already an especially time-laden space." In this sense, any walk in Rome necessarily evoked a multitude of ages and eras. Walking is used in this scene to generate a narrative, to explain monuments, and, ultimately, to animate history; for Romans walking through an urban landscape dominated by the monuments, inscriptions, statues, and buildings of their past, much the same process went on.[3] Virgil was not required to include a walking tour in his introduction of the city: Evander could have pointed out the sights to his guest from a high vantage point, like Helen at the walls of Troy. But, for the Roman reader, the walk itself is part of the appeal of this scene, part of what makes it so intimately familiar.

As we have seen in earlier chapters, Roman readers would have intuitively understood the larger social context of two men of equal standing conversing while they stroll. The tour in fact straddles the line between two distinct types of "walks with friends" that we have explored in this book: the domestic *ambulatio* and the urban *deductio*. The leisurely walk is part of a

---

[1] Fowler 1918, 71–6; Gransden 1976, 30–6; Edwards 1996, 31–2.
[2] See e.g. George 1974, 84–7; Edwards 1996, 31.
[3] Cf. Dupont 1992, 74 (cited in Edwards 1996, 30): "To walk around Rome was to travel through its memory." On how Roman topography created "a kind of non-sequential history," see Edwards 1996, 42. On movement through the Augustan cityscape, see Favro 1996, 227–50.

gradual negotiation between Evander and Aeneas, essential to the plot of the *Aeneid*; the walk, Evander's stories, and his hospitality are all acts that establish the bond of *amicitia* that will form the basis of their political pact. Moreover, given the Hellenizing associations of such walks in the domestic context, the Greek Evander here initiates the Trojan Aeneas in the ritual that will become an integral part of Greco-Roman leisure.[4] Just as the domestic *ambulatio* involved cultural negotiation and the creation of something new and distinctly Roman, Aeneas and Evander's stroll is an encounter that enables the creation of a new and distinctly Roman identity. But this tour is also, pointedly, taking its participants through the future political center of the city – the *forum Romanum*. Evander walks in the middle between his son and his guest (*Aen.* 8.307–9), and the men testify to their burgeoning alliance to any citizens (or cows) who may be watching – a prototype, then, of the republican *deductio in forum*.

Aeneas and Evander's walk is multivalent, bringing together many of the themes we have explored throughout this book: it serves as a venue for conversation, a confirmation of friendship, a display of political support, an occasion for viewing monuments and sights, and an opportunity to imagine other places and times. Furthermore, the story is in many ways foundational: we are encouraged to see this walk as a prototype for later encounters with the city and even as a quintessentially Roman experience of place. And indeed the process Virgil alludes to, walking through the city and experiencing a kind of metaphorical travel, has been a persistent motif for visitors through the ages.[5] That Rome was largely abandoned in late antiquity and returned to a state not dissimilar to Evander's city, a small settlement populated with ruins, only added to the resonance of this scene to later readers, for whom Virgil's vision became prophetic not only of the rise of Rome but also of its fall.[6]

As millions of tourists would attest, the power of walking to reanimate Roman history endures. Yet the emergence of a vibrant and sprawling city with mass transit and other mechanized forms of transport has obviously altered the experience of movement through modern Rome. By way of conclusion, let us briefly turn to a modern visual meditation on the relationship between movement and the experience of Rome – Federico Fellini's

---

[4] Papaioannou 2003 reads the entire Evander episode as Virgil's argument that Roman culture was Hellenized from very beginning.
[5] For a few salient examples, see Edwards 1996, 8–10 and 129–33. Cf. Larmour and Spencer 2007b, 30–2.
[6] See Edwards 1996, 14 and 31.

Roma (1972).[7] An analysis of two scenes from the film will highlight what has changed, and what has endured, in the culture of Roman walking.

Roma is a loosely autobiographical film, presenting a history of Fellini's relationship with his adopted home town. The film shuttles back and forth between the 1930s, as the young Fellini arrives in Rome on the cusp of world war, and the 1970s, as a film crew, led by the director himself, films a documentary about the modern city. The very act of contrasting different points of time in the same place evokes the similar move of *Aeneid* 8; as we have seen, movement through Rome always invites this sort of metaphorical time travel.[8] Yet the director also teases the viewer who might expect the documentary crew to produce the usual grand tour through the city's monuments.[9] The most explicitly historical tour of the city is not a walking tour at all but a tour of the subway tunnels under the city: the chief engineer points out the archaeological strata as the film crew rides deeper and deeper. Even without the engineer's somewhat jaded comments about the archaeological finds that delay the progress of technology, the antagonistic relationship between modern forms of movement and the ancient topography is clear enough. On the one hand, as the crew moves through the layers of history, their downward trajectory is yet another form of metaphorical time travel, the sort which Rome has always invited; the crew even travels underneath the Via Appia Antica for a stretch. Yet by the late twentieth century historical monuments are so abundant that one must travel *under* the city to get anywhere – and even the creation of such evasive tunnels is a destructive process.

In the scene's climax, the chief engineer casually orders a huge drill to cut into the perfectly preserved remains of a Roman house. Inside the *domus*, the film and construction crews come face to face with a wall painting depicting a procession of Romans making their way up a staircase, some of whom stare directly out at the viewers (Fig. 16). As the film crew gazes in wonder at what they have found, we finally get the ambulatory encounter with ancient spaces that the movie has been promising for so long, with ancient and modern Romans watching one another walk in the same space. But this tour has no happy ending: the modern air entering from the outside

---

[7] Both Foreman 1980 and Theodorakopoulos 2007 deal extensively with the theme of movement in Fellini's *Roma*.

[8] For further points of contact between *Roma* and the *Aeneid*, see Foreman 1980.

[9] Theodorakopoulos 2007, 361–9 aptly situates this move in the larger context of Fellini's ambivalence about an authoritative "view from above" (an ambivalence he inherits from his predecessors Rossellini and De Sica); such a view was associated not only with tourism but also with Nazi and Fascist appropriations of Roman topography.

Figure 16 Fellini's *Roma*. A documentary film crew explores an ancient Roman house.

quickly destroys the murals, which fade away in seconds as the horrified film crew looks on.

The question about how one moves through Rome is posed even more explicitly by the film's narrator in an earlier scene, as Fellini's documentary crew enters the city for the first time:

E la Roma di oggi? Che effetto fa a chi arriva per la prima volta? Proviamo entrarci in macchina dall'autostrada, attraverso l'inevitabile grande raccordo anulare – questo raccordo che circonda tutta la città come un anello di Saturno.

And the Rome of today? What effect does it have on someone arriving for the first time? Let's try to enter it by car on the highway, through the unavoidable great ring road – this road that encircles the entire city like a ring of Saturn.

The scene that follows is a hellish drive on a crowded, rainy highway. The sequence is an obvious counterpart to the young Fellini's first (ambulatory) encounters with the boisterous, carnivalesque Rome of the 1930s, where everyone is thrown together in boardinghouses, theaters, and on the streets. 1930s Rome is, above all, still human-scaled, with an emphasis on community and human interaction still perceptible through the bizarre spectacle of urban life. There are even signs of Rome's pastoral past: an empty streetscape at night hosts a flock of sheep making its way down cobblestoned streets – like the cattle lowing in the forum in Evander's Rome. By contrast, the highway scene through which we encounter the Rome of the 1970s is decidedly anti-pastoral.[10] Individuals still gather in groups, interacting with one another, but these groups are now separated from one another in tiny cars. The noises of Rome in the 1930s – boisterous back-and-forth on streets and piazzas – have been replaced by the noise of machines. The only Romans on foot in this scene are prostitutes, protesters, and hitchhiking hippies, and the few historical monuments encountered compete with the much more prominent industrial fires, grim apartment blocks, and overturned trucks – the new "ruins" of modern Rome. An accident on the side of the road even includes a small herd of slaughtered cows, representing the death of the earlier pastoral setting (both of Evander's Rome and of young Fellini's Rome).[11] And when we do finally get a shot of something that is recognizably Roman – the Colosseum glowing at night, the very symbol of the *città eterna* – it serves as the backdrop to a ring of cars stuck in traffic, with not a pedestrian in sight. If walking in spaces that have existed for millennia unites modern Romans with their ancient brethren – the idea at play in *Aeneid* 8, and in so many other scenes – then Fellini presents us with a very different Rome, with Romans no longer able to make that same connection to their past.

This is a modern, pessimistic view of what has happened to Rome and its past, and it may seem quite far from Virgil's cheery portrait of Evander's Rome.[12] Yet even if Fellini seems to offer an elegy for the disappearance of simpler modes of movement through the city, he shares with Virgil the impulse to characterize the city as a place that invites movement through it. For both artists, moving through Rome is an act of historical inquiry; just as the city sees itself as a palimpsest of artifacts and monuments, anyone who hopes to understand the city must move through its layers.[13] Juxtaposing Virgil and Fellini allows us to appreciate how Rome has always inspired a careful attention to how people move through it. It also allows us to

---

[10] The reference to Saturn's rings makes the approach to modern Rome a form of space travel, yet it also conveys an ironic allusion, perhaps, to the Saturnian golden age (also at play in Evander's Rome), which this is decidedly not.

[11] As Theodorakopoulos 2007, 363 points out, the dead cows look "suspiciously like sacrifical animals."

[12] To be fair, as Theodorakopoulos 2007, 374–9 shows in her excellent analysis of the final scene, Fellini's *Roma* is not entirely pessimistic about modern mobile encounters with the city. In the final scene, we are suddenly treated to the multiple camera shots of monuments ancient and modern that the film had been rejecting throughout – something more akin to Aeneas and Evander's tour – but the mobile viewers are not pedestrians or tourists, but rather a pack of motorcyclists zooming through empty city streets at night. We share their point of view, experiencing the classic tour of the *città eterna* at a frantic pace.

[13] For the palimpsest metaphor, see Edwards 1996, 28; Larmour and Spencer 2007b, 2–3.

appreciate what, in the end, makes Roman walking distinct: the uniqueness of ancient Rome itself. The city's imperial reach rendered it not only the center of the (Western) world but also a microcosm of it, a place that conquered and coopted countless other places and ideas.[14] As Edwards and Woolf (2003, 2) note, Rome's imperial might created a powerful experience for visitors and immigrants who arrived from the empire's furthest reaches:

> Its enormous size was unparalleled; no human eye could comprehend it. The splendour of its buildings, constructed from gleaming marbles brought from distant lands, was incomparable. The marketplaces of the city were crammed with more transitory reminders of Rome's dominance over the world ... Everywhere in the city elements of the conquered world had been appropriated and recontextualized; the city had absorbed the world.

Just as Rome was no ordinary city, a walk through it was no ordinary walk. For migrants to the city, a walk through Rome recreated the very journey that brought them there; for native Romans, the walk through Rome was a substitute for the world tour they no longer needed to take. Movement through Rome thus inspired not only historical inquiry but also geographical exploration.

The vast size of the city, as Edwards and Woolf observe, also made it impossible to comprehend by sight alone; despite the vantage points afforded by her famous hills, one had to move through Rome to take it all in.[15] Rome's cosmic scale, a result of its imperial reach, thus encouraged (and still encourages) visitors and residents to imagine and experience individual versions of the city – paradoxically, the seat of the first world empire has long invited individual acts of possession. We speak of Evander's Rome, Aeneas' Rome, Goethe's Rome, Lanciani's Rome, Mussolini's Rome, Fellini's Rome. Visitors to the eternal city have long asserted ownership of the city by looking at it, moving through it, and then writing and talking about it.[16] As Aeneas and Evander show us, this is a process that Romans imagined was inherent to the experience of their city.

More to the point, by positioning itself at the center, and casting the rest of the world as periphery, Rome extended its imperial reach outwards but

---

[14] See Edwards 1996, 98–100; Edwards and Woolf 2003, 1–6.

[15] Though a view from one of Rome's hills was of course the closest any ancient viewer could get to a "glimpse of totality," as Vout 2007 points out in her essay on the hills of Rome (quote at 296). Cf. Larmour and Spencer 2007b, 20 for the notion of Rome as "a vast mosaic [which] defies physical attempts to take it all in at once." On the topos of Rome's vastness, see also Purcell 1992, 422–6.

[16] On the notion of a "multiplicity of Romes," see Edwards 1996, 1; Larmour and Spencer 2007b, 44. As Edwards 1996, 112–13 and 129–33 has shown, such a process has long allowed non-Romans to present themselves as more Roman than the native-born residents.

also became the quintessentially self-conscious city. In the Roman imagination, the entire world was looking at Rome, looking at what Romans did – including how they moved. Thus ancient Rome created not only intense opportunities for watching (true of any pre-modern, face-to-face society) but also an intense awareness of being watched by others – indeed by the entire world.[17] The movement and mobility that enabled their world empire (and which their empire in turn enabled) brought with it a consciousness of the more quotidian forms of movement that defined their experience of their city.

Both Virgil and Fellini thus call our attention to a thread that unites the various themes explored in this book: not just the act of walking, but the act of *looking* at walking. What makes Roman walking distinctive is how self-conscious and self-reflective this culture became about a basic human activity: Romans spent significant time and energy not only watching themselves walk but also talking and writing about it. And this self-awareness took a specifically visual form – throughout this book we have seen Romans walking, aware of being looked at all the while. We have seen gaits evaluated, mental modes deduced, friends and allies confirmed, leisure time performed. We have seen how in virtually every social situation there was ample opportunity for assessing others simply by the way that they moved through life: the story of walking in Roman culture leads through the heart of Roman culture itself.

---

[17] Cf. Elsner 2007, xvii, who notes that "Roman eyes were trained" not only in "looking as such" but also in "being aware of being looked at while looking."

Bibliography

Adams, J. N. (1993) "The Generic Use of *mula* and the Status and Employment of Female Mules in the Roman World." *Rheinisches Museum für Philologie* 136: 35–61.

Adkin, N. (1983) "The Teaching of the Fathers concerning Footwear and Gait." *Latomus* 42: 885–6.

Africa, T. W. (1971) "Urban Violence in Imperial Rome." *Journal of Interdisciplinary Hcistory* 2: 3–21.

Alcock, S. E., J. F. Cherry, and J. Elsner, eds. (2001) *Pausanias: Travel and Memory in Roman Greece.* Oxford and New York.

Aldrete, G. S. (1999) *Gestures and Acclamations in Ancient Rome.* Baltimore.

Amato, J. A. (2004) *On Foot: A History of Walking.* New York.

Anderson, J. C. (1997) *Roman Architecture and Society.* Baltimore.

André, J.-M. (1966) *L'otium dans la vie morale et intellectuelle romaine des origines à l'époque augustéenne.* Paris.

(1989) "Sénèque: 'De breuitate uitae,' 'De constantia sapientis,' 'De tranquillitate animi,' 'De otio'." In *Aufstieg und Niedergang der römischen Welt* II.36.3: 1724–78.

Andreae, B. (1962) "Der Zyklus der Odysseefresken im Vatikan." *Mitteilungen des Deutschen Archäologischen Instituts, Römische Abteilung* 69: 106–17.

(1974) "Die römischen Repliken der mythologischen Skulpturengruppen von Sperlonga." In Conticello and Andreae (1974), 61–105.

(1988) "Wandmalerei augusteischer Zeit." In *Kaiser Augustus und die verlorene Republik: Eine Ausstellung im Martin-Gropius-Bau, Berlin, 7. Juni – 14. August 1988,* 273–90. Mainz.

Andronicos, M. (1984) *Vergina: The Royal Tombs and the Ancient City.* Athens.

Armstrong, D. (2004) "Horace's *Epistles* 1 and Philodemus." In Armstrong, Fish, Johnston, and Skinner (2004), 267–98.

Armstrong, D., J. Fish, P. A. Johnston, and M. B. Skinner, eds. (2004) *Vergil, Philodemus, and the Augustans.* Austin, Tex.

Asmis, E. (1991) "Philodemus's Poetic Theory and *On the Good King According to Homer.*" *Classical Antiquity* 10: 1–45.

(1995) "Epicurean Poetics." In *Philodemus and Poetry: Poetic Theory and Practice in Lucretius, Philodemus, and Horace,* ed. D. Obbink, 15–34. Oxford.

Baldassarre, I., A. Pontrandolfo, A. Rouveret, and M. Salvadori (2002) *Pittura romana: Dall'ellenismo al tardo antico*. Milan.

Barbet, A. (1985) *La peinture murale romaine: Les styles décoratifs pompéiens*. Paris.

Baroin, C. (1998) "La maison romaine comme image et lieu de mémoire." In *Images romaines: Actes de la table ronde organisée à l'École normale supérieure*, ed. C. Auvray-Assayas, 177–91. Paris.

Barta, P. I. (1996) *Bely, Joyce, and Döblin: Peripatetics in the City Novel*. Gainesville, Fla.

Bartman, E. (1991) "Sculptural Collecting and Display in the Private Realm." In Gazda (1991), 71–88.

Barton, T. S. (1994) *Power and Knowledge: Astrology, Physiognomics, and Medicine under the Roman Empire*. Ann Arbor, Mich.

Bartsch, S. (1994) *Actors in the Audience: Theatricality and Doublespeak from Nero to Hadrian*. Cambridge, Mass. and London.

Beagon, M. (1992) *Roman Nature: The Thought of Pliny the Elder*. Oxford.

Beard, M. (1980) "The Sexual Status of Vestal Virgins." *Journal of Roman Studies* 70: 12–27.

(2007) *The Roman Triumph*. Cambridge, Mass.

Beard, M. and J. Henderson (2001) *Classical Art: From Greece to Rome*. Oxford.

Bek, L. (1980) *Towards Paradise on Earth: Modern Space Conception in Architecture: A Creation of Renaissance Humanism*. Odense.

Bell, A. (2004) *Spectacular Power in the Greek and Roman City*. Oxford.

Beltrán Fortes, J. (1995) "La incorporación de los modelos griegos por las élites romanas en ámbito privado: Una aproximación arqueológica." In *Graecia capta: De la conquista de Grecia a la helenización de Roma*, ed. E. Falque Rey and F. Gascó, 201–32. Huelva.

Benjamin, W. (1999) *The Arcades Project*. Trans. H. Eiland and K. McLaughlin. Ed. R. Tiedemann. Cambridge, Mass.

Bergmann, B. (1991) "Painted Perspectives of a Villa Visit: Landscape as Status and Metaphor." In Gazda (1991), 49–70.

(1992) "Exploring the Grove: Pastoral Space on Roman Walls." In *The Pastoral Landscape*, ed. J. D. Hunt, 21–46. Washington, DC.

(1994) "The Roman House as Memory Theater: The House of the Tragic Poet at Pompeii." *Art Bulletin* 76: 225–56.

(1995a) "Greek Masterpieces and Roman Recreative Fictions." *Harvard Studies in Classical Philology* 97: 79–120.

(1995b) "Visualizing Pliny's Villas." *Journal of Roman Archaeology* 8: 406–20.

(1999) "Rhythms of Recognition: Mythological Encounters in Roman Landscape Painting." In *Im Spiegel des Mythos: Bilderwelt und Lebenswelt = Lo specchio del mito: Immaginario e realtà*, ed. F. de Angelis and S. Muth, 81–107. Wiesbaden.

(2001) "Meanwhile, Back in Italy...: Creating Landscapes of Allusion." In Alcock, Cherry, and Elsner (2001), 154–66.

(2002) "Art and Nature in the Villa at Oplontis." In *Pompeian Brothels, Pompeii's Ancient History, Mirrors and Mysteries, Art and Nature at Oplontis, and the*

Herculaneum "Basilica," ed. T. A. J. McGinn, P. Carafa, N. T. de Grummond, B. Bergmann, and T. Najbjerg, 87–120. Portsmouth, RI.

Bergmann, B. and C. Kondoleon, eds. (1999) *The Art of Ancient Spectacle.* Washington, DC.

Bettini, M. (1991) *Anthropology and Roman Culture: Kinship, Time, Images of the Soul.* Trans. J. V. Sickle. Baltimore.

Beyen, H. G. (1960) *Die pompejanische Wanddekoration vom zweiten bis zum vierten Stil.* Vol. II.1. The Hague.

Biering, R. (1995) *Die Odysseefresken vom Esquilin.* Munich.

Bloomer, W. M. (2006) "The Technology of Child Production: Eugenics and Eulogics in the *De liberis educandis." Arethusa* 39: 71–99.

Bodel, J. (1997) "Monumental Villas and Villa Monuments." *Journal of Roman Archaeology* 10: 5–35.

  (1999) "Death on Display: Looking at Roman Funerals." In Bergmann and Kondoleon (1999), 259–81.

Boëthius, A. (1960) *The Golden House of Nero: Some Aspects of Roman Architecture.* Ann Arbor, Mich.

Boyle, A. J. (1997) *Tragic Seneca: An Essay in the Theatrical Tradition.* London and New York.

Braun, E. (1849) "Römische Ausgrabungen: Scenen aus dem Abenteuer der Lästrygonen." *Archäologische Zeitung* 7 (*Archäologischer Anzeiger* 2, Feb. 1849): 27–32.

Bremmer, J. (1991) "Walking, Standing, and Sitting in Ancient Greek Culture." In Bremmer and Roodenburg (1991), 15–35.

Bremmer, J. and H. Roodenburg, eds. (1991) *A Cultural History of Gesture: From Antiquity to the Present Day.* Cambridge.

Brilliant, R. (1984) *Visual Narratives: Storytelling in Etruscan and Roman Art.* Ithaca, NY.

Brown, P. (1988) *The Body and Society: Men, Women, and Sexual Renunciation in Early Christianity.* New York.

Brown, R. D. (1983) "The Litter: A Satirical Symbol in Juvenal and Others." In *Studies in Latin Literature and Roman History.* Vol. III, ed. C. Deroux, 266–82. Brussels.

Bruno, V. J. (1969) "Antecedents of the Pompeian First Style." *American Journal of Archaeology* 73: 305–17.

Buck-Morss, S. (1989) *The Dialectics of Seeing: Walter Benjamin and the Arcades Project.* Cambridge, Mass.

Buffière, F. (1956) *Les mythes d'Homère et la pensée grecque.* Paris.

Butler, S. (2002) *The Hand of Cicero.* London and New York.

Camp, J. M. (1986) *The Athenian Agora: Excavations in the Heart of Classical Athens.* London and New York.

Carettoni, G. (1983) "La decorazione pittorica della casa di Augusto sul Palatino." *Mitteilungen des Deutschen Archäologischen Instituts, Römische Abteilung* 90: 373–419.

Chambert, R. (2005) *Rome: Le mouvement et l'ancrage. Morale et philosophie du voyage au début du Principat.* Brussels.

Champlin, E. (1982) "The *Suburbium* of Rome." *American Journal of Ancient History* 7: 97–117.

Church, F. F. (1975) "Sex and Salvation in Tertullian." *Harvard Theological Review* 68: 83–101.

Clarke, J. R. (1991) *The Houses of Roman Italy, 100 BC–AD 250: Ritual, Space, and Decoration*. Berkeley.

Clay, D. (2004) "Vergil's Farewell to Education (Catalepton 5) and Epicurus' Letter to Pythocles." In Armstrong, Fish, Johnston, and Skinner (2004), 25–36.

Coarelli, F. (1998) "The Odyssey Frescos of the Via Graziosa: A Proposed Context." *Papers of the British School at Rome* 66: 21–37.

Cohen, A. (2001) "Art, Myth, and Travel in the Hellenistic World." In Alcock, Cherry, and Elsner (2001), 93–126.

Connolly, J. (2007) "Virile Tongues: Rhetoric and Masculinity." In *A Companion to Roman Rhetoric*, ed. W. Dominik and J. Hall, 83–97. Malden, Mass. and Oxford.

Conticello, B. and B. Andreae (1974) *Die Skulpturen von Sperlonga: I gruppi scultorei di soggetto mitologico a Sperlonga*. Berlin.

Cook, E. F. (1995) *The Odyssey in Athens: Myths of Cultural Origins*. Ithaca, NY.

Cooper, J. M. (2006) "Seneca on Moral Theory and Moral Improvement." In Volk and Williams (2006), 43–55.

Corbeill, A. (2004) *Nature Embodied: Gesture in Ancient Rome*. Princeton.

Coulton, J. J. (1976) *The Architectural Development of the Greek Stoa*. Oxford.

Csapo, E. (1987) "Is the Threat-Monologue of the 'Servus Currens' an Index of Roman Authorship?" *Phoenix* 41: 399–419.

   (1989) "Plautine Elements in the Running-Slave Entrance Monologues?" *Classical Quarterly* 39: 148–63.

D'Arms, J. H. (1970) *Romans on the Bay of Naples: A Social and Cultural Study of the Villas and Their Owners from 150 BC to AD 400*. Cambridge, Mass.

David, J.-M. (1992) *Le patronat judiciaire au dernier siècle de la république romaine*. Rome.

Davidson, J. N. (1997) *Courtesans and Fishcakes: The Consuming Passions of Classical Athens*. New York.

Davies, J. C. (1971) "Was Cicero Aware of Natural Beauty?" *Greece and Rome* 18: 152–65.

Decleva Caizzi, F., ed. (1966) *Antisthenis fragmenta*. Milan.

Delorme, J. (1960) *Gymnasion: Étude sur les monuments consacrés à l'éducation en Grèce (des origines à l'empire romain)*. Paris.

Deniaux, E. (1987) "De l'*ambitio* à l'*ambitus*: Les lieux de la propagande et de la corruption électorale à la fin de la République" In *L'Urbs: Espace urbain et histoire (1er siècle av. J.-C.–IIIe siècle ap. J.-C.)*, 279–304. Rome.

Dickmann, J.-A. (1997) "The Peristyle and the Transformation of Domestic Space in Hellenistic Pompeii." In Laurence and Wallace-Hadrill (1997), 121–36.

   (1999) *Domus frequentata: Anspruchsvolles Wohnen im pompejanischen Stadthaus*. Munich.

Dilke, O. A. W. (1998) *Greek and Roman Maps*. Baltimore.
Dillon, M. (1997) *Pilgrims and Pilgrimage in Ancient Greece*. London and New York.
Dillon, S. (2000) "Subject Selection and Viewer Reception of Greek Portraits from Herculaneum and Tivoli." *Journal of Roman Archaeology* 13: 21–40.
Doherty, J. K. (2010) "Roman Landscape Painting and Ancient Cartography." Ph.D. diss., Boston University.
Dolansky, F. (2008) "*Togam virilem sumere*: Coming of Age in the Roman World." In *Roman Dress and the Fabrics of Roman Culture*, ed. J. Edmondson and A. Keith, 47–70. Toronto.
Drerup, H. (1959) "Bildraum und Realraum in der römischen Architektur." *Mitteilungen des Deutschen Archäologischen Instituts, Römische Abteilung* 66: 147–74.
Dudley, D. R. (1937) *A History of Cynicism: From Diogenes to the 6th Century* AD. London.
Dupont, F. (1992) *Daily Life in Ancient Rome*. Trans. C. Woodall. Oxford and Cambridge, Mass.
Dyck, A. R. (2004) *A Commentary on Cicero, De Legibus*. Ann Arbor, Mich.
Edwards, C. (1993) *The Politics of Immorality in Ancient Rome*. Cambridge.
(1996) *Writing Rome: Textual Approaches to the City*. Cambridge.
Edwards, C. and G. Woolf (2003) "Cosmopolis: Rome as World City." In *Rome the Cosmopolis*, ed. C. Edwards and G. Woolf, 1–20. Cambridge.
Ehrhardt, W. (1987) *Stilgeschichtliche Untersuchungen an römischen Wandmalereien: Von der späten Republik bis zur Zeit Neros*. Mainz.
(1991) "Bild und Ausblick in Wandbemalungen zweiten Stils." *Antike Kunst* 34: 28–65.
Ellis, S. J. (2004) "The Distribution of Bars at Pompeii: Archaeological, Spatial, and Viewshed Analyses." *Journal of Roman Archaeology* 17: 371–84.
Ellis, S. P. (2000) *Roman Housing*. London.
Elsner, J. (1995) *Art and the Roman Viewer: The Transformation of Art from the Pagan World to Christianity*. Cambridge.
(2007) *Roman Eyes: Visuality and Subjectivity in Art and Text*. Princeton and Oxford.
Elsner, J. and I. Rutherford (2005) "Introduction." In *Pilgrimage in Graeco-Roman and Early Christian Antiquity: Seeing the Gods*, ed. J. Elsner and I. Rutherford, 1–38. Oxford and New York.
Engemann, J. (1967) *Architekturdarstellungen des frühen zweiten Stils: Illusionistische römische Wandmalerei der ersten Phase und ihre Vorbilder in der realen Architektur*. Heidelberg.
Evans, E. C. (1935) "Roman Descriptions of Personal Appearance in History and Biography." *Harvard Studies in Classical Philology* 46: 43–84.
(1969) *Physiognomics in the Ancient World*. Philadelphia.
Farrell, J. (2001) *Latin Language and Latin Culture: From Ancient to Modern Times*. Cambridge.
(2004) "Roman Homer." In *The Cambridge Companion to Homer*, ed. R. Fowler, 254–71. Cambridge.

Favro, D. G. (1996) *The Urban Image of Augustan Rome*. Cambridge and New York.

Feldherr, A. (1998) *Spectacle and Society in Livy's History*. Berkeley and Los Angeles.

Ferri, R. (2003) *Octavia: A Play Attributed to Seneca*. Cambridge.

Ferrill, A. (1966) "Seneca's Exile and the *Ad Helviam*: A Reinterpretation." *Classical Philology* 61: 253–7.

Fish, J. (2004) "Anger, Philodemus' Good King, and the Helen Episode of Aeneid 2.567–589: A New Proof of Authenticity from Herculaneum." In Armstrong, Fish, Johnston, and Skinner (2004), 111–38.

Fisher, N. (1998) "Gymnasia and the Democratic Values of Leisure." In *Kosmos: Essays in Order, Conflict, and Community in Classical Athens*, ed. P. Cartledge, P. Millett, and S. von Reden, 84–104. Cambridge.

Fitch, J. G., ed. (1987) *Seneca's Hercules Furens: A Critical Text with Introduction and Commentary*. Ithaca, NY.

  (2000) "Playing Seneca?" In *Seneca in Performance*, ed. G. W. M. Harrison, 1–12. London.

Fitzgerald, W. (2000) *Slavery and the Roman Literary Imagination*. Cambridge.

Flower, H. I. (1996) *Ancestor Masks and Aristocratic Power in Roman Culture*. Oxford.

Foerster, R., ed. (1893) *Scriptores physiognomonici graeci et latini*. Leipzig.

Ford, A. (1999) "Performing Interpretation: Early Allegorical Exegesis of Homer." In *Epic Traditions in the Contemporary World: The Poetics of Community*, ed. M. H. Beissinger, J. Tylus, and S. L. Wofford, 33–53. Berkeley.

Foreman, W. C. (1980) "Fellini's Cinematic City: *Roma* and Myths of Foundation." *Forum Italicum* 14: 78–98.

Fowler, D. (2007) "Laocoon's Point of View: Walking the Roman Way." In *Classical Constructions: Papers in Memory of Don Fowler, Classicist and Epicurean*, ed. S. J. Heyworth, P. G. Fowler, and S. J. Harrison, 1–17. Oxford.

Fowler, W. W. (1918) *Aeneas at the Site of Rome: Observations on the Eighth Book of the Aeneid*. 2nd edn. Oxford.

Frakes, J. F. D. (2009) *Framing Public Life: The Portico in Roman Gaul*. Vienna.

Frier, B. W. and T. A. J. McGinn (2004) *A Casebook on Roman Family Law*. Oxford.

Fuchs, R. H. (1986) *Richard Long*. London and New York.

Garbarino, G. (1996) "*Secum peregrinari*: Il tema del viaggio in Seneca." In *De tuo tibi: Omaggio degli allievi a Italo Lana*, 263–85. Bologna.

Gargiulo, T. (1981) "P. Herc. 222: Filodemo sull'adulazione." *Cronache ercolanesi* 11: 103–27.

Garland, R. (1995) *The Eye of the Beholder: Deformity and Disability in the Graeco-Roman World*. Ithaca, NY.

Gazda, E. K., ed. (1991) *Roman Art in the Private Sphere: New Perspectives on the Architecture and Decor of the Domus, Villa, and Insula*. Ann Arbor, Mich.

  (1995) "Roman Sculpture and the Ethos of Emulation: Reconsidering Repetition." *Harvard Studies in Classical Philology* 97: 121–56.

  ed. (2002) *The Ancient Art of Emulation: Studies in Artistic Originality and Tradition from the Present to Classical Antiquity*. Ann Arbor, Mich.

Geffcken, K. A. (1973) *Comedy in the Pro Caelio*. Leiden.
George, E. V. (1974) *Aeneid* VIII *and the Aitia of Callimachus*. Leiden.
Gigante, M. (1984) "Per l'interpretazione del libro di Filodemo *Del buon re secondo Omero*." *La Parola del Passato* 217: 285–98.
Gilbert, R. (1991) *Walks in the World: Representation and Experience in Modern American Poetry*. Princeton.
Gill, C. (1983) "The Question of Character-Development: Plutarch and Tacitus." *Classical Quarterly* 33: 469–87.
(1996) *Personality in Greek Epic, Tragedy, and Philosophy: The Self in Dialogue*. Oxford.
Ginouvès, R. (1992) *Dictionnaire méthodique de l'architecture grecque et romaine*. Vol. II: *Éléments constructifs: Supports, couvertures, aménagements intérieurs*. Rome.
Gleason, K. L. (1990) "The Garden Portico of Pompey the Great: An Ancient Public Park Preserved in the Layers of Rome." *Expedition* 32.2: 4–13.
Gleason, M. W. (1995) *Making Men: Sophists and Self-Presentation in Ancient Rome*. Princeton.
(1999) "Elite Male Identity in the Roman Empire." In *Life, Death, and Entertainment in the Roman Empire*, ed. D. S. Potter and D. J. Mattingly, 67–84. Ann Arbor, Mich.
Glucker, J. (1988) "Cicero's Philosophical Affiliations." In *The Question of "Eclecticism": Studies in Later Greek Philosophy*, ed. J. M. Dillon and A. A. Long, 34–69. Berkeley, Los Angeles, and London.
Görler, W. (1988) "From Athens to Tusculum: Gleaning the Background of Cicero's *De oratore*." *Rhetorica* 6: 215–35.
(1990) "Syracusae auf dem Palatin; Syracuse, New York: Sentimentale Namengebung in Rom und später." In *Pratum Saraviense: Festgabe für Peter Steinmetz*, ed. W. Görler and S. Koster, 169–88. Stuttgart.
Gourevitch, D. (1995) "Comment rendre à sa véritable nature le petit monstre humain?" In *Ancient Medicine in its Socio-Cultural Context: Papers Read at the Congress Held at Leiden University, 13–15 April 1992*, ed. P. J. v. d. Eijk, H. F. J. Horstmanshoff, and P. H. Schrijvers, 239–60. Amsterdam and Atlanta.
Gowing, A. M. (2005) *Empire and Memory: The Representation of the Roman Republic in Imperial Culture*. Cambridge and New York.
Graf, F. (1991) "Gestures and Conventions: The Gestures of Roman Actors." In Bremmer and Roodenburg (1991), 36–58.
Grahame, M. (1997) "Public and Private in the Roman House: The Spatial Order of the *Casa del Fauno*." In Laurence and Wallace-Hadrill (1997), 137–64.
Gransden, K. W. (1976) *Virgil: Aeneid, Book* VIII. Cambridge.
Graver, M. (1998) "The Manhandling of Maecenas: Senecan Abstractions of Masculinity." *American Journal of Philology* 119: 607–32.
Griffin, M. T. (1976) *Seneca: A Philosopher in Politics*. Oxford.
Grimal, P. (1984) *Les jardins romains*. 3rd edn. Paris.
Gruen, E. S. (1992) *Culture and National Identity in Republican Rome*. Ithaca, NY.

Gummere, R. M., trans. (1918) *Seneca: Ad Lucilium epistulae morales*. Vol. 1. London.

Gunderson, E. (1998) "Discovering the Body in Roman Oratory." In Wyke (1998), 169–89.

Habinek, T. N. (2005) *The World of Roman Song: From Ritualized Speech to Social Order*. Baltimore.

Hadot, P. (1995) *Philosophy as a Way of Life: Spiritual Exercises from Socrates to Foucault*. Trans. M. Chase. Ed. A. I. Davidson. Oxford and New York.

Hales, S. (2003) *The Roman House and Social Identity*. Cambridge.

Halperin, D. M. (2002) "Forgetting Foucault: Acts, Identities, and the History of Sexuality." In *The Sleep of Reason: Erotic Experience and Sexual Ethics in Ancient Greece and Rome*, ed. M. C. Nussbaum and J. Sihvola, 21–54. Chicago.

Hamilton, H. C. and W. Falconer, trans. (1854) *The Geography of Strabo*. Vol. 1. London.

Hardie, A. (1998) "Juvenal, the *Phaedrus*, and the Truth about Rome." *Classical Quarterly* 48: 234–51.

Hardie, P. R. (1986) *Virgil's Aeneid: Cosmos and imperium*. Oxford.

Harlow, M. and R. Laurence (2002) *Growing Up and Growing Old in Ancient Rome: A Life Course Approach*. London and New York.

Hartnett, J. (2007) "*Si quis hic sederit*: Streetside Benches and Urban Society in Pompeii." *American Journal of Archaeology* 112: 91–119.

Hartog, F. (2001) *Memories of Odysseus: Frontier Tales from Ancient Greece*. Trans. J. Lloyd. Chicago.

Hauken, T. (1998) *Petition and Response: An Epigraphic Study of Petitions to Roman Emperors, 181–249*. Bergen.

Heine, H. (1882) *Religion and Philosophy in Germany: A Fragment*. Trans. J. Snodgrass. London.

Henderson, J. (1997) "The Name of the Tree: Recounting *Odyssey* XXIV 340–2." *Journal of Hellenic Studies* 117: 87–116.

(2002) "Knowing Someone Through Their Books: Pliny on Uncle Pliny (*Epistles* 3.5)." *Classical Philology* 97: 256–84.

(2004) *Morals and Villas in Seneca's Letters: Places to Dwell*. Cambridge and New York.

(2006) "Journey of a Lifetime: Seneca, *Epistle* 57 in Book VI in *EM*." In Volk and Williams (2006), 123–46.

Henzen, W. (1850) "Römische Ausgrabungen." *Archäologische Zeitung* 8 (*Archäologischer Anzeiger* 15, Feb. 1850): 165–8.

Heurgon, J. (1978) *Varron: Économie rurale*. Vol. 1: *Livre premier*. Paris.

Höistad, R. (1948) *Cynic Hero and Cynic King: Studies in the Cynic Conception of Man*. Uppsala.

Hölkeskamp, K.-J. (2004) *Rekonstruktionen einer Republik: Die politische Kultur des antiken Rom und die Forschung der letzten Jahrzehnte*. Munich.

Holliday, P. J. (2002) *The Origins of Roman Historical Commemoration in the Visual Arts*. Cambridge.

Holzberg, N. (1997) *Ovid: Dichter und Werk*. Munich.

Hopkins, K. (1983) *Death and Renewal*. Cambridge.

Horsfall, N. (1971) "Incedere and incessus." *Glotta* 49: 145–7.

Housman, A. E. (1918) "Jests of Plautus, Cicero, and Trimalchio." *Classical Review* 32: 162–4.

Hoyland, R. (2007) "A New Edition and Translation of the Leiden Polemon." In Swain (2007a), 329–463.

Hunter, R. and I. Rutherford, eds. (2009) *Wandering Poets in Ancient Greek Culture: Travel, Locality and Pan-Hellenism*. Cambridge.

Inwood, B. (2007) *Seneca: Selected Philosophical Letters*. Oxford.

Itgenshorst, T. (2008) "Der Princeps triumphiert nicht: Vom Verschwinden des Siegesrituals in augusteischer Zeit." In *Triplici invectus triumpho: Der römische Triumph in augusteischer Zeit*, ed. H. Krasser, D. Pausch, and I. Petrovic, 27–54. Stuttgart.

Jaeger, M. (1997) *Livy's Written Rome*. Ann Arbor, Mich.

Janko, R. (1992) *The Iliad: A Commentary*. Vol. iv: *Books 13–16*. Ed. G. S. Kirk. Cambridge.

(2000) *Philodemus: On Poems, Book 1*. Oxford.

Jarvis, R. (1997) *Romantic Writing and Pedestrian Travel*. London.

Jashemski, W. (1979) *The Gardens of Pompeii, Herculaneum and the Villas Destroyed by Vesuvius*. New Rochelle, NY.

Jenkins, T. E. (2006) *Intercepted Letters: Epistolarity and Narrative in Greek and Roman Literature*. Lanham, Md.

Johnson, W. A. (2000) "Toward a Sociology of Reading in Classical Antiquity." *American Journal of Philology* 121: 593–627.

Jones, R. M. (1926) "Posidonius and the Flight of the Mind through the Universe." *Classical Philology* 21: 97–113.

Kaiser, E. (1964) "Odyssee-Szenen als Topoi." *Museum Helveticum* 21: 109–36, 197–224.

Kajanto, I. (1982) *The Latin Cognomina*. Rome.

Kellum, B. (1999) "The Spectacle of the Street." In Bergmann and Kondoleon (1999), 283–99.

Ker, J. (2002) "Nocturnal Letters: Roman Temporal Practices and Seneca's *Epistulae morales*." Ph.D. diss., University of California, Berkeley.

(2006) "Seneca, Man of Many Genres." In Volk and Williams (2006), 19–41.

(2009) *The Deaths of Seneca*. Oxford and New York.

Keuls, E. C. (1974) *The Water Carriers in Hades: A Study of Catharsis through Toil in Classical Antiquity*. Amsterdam.

Kragelund, P. (1999) "Senecan Tragedy: Back on Stage?" *Classica et Mediaevalia* 50: 235–47.

Krostenko, B. A. (2001) *Cicero, Catullus, and the Language of Social Performance*. Chicago.

Kubitschek, W. (1919) "Karten." In *RE* x.2: cols. 2022–149.

Kuttner, A. (1995) "Republican Rome Looks at Pergamon." *Harvard Studies in Classical Philology* 97: 157–78.

(1999) "Culture and History at Pompey's Museum." *Transactions of the American Philological Association* 129: 343–73.

(2003) "Delight and Danger in the Roman Water Garden: Sperlonga and Tivoli." In *Landscape Design and the Experience of Motion*, ed. M. Conan, 103–56. Washington, DC.

La Porte du Theil, F. J. G. d., A. Koraes, A. J. Letronne, and P. F. J. Gosselin, trans. (1805–19) *Géographie de Strabon*. 5 vols. Paris.

Lamberton, R. (1986) *Homer the Theologian: Neoplatonist Allegorical Reading and the Growth of the Epic Tradition*. Berkeley, Los Angeles, and London.

Lamberton, R. and J. J. Keaney, eds. (1992) *Homer's Ancient Readers: The Hermeneutics of Greek Epic's Earliest Exegetes*. Princeton.

Langan, C. (1995) *Romantic Vagrancy: Wordsworth and the Simulation of Freedom*. Cambridge.

Langlands, R. (2007) *Sexual Morality in Ancient Rome*. Cambridge.

Larmour, D. H. J. (2007) "Holes in the Body: Sites of Abjection in Juvenal's Rome." In Larmour and Spencer (2007a), 168–210.

Larmour, D. H. J. and D. Spencer, eds. (2007a) *The Sites of Rome: Time, Space, Memory*. Oxford and New York.

(2007b) "Introduction – *Roma, recepta*: A Topography of the Imagination." In Larmour and Spencer (2007a), 1–60.

Laurence, R. (1994) *Roman Pompeii: Space and Society*. London and New York.

(1999) *The Roads of Roman Italy: Mobility and Cultural Change*. London.

Laurence, R. and D. J. Newsome, eds. (forthcoming) *Rome, Ostia, Pompeii: Movement and Space*. Oxford.

Laurence, R. and A. Wallace-Hadrill (1997) *Domestic Space in the Roman World: Pompeii and Beyond*. Portsmouth, RI.

Lavery, G. B. (1980) "Metaphors of War and Travel in Seneca's Prose Works." *Greece and Rome* 27: 147–57.

Leach, E. W. (1981) "Metamorphoses of the Acteon Myth in Campanian Painting." *Mitteilungen des Deutschen Archäologischen Instituts, Römische Abteilung* 88: 307–27.

(1986) "The Punishment of Dirce: A Newly Discovered Painting in the Casa di Giulio Polibio and its Significance within the Visual Tradition." *Mitteilungen des Deutschen Archäologischen Instituts, Römische Abteilung* 93: 157–82.

(1988) *The Rhetoric of Space: Literary and Artistic Representations of Landscape in Republican and Augustan Rome*. Princeton.

(1997) "Oecus on Ibycus: Investigating the Vocabulary of the Roman House." In *Sequence and Space in Pompeii*, ed. S. E. Bon and R. Jones, 50–72. Oxford.

(1999) "Viewing the *Spectacula* of Aeneid 6." In *Reading Vergil's Aeneid: An Interpretive Guide*, ed. C. Perkell, 111–27. Norman, Okla.

(2003) "*Otium* as *luxuria*: Economy of Status in the Younger Pliny's *Letters*." *Arethusa* 36: 147–65.

(2004) *The Social Life of Painting in Ancient Rome and on the Bay of Naples*. Cambridge.

Leeman, A. D., H. Pinkster, and H. L. W. Nelson (1985) *M. Tullius Cicero, De oratore libri III: Kommentar.* Vol. II: *Buch I, 166–265; Buch II, 1–98.* Heidelberg.

Lehnen, J. (1997) *Adventus principis: Untersuchungen zu Sinngehalt und Zeremoniell der Kaiserankunft in den Städten des Imperium Romanum.* Frankfurt am Main.

Levick, B. (1990) *Claudius.* New Haven, Conn.

Ling, R. (1977) "Studius and the Beginnings of Roman Landscape Painting." *Journal of Roman Studies* 67: 1–16.

(1991) *Roman Painting.* Cambridge.

Lintott, A. (1999) *Violence in Republican Rome.* 2nd edn. Oxford.

Long, A. A. (1974) *Hellenistic Philosophy: Stoics, Epicureans, Sceptics.* London.

(1992) "Stoic Readings of Homer." In Lamberton and Keaney (1992), 41–66.

Lowenstam, S. (1995) "The Sources of the *Odyssey Landscapes.*" *Echos du Monde Classique/Classical Views* 39 (n.s. 14): 193–226.

Lydakis, S. (2004) *Ancient Greek Painting and its Echoes in Later Greek Art.* Los Angeles.

Macaulay-Lewis, E. (2009) "Political Museums: Porticos, Gardens and the Public Display of Art in Ancient Rome." In *Collecting and Dynastic Ambition,* ed. S. Bracken, A. M. Gáldy, and A. Turpin, 1–21. Newcastle.

MacCormack, S. G. (1981) *Art and Ceremony in Late Antiquity.* Berkeley, Los Angeles, and London.

MacDonald, W. L. (1986) *The Architecture of the Roman Empire.* Vol. II: *An Urban Appraisal.* Rev. edn. New Haven, Conn.

MacDonald, W. L. and J. A. Pinto (1995) *Hadrian's Villa and its Legacy.* New Haven, Conn.

Maiuri, A. (1946) "Portico e peristilio." *La Parola del Passato* 3: 306–22.

Malcovati, E. (1976) *Oratorum Romanorum fragmenta liberae rei publicae.* 4th edn. Turin, Milan, and Padua.

Marvin, M. (2008) *The Language of the Muses: The Dialogue between Roman and Greek Sculpture.* Los Angeles.

Marzano, A. (2007) *Roman Villas in Central Italy: A Social and Economic History.* Leiden and Boston.

Matranga, P. (1852) *La città di Lamo stabilita in Terracina secondo la descrizione di Omero e due degli antichi dipinti già ritrovati sull'Esquilino.* Rome.

Mattusch, C. C. (2005) *The Villa dei Papiri at Herculaneum: Life and Afterlife of a Sculpture Collection.* Los Angeles.

Mayer, R. (1986) "Horace's *Epistles* I and Philosophy." *American Journal of Philology* 107: 55–73.

Mayor, J. E. B. (1878) *Thirteen Satires of Juvenal.* Vol. II. London.

McGinn, T. A. J. (1998) "*Feminae probrosae* and the Litter." *Classical Journal* 93: 241–50.

Mielsch, H. (1987) *Die römische Villa: Architektur und Lebensform.* Munich.

(2001) *Römische Wandmalerei.* Stuttgart.

Millar, F. (1977) *The Emperor in the Roman World (31 BC–AD 337).* Ithaca, NY.

(1998) *The Crowd in Rome in the Late Republic.* Ann Arbor, Mich.

Miller, P. A. (2007) "'I Get Around': Sadism, Desire, and Metonymy on the Streets of Rome with Horace, Ovid, and Juvenal." In Larmour and Spencer (2007a), 138–67.

Miller, P. C. (2004) "Visceral Seeing: The Holy Body in Late Ancient Christianity." *Journal of Early Christian Studies* 12: 391–411.

Milligan, S. (2004) "Kerry Criticized for French Connection: Republican Strategy Hits Culture, Image." *Boston Globe*, 12 April.

Möller, M. (2004) *Talis oratio – qualis vita: Zu Theorie und Praxis mimetischer Verfahren in der griechisch-römischen Literaturkritik*. Heidelberg.

Monoson, S. S. (2000) *Plato's Democratic Entanglements: Athenian Politics and the Practice of Philosophy*. Princeton.

Montiglio, S. (2005) *Wandering in Ancient Greek Culture*. Chicago.

(2006) "Should the Aspiring Wise Man Travel? A Conflict in Seneca's Thought." *American Journal of Philology* 127: 553–86.

Montserrat, D., ed. (1998) *Changing Bodies, Changing Meanings: Studies on the Human Body in Antiquity*. London and New York.

Moore, T. J. (1998) *The Theater of Plautus: Playing to the Audience*. Austin, Tex.

Moormann, E. M., ed. (1993) *Functional and Spatial Analysis of Wall Painting: Proceedings of the Fifth International Congress on Ancient Wall Painting, Amsterdam, 8–12 September 1992*. Leiden.

Morford, M. P. O. (1992) "*Iubes esse liberos*: Pliny's *Panegyricus* and Liberty." *American Journal of Philology* 113: 575–93.

Morstein-Marx, R. (1998) "Publicity, Popularity, and Patronage in the *Commentariolum petitionis*." *Classical Antiquity* 17: 259–88.

(2004) *Mass Oratory and Political Power in the Late Roman Republic*. Cambridge.

Motto, A. L. and J. R. Clark (1981) "*Maxima virtus* in Seneca's *Hercules Furens*." *Classical Philology* 76: 101–17.

(1993) *Essays on Seneca*. Frankfurt.

Mouritsen, H. (2001) *Plebs and Politics in the Late Roman Republic*. Cambridge.

Myerowitz, M. (1985) *Ovid's Games of Love*. Detroit.

Myers, K. S. (2000) "'Miranda fides': Poet and Patrons in Paradoxographical Landscapes in Statius' *Silvae*." *Materiali e discussioni per l'analisi dei testi classici*: 103–38.

Nagy, G. (1979) *The Best of the Achaeans: Concepts of the Hero in Archaic Greek Poetry*. Baltimore.

Neudecker, R. (1988) *Die Skulpturenausstattung römischer Villen in Italien*. Mainz.

Newlands, C. E. (2002) *Statius' Silvae and the Poetics of Empire*. Cambridge.

Nicholson, G. (2008) *The Lost Art of Walking: The History, Science, and Literature of Pedestrianism*. New York.

Nicolet, C. (1980) *The World of the Citizen in Republican Rome*. Trans. P. S. Falla. Berkeley and Los Angeles.

Nightingale, A. W. (2001) "On Wandering and Wondering: *Theôria* in Greek Philosophy and Culture." *Arion* 9.2: 23–58.

(2004) *Spectacles of Truth in Classical Greek Philosophy: Theoria in its Cultural Context*. Cambridge.

Nippel, W. (1988) *Aufruhr und "Polizei" in der römischen Republik.* Stuttgart.

Nisbet, G. (2003) "A Sickness of Discourse: The Vanishing Syndrome of *Leptosune.*" *Greece and Rome* 50: 191–205.

Norden, E., ed. (1957) *P. Vergilius Maro: Aeneis, Buch* VI. 4th edn. Stuttgart.

O'Gorman, E. (2000) *Irony and Misreading in the Annals of Tacitus.* Cambridge.

Osborne, R. (1987) "The Viewing and Obscuring of the Parthenon Frieze." *Journal of Hellenic Studies* 107: 98–105.

Östenberg, I. (2009) *Staging the World: Spoils, Captives, and Representations in the Roman Triumphal Procession.* Oxford and New York.

O'Sullivan, T. M. (2006) "The Mind in Motion: Walking and Metaphorical Travel in the Roman Villa." *Classical Philology* 101: 133–52.

(2007) "Walking with Odysseus: The Portico Frame of the Odyssey Landscapes." *American Journal of Philology* 128: 497–532.

Pandermalis, D. (1971) "Zur Programm der Statuenausstattung in der Villa dei Papiri." *Mitteilungen des Deutschen Archäologischen Instituts, Athenische Abteilung* 86: 173–209.

Papaioannou, S. (2003) "Founder, Civilizer, and Leader: Vergil's Evander and his Role in the Origins of Rome." *Mnemosyne* 56: 680–702.

Parker, H. (1989) "Crucially Funny or Tranio on the Couch: The *servus callidus* and Jokes about Torture." *Transactions of the American Philological Association* 119: 233–46.

Parslow, C. C. (1989) "The Praedia Iuliae Felicis in Pompeii." Ph.D. diss., Duke University.

Pattison, G. (2005) *The Philosophy of Kierkegaard.* Montreal, Que. and Kingston, Ont.

Perry, E. (2005) *The Aesthetics of Emulation in the Visual Arts of Ancient Rome.* Cambridge.

Platt, V. (2002) "Viewing, Desiring, Believing: Confronting the Divine in a Pompeian House." *Art History* 25: 87–112.

Pollitt, J. J. (1986) *Art in the Hellenistic Age.* Cambridge.

Porter, J. I., ed. (1999) *Constructions of the Classical Body.* Ann Arbor, Mich.

Pugliese Carratelli, G., ed. (1990–2003) *Pompei: Pitture e mosaici.* Rome.

Purcell, N. (1992) "The City of Rome." In *The Legacy of Rome: A New Appraisal,* ed. R. Jenkyns, 421–53. Oxford.

(1995) "The Roman *villa* and the Landscape of Production." In *Urban Society in Roman Italy,* ed. T. Cornell and K. Lomas, 151–79. New York.

Raaflaub, K. A. (1986) "From Protection and Defense to Offense and Participation: Stages in the Conflict of the Orders." In *Social Struggles in Archaic Rome: New Perpectives on the Conflict of the Orders,* ed. K. A. Raaflaub, 198–237. Berkeley, Los Angeles, and London.

Rackham, H., trans. (1931) *Cicero: De finibus bonorum et malorum.* Cambridge, Mass.

Ramage, E. S. (1983) "Urban Problems in Ancient Rome." In *Aspects of Graeco-Roman Urbanism: Essays on the Classical City,* ed. R. T. Marchese, 61–92. Oxford.

Rausch, H. (1982) *Theoria: Von ihrer sakralen zur philosophischen Bedeutung.* Munich.

Rawson, E. (1975) "Caesar's Heritage: Hellenistic Kings and their Roman Equals." *Journal of Roman Studies* 65: 148–59.

Reay, B. (1998) "Cultivating Romans: Republican Agricultural Writing and the Invention of the *Agricola.*" Ph.D. diss., Stanford University.

Redfield, J. (1985) "Herodotus the Tourist." *Classical Philology* 80: 97–118.

Rehm, R. (1994) *Marriage to Death: The Conflation of Wedding and Funeral Rituals in Greek Tragedy.* Princeton.

Repath, I. (2007) "Anonymus Latinus, *Book of Physiognomy.*" In Swain (2007a), 549–635.

Richardson, J. S. (1975) "The Triumph, the Praetors and the Senate in the Early Second Century BC." *Journal of Roman Studies* 65: 50–63.

Richardson, L., Jr. (1977) "Hercules Musarum and the Porticus Philippi in Rome." *American Journal of Archaeology* 81: 355–61.

Richlin, A. (1993) "Not before Homosexuality: The Materiality of the *Cinaedus* and the Roman Law against Love between Men " *Journal of the History of Sexuality* 3: 523–73.

  (1997) "Gender and Rhetoric: Producing Manhood in the Schools." In *Roman Eloquence: Rhetoric in Society and Literature,* ed. W. J. Dominik, 90–110. London.

  (1999) "Cicero's Head." In Porter (1999), 190–211.

Ridley, A. and J. Norman, eds. (2005) *Nietzsche: The Anti-Christ, Ecce Homo, Twilight of the Idols, and Other Writings.* Cambridge.

Riggsby, A. M. (1997) "'Public' and 'Private' in Roman Culture: The Case of the *cubiculum.*" *Journal of Roman Archaeology* 10: 36–56.

  (2003) "Pliny in Space (and Time)." *Arethusa* 36: 167–86.

Robert, C. (1881) *Bild und Lied: Archäologische Beiträge zur Geschichte der griechischen Heldensage.* Berlin.

Robertson, M. (1955) "The Boscoreale Figure-Paintings." *Journal of Roman Studies* 45: 58–67.

Robinson, J. C. (1989) *The Walk: Notes on a Romantic Image.* Norman, Okla. and London.

Rogers, P. M. (1980) "Titus, Berenice and Mucianus." *Historia* 29: 86–95.

Roller, M. B. (2001) *Constructing Autocracy: Aristocrats and Emperors in Julio-Claudian Rome.* Princeton.

  (2006) *Dining Posture in Ancient Rome: Bodies, Values, and Status.* Princeton.

Rosenmeyer, T. G. (1989) *Senecan Drama and Stoic Cosmology.* Berkeley, Los Angeles, and London.

Roskam, G. (2005) *On the Path to Virtue: The Stoic Doctrine of Moral Progress and its Reception in (Middle-)Platonism.* Leuven.

Russell, D. A. (1964) *"Longinus" on the Sublime.* Oxford.

Rutherford, I. (1998) "Theoria as Theatre: Pilgrimage in Greek Drama." *Papers of the Leeds International Latin Seminar* 10: 131–56.

  (2000) "Theoria and Darśan: Pilgrimage and Vision in Greece and India." *Classical Quarterly* 50: 133–46.

Rutherford, R. B. (1986) "The Philosophy of the *Odyssey.*" *Journal of Hellenic Studies* 106: 145–62.

Sailor, D. (2008) *Writing and Empire in Tacitus.* Cambridge.

Saller, R. P. (1982) *Personal Patronage under the Early Empire.* Cambridge.

(1989) "Patronage and Friendship in Early Imperial Rome: Drawing the Distinction." In Wallace-Hadrill (1989a), 49–62.

(1994) *Patriarchy, Property, and Death in the Roman Family.* Cambridge.

Sassi, M. M. (1991) "Il viaggio e la festa: Note sulla rappresentazione dell'ideale filosofico della vita." In *Idea e realtà del viaggio: Il viaggio nel mondo antico,* ed. G. Camassa and S. Fasce, 17–36. Genoa.

Sauron, G. (1980) "Templa Serena: A propos de la 'villa des Papyri' d'Herculanum. Contribution à l'étude des comportements aristocratiques romains à la fin de la république." *Mélanges de l'École Française de Rome: Antiquité* 92: 277–301.

Saylor, C. (2002) "Thinking about Friends: Seneca, *Epist.* 55." *Latomus* 61: 102–5.

Scagliarini Corlàita, D. (1974–6) "Spazio e decorazione nella pittura pompeiana." *Palladio* 23–5: 3–44.

(1997) "*Propter spatia longitudinis*: Cicli e serie figurative nelle *ambulationes* del secondo e del quarto 'stile pompeiano'." In *I temi figurativi nella pittura parietale antica (IV sec. a.C.–IV sec. d.C.): Atti del VI Convegno Internazionale sulla Pittura Parietale Antica,* ed. D. Scagliarini Corlàita, 119–23. Imola.

Schafer, J. (2009) *Ars didactica: Seneca's 94th and 95th Letters.* Göttingen.

Schiesaro, A. (2003) *The Passions in Play: Thyestes and the Dynamics of Senecan Drama.* Cambridge.

Schmidt, O. E. (1899) "Ciceros Villen." *Neue Jahrbücher für das klassische Altertum, Geschichte und deutsche Literatur* 3: 328–55; 466–97.

Schofield, M. (1991) *The Stoic Idea of the City.* Cambridge.

Scobie, A. (1986) "Slums, Sanitation, and Mortality in the Roman World." *Klio* 68: 399–433.

Scullard, H. H. (1973) *Roman Politics: 220–150 BC.* 2nd edn. Oxford.

Shackleton Bailey, D. R. (1966) *Cicero's Letters to Atticus.* Vol. V. Cambridge.

(1968) *Cicero's Letters to Atticus.* Vol. III. Cambridge.

Shaw, B. D. (1985) "The Divine Economy: Stoicism as Ideology." *Latomus* 44: 16–54.

Sherman, N. (2005) "The Look and Feel of Virtue." In *Virture, Norms, and Objectivity: Issues in Ancient and Modern Ethics,* ed. C. Gill, 59–82. Oxford.

Short, W. M. (2008) "Thinking Places, Placing Thoughts: Spatial Metaphors of Mental Activity in Roman Culture." *Quaderni del Ramo d'Oro* 1: 106–29.

Skard, E. (1965) "Die Heldenschau in Vergils Aeneis." *Symbolae Osloenses* 40: 53–65.

Slater, N. W. (2000) *Plautus in Performance: The Theatre of the Mind.* 2nd rev. edn. Amsterdam.

Small, J. P. (1999) "Time *in* Space: Narrative in Classical Art." *Art Bulletin* 81: 562–75.

Solnit, R. (2000) *Wanderlust: A History of Walking.* New York.

Squire, M. (2003) "Giant Questions: Dining with Polyphemus at Sperlonga and Baiae." *Apollo* (July): 29–37.

Stanford, W. B. (1963) *The Ulysses Theme: A Study in the Adaptability of a Traditional Hero.* 2d edn. Oxford.

Stansbury-O'Donnell, M. (1999) *Pictorial Narrative in Ancient Greek Art.* Cambridge.

Star, C. (2006) "Commanding *constantia* in Senecan Tragedy." *Transactions of the American Philological Association* 136: 207–44.

Starr, R. J. (1991) "Reading Aloud: *Lectores* and Roman Reading." *Classical Journal* 86: 337–43.

Stewart, A. (1977) "To Entertain an Emperor: Sperlonga, Laokoon and Tiberius at the Dinner-Table." *Journal of Roman Studies* 67: 76–90.

  (1996) "A Hero's Quest: Narrative and the Telephos Frieze." In *Pergamon: The Telephos Frieze from the Great Altar.* Vol. 1, ed. R. Dreyfus and E. Schraudolph, 39–52. San Francisco.

Stone, S. (1994) "The Toga: From National to Ceremonial Costume." In *The World of Roman Costume,* ed. J. L. Sebesta and L. Bonfante, 13–45. Madison, Wis.

Sumi, G. S. (2005) *Ceremony and Power: Performing Politics in Rome between Republic and Empire.* Ann Arbor, Mich.

Sutton, D. F. (1986) *Seneca on the Stage.* Leiden.

Swain, S., ed. (2007a) *Seeing the Face, Seeing the Soul: Polemon's Physiognomy from Classical Antiquity to Medieval Islam.* Oxford.

  (2007b) "Polemon's *Physiognomy.*" In Swain (2007a), 125–201.

Taladoire, B.-A. (1951) *Commentaires sur la mimique et l'expression corporelle du comédien romain.* Montpellier.

Taplin, O. (1978) *Greek Tragedy in Action.* Berkeley.

Tarrant, R. (2006) "Seeing Seneca Whole?" In Volk and Williams (2006), 1–17.

Tester, K., ed. (1994) *The Flâneur.* London and New York.

Theodorakopoulos, E. (2007) "The Sites and Sights of Rome in Fellini's Films: 'Not a Human Habitation but a Psychical Entity'." In Larmour and Spencer (2007a), 353–84.

Thomas, E. (1995) "Zum Zeugniswert griechischer Beischriften auf römischen Wandgemälden der späten Republik und frühen Kaiserzeit." *Mededelingen van het Nederlands Instituut te Rome* 54: 110–23.

Tilburg, C. van (2007) *Traffic and Congestion in the Roman Empire.* Abingdon and New York.

Tozer, H. F. (1893) *Selections from Strabo.* Oxford.

Treggiari, S. (1991) *Roman Marriage: Iusti coniuges from the Time of Cicero to the Time of Ulpian.* Oxford.

Tybout, R. A. (1989) *Aedificiorum figurae: Untersuchungen zu den Architekturdarstellungen des frühen zweiten Stils.* Amsterdam.

  (2001) "Roman Wall-painting and Social Significance." *Journal of Roman Archaeology* 14: 33–56.

Valakas, K. (2002) "The Use of the Body by Actors in Tragedy and Satyr-Play." In *Greek and Roman Actors: Aspects of an Ancient Profession*, ed. P. Easterling and E. Hall, 69–92. Cambridge.

Vasaly, A. (1993) *Representations: Images of the World in Ciceronian Oratory*. Berkeley.

Versnel, H. S. (1970) *Triumphus: An Inquiry into the Origin, Development and Meaning of the Roman Triumph*. Leiden.

Vlad Borrelli, L. (1956) "Un nuovo frammento dei 'paesaggi dell'Odissea'." *Bollettino d'Arte del Ministero per i Beni Culturali e Ambientali* 41: 289–300.

Volk, K. and G. D. Williams, eds. (2006) *Seeing Seneca Whole: Perspectives on Philosophy, Poetry and Politics*. Leiden and Boston.

von Blanckenhagen, P. H. (1957) "Narration in Hellenistic and Roman Art." *American Journal of Archaeology* 61: 78–83.

   (1963) "The Odyssey Frieze." *Mitteilungen des Deutschen Archäologischen Instituts, Römische Abteilung* 70: 100–46.

von Staden, H. (2000) "The Dangers of Literature and the Need for Literacy: A. Cornelius Celsus on Reading and Writing." In *Les textes médicaux latins comme littérature: Actes du VIe colloque international sur les textes médicaux latins du 1er au 3 septembre 1998 à Nantes*, ed. A. Pigeaud and J. Pigeaud, 355–68. Nantes.

Vout, C. (2007) "Sizing Up Rome, or Theorizing the Overview." In Larmour and Spencer (2007a), 295–322.

Wallace, A. D. (1993) *Walking, Literature, and English Culture: The Origins and Uses of the Peripatetic in the Nineteenth Century*. Oxford.

Wallace-Hadrill, A., ed. (1989a) *Patronage in Ancient Society*. London and New York.

   (1989b) "Patronage in Roman Society: From Republic to Empire." In Wallace-Hadrill (1989a), 63–87.

   (1994) *Houses and Society in Pompeii and Herculaneum*. Princeton.

   (1997) "Rethinking the Roman Atrium House." In Laurence and Wallace-Hadrill (1997), 219–40.

   (1998) "To Be Roman, Go Greek: Thoughts on Hellenization at Rome." In *Modus operandi: Essays in Honour of Geoffrey Rickman*, ed. M. Austin, J. Harries, and C. J. Smith, 79–91. London.

Warden, P. G. and D. G. Romano (1994) "The Course of Glory: Greek Art in a Roman Context at the Villa of the Papyri at Herculaneum." *Art History* 17: 228–54.

Weeber, K.-W. (1995) *Alltag im alten Rom: Ein Lexikon*. Zurich.

Williams, C. A. (1999) *Roman Homosexuality: Ideologies of Masculinity in Classical Antiquity*. Oxford and New York.

   (2004) *Martial: Epigrams Book Two*. Oxford.

Williams, G. D. (1994) *Banished Voices: Readings in Ovid's Exile Poetry*. Cambridge.

   (2003) *Seneca: De otio; De brevitate vitae*. Cambridge.

   (2006) "States of Exile, States of Mind: Paradox and Reversal in Seneca's *Consolatio ad Helviam matrem*." In Volk and Williams (2006), 147–73.

Winkler, J. J. (1990) "Laying Down the Law: The Oversight of Men's Sexual Behavior in Classical Athens." In *Before Sexuality: The Construction of Erotic Experience in the Ancient Greek World*, ed. D. M. Halperin, J. J. Winkler, and F. I. Zeitlin, 171–209. Princeton.

Wlosok, A. (1967) *Die Göttin Venus in Vergils Aeneis*. Heidelberg.

Wojcik, M. R. (1986) *La villa dei papiri ad Ercolano: Contributo alla ricostruzione dell'ideologia della nobilitas tardorepubblicana*. Rome.

Wright, J. (1974) *Dancing in Chains: The Stylistic Unity of the comoedia palliata*. Rome.

Wyke, M., ed. (1998) *Parchments of Gender: Deciphering the Body in Antiquity*. Oxford.

Yakobson, A. (1999) *Elections and Electioneering in Rome: A Study in the Political System of the Late Republic*. Stuttgart.

Yates, F. A. (1966) *The Art of Memory*. Chicago.

Zanker, G. (2004) *Modes of Viewing in Hellenistic Poetry and Art*. Madison, Wis.

Zanker, P. (1998) *Pompeii: Public and Private Life*. Trans. D. L. Steiner. Cambridge, Mass.

Zeiner, N. K. (2005) *Nothing Ordinary Here: Statius as Creator of Distinction in the Silvae*. New York and London.

Zetzel, J. (2003) "Plato with Pillows: Cicero on the Uses of Greek Culture." In *Myth, History and Culture in Republican Rome: Studies in Honour of T. P. Wiseman*, ed. D. Braund and C. Gill, 119–38. Exeter.

Zwierlein, O. (1966) *Die Rezitationsdramen Senecas, mit einem kritisch-exegetischen Anhang*. Meisenheim.

Subject index

absent-mindedness, 100, 102
Academy (Cicero's), 93, 94, 105, 107
Academy (Plato's), 93, 104, 107
adsectatores, 60
    see also escorts
Aeneas, 12, 74, 150–2
Aeneid (Virgil), 11–12, 74–5, 150–2
Agricola, 67–8
Agrippina, 46, 65–6
Alcibiades, 93
allegoresis, 143
allegory of Hades, 146
Amaltheum, 110
Amato, Joseph, 5
ambassadors, 99
ambulatio (leisurely walking*)*
    Aeneas and, 150–2
    and business meetings, 87–8
    of elite males, 79, 142
    and friendship, 6, 83–5, 86, 152
    and the Odyssey Landscapes, 122, 148
    and reading, 89
    as social and intellectual activity, 9, 78–9
    and *theoria*, 9, 104, 111
ambulatory spaces
    and display of art, 114, 132–4
    and intellectual activity, 77–8, 87–8
    as reminders of Greek architecture and
        philosophy, 94–6
    and *theoria*, 9, 112–13
amicitia, 83–5, 86, 88, 152
    see also ambulatio, and friendship
Andromache, 39–40
Antiochus, 61
Antisthenes, 143
Antony, 62, 72
Apuleius, 20, 79
Ara Pacis (Rome), 76
Arctic, 99
Argiletum (Rome), 151
Aristo, 16

aristocrats, *see* elite males
Aristophanes, 92, 93, 100
Aristotle, 20–1, 92, 98, 99–100
art collections, 113, 114–15, 132–4
Astyanax, 16
ataraxia (freedom from anxiety), 114
Athens, 104–5
atria, 87
atrium houses, 95
Attalus, 92
Atticus, 5, 6, 83, 105, 108, 109, 110
Augustus
    on Claudius, 29
    funeral procession of, 75
    on gait, 19
    and grandsons' *deductio in forum*, 57
    modesty of, 68
    and walking, 57
Aulus Gellius, 92

barbarians, 1–2
Bennicelli, Filippo, 124
Bergmann, Bettina, 107, 116
Biering, Ralf, 125, 134
Bloomer, W. Martin, 30
Bodel, John, 107
bodily comportment, 14–15
body movement
    and knowledge, 97–9
    and mindset, 8
    and narrative art, 132–3, 134,
        135–42
    walking for exercise, 80–3
Braun, Emil, 124
bridal processions, 58
broken gait, 22, 26, 32
Brutus, 106
bucolic poetry, 126

Caelius Rufus, M., 83
Caesarion, 15–16

Casa del Frutetto (Pompeii), Diana and
  Actaeon panel, 141
Catiline, 20, 36
Cato the Elder, 79
Cato the Younger, 56, 82
Catullus, 22, 73
Catulus, Q. Lutatius, 77–8, 94
Celsus, 80–1
Christianity and modesty, 25–6
chronological viewpoints, 151
Cicero, Lucius Tullius, 104
Cicero, Marcus Tullius
  Academy of, 93, 94, 105, 107
  on Antiochus, 61
  on conversing while walking, 6, 83–5, 93–5
  on *deductio in forum*, 55–6
  dictation while walking, 83
  on equalizing power of walking, 70
  on escorts, 60–1
  on face and gait, 12, 14, 15
  on gait, 19, 47–8, 49–50
  and honorable leisure, 103
  on letters, 87
  on litters, 72, 73
  Lyceum of, 93, 94, 105, 107
  on walking, in history, 105; in nature, 5
  on non-conversational walking, 88–9
  on *otium*, 77–8
  on remembering the past and walking,
    108–9
  villa of, 93, 95, 105, 108–9
  on women, 24–5
  writings of
    De divinatione, 93
    De finibus, 93, 104–5, 107
    De legibus, 93, 108
    De oratore, 70, 77–8, 93, 94
    Tusculan Disputations, 93
Cicero, Quintus Tullius, 59–60, 108
cinaedus (effeminate male), 21–2
  see also effeminacy
Circe, 140, 146
Claudia, 23–4
Claudius, 29, 46
Claudius (decemvir), 58
clients, 52, 61, 85, 87, 111–12
  see also escorts
Clodia, 24–5
clothing and identity, 51–2
  see also togas
Clouds (Aristophanes), 93
Coarelli, Filippo, 124
Colosseum (Rome), 155
comedic plays and gait, 36–7
comitatus (retinue), 62

see also escorts
Commentariolum petitionis (Q. Cicero), 59–60
contemplative mind, 100, 101–4, 108
contemplative walking, *see ambulatio*
continuous narrative, 140, 141
Corbeill, Anthony, 16, 18, 20, 33, 47
cosmopolitanism, Stoic, 43–4
Crassus, 70, 77–8
Croesus, 99
Cupid, 12
Cynic philosophy, 143

Danaids, 144
decadence, 71–2
deductio in forum (escort to the forum), 55–7, 58,
  59–60, 151–2
deductores (escorts), 60
  see also escorts
Demetrius of Phaleron, 22
Diogenes, 4
disguises, 15, 37
Domitian, 67, 69
dress, *see* clothing and identity

education
  by slaves, 30
  tirocinium fori, 17, 56–7
Edwards, Catharine, 151, 156
effeminacy, 21–2, 27, 32, 52, 80, 81
elite males
  and *ambulatio*, 79, 142
  education by slaves, 30
  escorts of, 54
  gait of, 13, 17–21, 35
  initiation into adulthood, 56–7
  in plays, 37
  see also togas
emperors and escorts, 61–2, 67, 76
entourage, *see* escorts
Epicureanism, 113–14, 143–4, 146
Epicurus, 100, 144
equalizing power of walking, 70, 87
escorts
  adsectatores, 60
  of Agricola, 67–8
  of Agrippina, 65–6
  Cicero on, 60–1
  deductores, 60
  as democratic institution, 61
  elite males and, 8–9, 54
  funeral processions as, 74–5
  of kings, 61–2, 67, 76
  lawyers and, 54
  of Messalina, 65
  militarization of, 66

escorts (cont.)
  of Pallas, 66–7
  parade of heroes and, 74–5
  of philosophers, 112
  Pliny on, 68–9
  ranking of, 60
  and republican politics, 65–71, 76
  salutatores, 60, 66
  Tacitus on, 65–8
  of Trajan, 68–70
  and violence, 62
  see also deductio in forum; lictors
Euripus, 105
Eurotas, 106
Evander, 150–2
exercise, walking for, *see* walking, for exercise

Fabii, the, 75–6
facial characteristics and identity, 14–15
family identity, *see* identity, family
family names, 16, 25
fathers, 110
Fellini, Federico, 152–5, 157
fercula (floats), 20
festina lente (hurry up slowly), 19
Fibrenus, 109
flânerie, 6
Flaubert, Gustave, 4
floats, *see fercula* (floats)
Fowler, Don, 18–19
friendship and *ambulatio, see ambulatio* and
    friendship
  see also amicitia
funeral and marriage rituals, conflation of, 58
funeral processions
  as ambulatory ritual, 9, 52–4
  as escort, 74–5
  and gait, *see* gait, funeral processions and
  and parade of heroes, 74, 75

gait, 13
  broken, 22, 26, 32
  and effeminacy, 21–2, 27, 32, 52
  of elite males, 13, 17–21, 35
  expressive, 20
  and family identity, 15–16
  and family names, 25
  fast, 38
  feigned, 22, 28, 32
  female, 13, 19, 25, 27–8
  funeral processions and, 16, 53
  gait instruction, 16–17, 28, 29–31, 45
  and gender identity, 8, 13, 17, 19, 27,
    31–2
  of gods and goddesses, 11, 12, 13

and identity, 8, 32, 52
measured, 18–21
and mindset, 34–6, 37–40, 45
and plays, 8, 18, 36–8
and politicians, 13, 47–8, 49–50
rule of, 13
and self-control, 13
slaves, 18
slow, 19–20, 38, 52
and status, 13, 17–18
and togas, 19
see also walking; *see also under specific*
  writers on
Gaius Caesar, 57
gender identity
  and *deductio in forum*, 58
  and *deductiones*, 58
  and gait, *see* gait, and gender identity
  see also effeminacy; elite males
Germanicus, 48, 90–1
Gigante, Marcello, 145–6
Gleason, Maud, 17, 20, 21, 31, 45
gods and goddesses, gait of, *see* gait, of gods and
  goddesses
Golden Verses (Homer), 144
  see also Odyssey (Homer)
Gracchus, C. Sempronius, 72
Greek culture
  Roman attitudes toward, 91
  Roman recreations of, 126
Greek philosophers and walking
  discussions of, 3–4, 91–3
  and *otium*, 77–8
  Plato and, 92
  and Roman culture, 4–5, 94
  Seneca and, 110–13
  Socrates and, 93
  and Stoic school, 92
Greek walking, *see* walking, Greek

Hades, 144, 146
Hadrian, 97, 106, 129
Hall of the Doric Pillars (Hadrian's villa), 129
Hector, 16
Heine, Heinrich, 4
Heliodorus, 11, 12
Helvia, 102
Hercules, 29, 40
Herodotus, 99
heroes, parade of, 53, 74–5
Hippocrates, 92
Historia Augusta, 106
history, non-sequential, 151
Homer, 142–3, 144, 145–6
  see also Odyssey Landscapes

homes, *see* villas
honorable leisure, 103
    see also otium
Horace, 5, 6–7, 36, 55, 145–6, 148
House of Augustus (Rome), 129, 130
House of the Cryptoporticus (Pompeii), 129
House of the Faun (Pompeii), 96
houses, *see* villas

identity
    and clothing, *see* clothing and identity
    family, 75–6
    and gait, *see* gait, and identity
    and mindset, 35
    and walking, *see* walking, and identity
    see also gender identity
Iliad (Homer), 145
Ilissus, 109
imagines (ancestor masks), 16, 107
inactivity, busy, 43
incessus (gait), 12–13
    see also gait
inconstancy, 36
initiation into adulthood, 56–7
Iris, 12

Jerome, 26
Josephus, 113
journeys, *see* travel
Julius Caesar, 39, 71
Juno, 12
Juvenal, 54–5, 71

Kant, Immanuel, 4
Kerry, John, 90
Kierkegaard, Søren, 4
knowledge gained by travel and movement, 97–9
Kuttner, Ann, 124

Laestrygonians, 135–8, 146–7
landscape painting, 133
lawyers, 54
Leach, Eleanor Winsor, 130
lector (reader), 89
Leeman, Anton D., 93
legs, economic potential of, 79
leisure, *see otium* (leisure)
    see also ambulatio
Lesbia, 22
letters as form of communication, 83, 85–6, 87
lictors, 65
    see also escorts
litters, 7, 71–4
Livia, 48
Livy, 61–2, 63–4
Long, Anthony A., 45

Long, Richard, 3
Lucilius, 34
Lucius Caesar, 57
Lucretius, 100, 144, 146
Lyceum (Athens), 92
Lyceum (Cicero's), *see* Cicero, Marcus Tullius, Lyceum of

Maecenas, 34
Manilius, 28, 32
maps, 97
Marcellus, 74–5
Marcius Philippus, Q., 61–2
marriage ceremonies, 58
Martial, 51–2
masks, 16, 36, 107
    see also disguises
Matranga, Pietro, 124
memorization, 107
Menander, 22
Messalina, 65
Metamorphoses (Apuleius), 79
modesty, 25–6
Montiglio, Silvia, 92, 93, 98
Morpheus, 14
Moschus, 126
Mucianus, C. Licinius, 49
Murena, L. Licinius, 60
Myerowitz, Molly, 28

Narcissus, 66
narrative art
    continuous, 140, 141
    and portico frame, 135–42
    and walking, *see* walking, and narrative art
nature, walking in, 5–6
    see also outdoors, walking
nature in art, 116, 133
    see also landscape painting
Nazis, 153
Nero, 46, 57, 65–6
Nicolet, Claude, 61–2
Nietzsche, Friedrich, 4
Nightingale, Andrea W., 99
noblemen, *see* elite males
non-walking, 53–4

Odysseus
    as symbol of Greek identity, 110
    as traveler, 142, 143–4, 146, 148
    wisdom of, 39–40, 99
    see also Odyssey Landscapes
Odysseus (Antisthenes), 143
Odyssey (Homer), 143, 144, 145–6
    see also Odyssey Landscapes

Odyssey Landscapes
  and the *ambulatio*, 122, 148
  as blending of Greek and Roman art, 125
  excavation, 122–5
  Laestrygonian episode, 135–8, 146–7
  and landscape painting, 133
  narrative, 135–42
  origins, 116, 124, 125–6
  panel 1, 125
  panel 2, 135
  panel 3, 135–7, 138
  panel 4, 137–8
  panel 5, 138–9
  panel 6 (Circe panel), 139–41, 146, 147–9
  panel 9, 146
  pastoral scenes, 135–6
  perspective, 127–8, 141
  philosophical interpretations, 146–9
  pillars, 127, 134–5
  restoration, 124
  and Second Style of Roman wall painting,
    130–2
  and walking, 146
  see also portico frame of Odyssey Landscapes
On the Good King according to Homer
    (Philodemus), 145–6
Oplontis, Villa at, 130
optical illusions, 116, 127, 130, 135
otium (leisure), 77–8, 94–6, 103
outdoors, walking, 5–6, 46, 80–3, 101
ovatio (lesser triumphal parade), 53–4
Ovid, 14–15, 27–8, 85–6

Pallas, 66–7
parade of heroes, 53, 74–5
parades, *see* bridal processions; funeral
    processions; parade of heroes; triumphal
    parades
Parthenon (Athens), 106
pastoral scenes, 135–6, 154–5
  see also Odyssey Landscapes, pastoral scenes
peragrare (to travel over or through), 101
perambulare (to walk through), 97, 100, 112
Peripatetic school, 4, 92
peristyles, 79, 87–8, 94, 95–6
Perpetua, 14
Perseus of Macedon, 61–2
Persike Porticus, 106
Petronius, 22, 39
Philodemus, 142, 144, 145–6
philosophers and philosophy
  definition of, 102
  European, 4
  Homer as father of, 142–3
  and the Odyssey Landscapes, 146–9

  and *theoria*, 98–100
  and walking, 3–5, 92, 93, 110–13
  see also Epicureanism; Greek philosophers and
    walking; Peripatetic school; Stoic philosophy;
    and individual philosophers
physiognomy, 20–1
pillars, 122, 126–7, 128–30, 134–5
  see also porticoes; Odyssey Landscapes,
    pillars
Plato
  Academy of, 93, 104, 107
  and *theoria*, 98, 99–100
  on travels in the mind, 9
  and walking, 4, 92–3
  writings of
    Laws, 92, 109–10
    Phaedrus, 93, 94, 109
    Protagoras, 92
    Symposium, 92
    Theages, 92
Plautus, 18, 91
Pliny the Elder, 6, 20, 73, 132
Pliny the Younger
  on escorts, 68–9
  on litters, 73
  Panegyricus, 68
  villas of, 87, 109
  on walking, 81–3, 88, 89
Plutarch, 30
Polemon, 21
politics and politicians, *see* gait, and politicians;
    Seneca the Younger, on political
    engagement; walking, and politicians
Pollio, C. Asinius, 85
Pollius Felix, 113–14
Polybius, 53
Pompeian domus, 95–6
Pompey the Younger, 56–7
portico frame of Odyssey Landscapes
  and continuous narrative, 135–42,
    147–9
  discussions of, 10, 122, 126–34
  and optical illusion, 127
  and Second Style of Roman wall
    paintings, 133
  and walking, 146
Portico of Livia (Rome), 88
Portico of Pompey (Rome), 95, 113, 132
porticoes, 77–8, 79, 94,
    129, 131–4
Porticus Philippi (Rome), 132
Poseidon, 11
practical etiquette, 16–17
practical instruction, 45
Praedia Iuliae Felicis (Pompeii), 129

processions, 75–6
  see also bridal processions; funeral processions;
    parade of heroes; triumphal parades
public art, 132
pudicitia (sexual modesty), 25–6
Pyrrho, 100
Pythagoras, 99, 102

Quintilian, 18, 22

remembering the past, 108–9
republican politics and escorts, 65–71, 76
retinues, *see* escorts
rites of passage, *see* bridal processions; initiation
  into adulthood; *tirocinium fori*; togas
Robert, Carl, 141
Roma, Fellini's film, 152–5
Roman Forum, 151
  see also deductio in forum; tirocinium fori
Rome, as center of the world, 156–7
Rome, modern, 152–5
Rousseau, Jean-Jacques, 5
Rullus, P. Servilius, 15
Rutherford, Richard, 143

Saepta Iulia (Rome), 52
salutatores (greeters), 60, 66
  see also escorts
Saturn's rings, 154, 155
Scipio Africanus, 63–4, 89–91, 107–8
secessio plebis (secession of the plebs), 62–4
self-reflection, 148
Seneca the Younger
  on allegory of Hades, 144
  on Attalus, 92
  on clients, 111–12
  on contemplation of the universe, 101–3
  and the contemplative mind, 103–4, 108
  on exercise, 83
  on gait, 22, 26–7, 31–2, 34–5, 37–40, 49–50
  on gait instruction, 45
  on journeys, 44
  on political engagement, 103–4
  on practical etiquette instruction, 16–17
  and *theoria*, 98
  on tranquility, 42–3, 45–6
  villa of, 108
  on villa of Scipio Africanus, 107–8
  on walking, 5–6, 8, 44, 46, 101, 110–13
  writings of
    De otio, 103
    De tranquillitate animi, 41, 112
    Phaedra, 38
Serenus, 41
servus currens (running slave), 18

Shackleton Bailey, D. R., 106
Silius, C., 65
Sirens, 144, 146, 148
slaves
  and education of children, 30
  names of, 18
  in plays, 37
  Pliny the Elder on, 73
  as readers, 89
  running (*servus currens*), 18
  and walking, 7, 79
  see also litters
Socrates
  absent-mindedness of, 100
  on contemplation, 100
  and the Golden Verses, 144
  and the Ilissus, 109
  and walking, 46–7, 92–3
Solnit, Rebecca, 5
Solon, 99
Sperlonga grotto (Italy), 146
Spurinna, T. Vestricius, 81–2, 88, 89
Statius, 113–14
stoa of Zeus Eleutherios (Athens), 92
Stoa Poikile (Athens), 92, 132
stoas, *see* porticoes
Stoic philosophy
  and contemplative mind, 103–4
  cosmopolitanism, 43–4
  on Hercules, 40
  and Homeric poetry, 142
  on mind and body unity, 39–40
  and the *Odyssey*, 143
  and politics, 46–7
  on practical instruction, 45
  and virtue, 43
  and walking, 4, 8, 43–4, 92
Strabo, 1–3
Suetonius, 29, 57, 71, 88
sumptuary laws, 71–2

Tacitus, 48, 65–8, 90–1
Tantalus, 38
Tarpeian Rock (Rome), 151
Telephos frieze (Pergamon),
  132, 141
Tellos, 99
Templum Pacis (Rome), 113
Tertullian, 25–6
Thales, 4, 100
Theagenes of Rhegium, 143
theater
  and architecture, 129
  see also gait, and plays
Theocritus, 126

theoria
and *ambulatio, see ambulatio,* and *theoria*
and Greek philosophers, 98–100
meaning of, 98–9
and walking, 106–7
Thoreau, Henry David, 5
Thyestes, 38
Tiberius, 48, 88
tirocinium fori (apprenticeship of the forum), 17, 56–7
togas, 19, 52, 56, 57
tomb of Philip at Vergina (Greece), 126
tourism, *see* travel
Tozer, H. F., 2
Trajan, 68–70
tranquility, 42–3, 45–6
travel
and *ambulatio*, 9
into history, 104–5, 107–10, 108–9, 113–14, 151
and journey of a hero, 143–4
and knowledge, 97–9
Seneca on, 44
theoretical, 99–100, 106–7, 111, 151
through time, 151, 153
visual emphasis of, 99
walking as metaphor for, 98
triumphal parades, 8, 52–4, 63–4
trompe l'oeil, *see* optical illusions
Turpilius, 36

underworld myths, 144
universe, Seneca on, 101–3
urban walking, 6–7
see also escorts

Varro, 97, 99, 100–1
Venus, 11, 13
Verginia, 58–9
Verres, 72
Vespasian, 49, 113
Vestal Virgins, 65
vestigia (footprints), 105
see also walking, in history
Vettonians, 1–2
Via Cavour (Rome), 124
Via Graziosa (Rome), 122
Villa of the Papyri (Herculaneum), 114–15
villas
economic benefits of, 78
evocations of famous places, 105–7
naming of, 106
optical illusions, 116
and *otium*, 77–9
and philosophical ideals, 94–6, 113

as repository of memory, 107
see also ambulatory spaces
violence, 37, 62, 137
Virgil, 53, 74–5, 150–2, 157
Vitellius, 48–9
Vitruvius, 80, 87–8, 128, 133–4
von Blanckenhagen, Peter, 125, 132–3, 134–5, 141
vultus (face), *see* facial characteristics and identity

walking
and art collections, 113, 114–15, 132–4
and conducting business, 87–8
and conversing, 82–9, 93–5
and dictating, 83
equalizing power of, 70, 87
for exercise, 80–3
Greek, 90–1
in history, *see* travel, into history
and identity, 7–8
as intellectual exercise, 82–3
for leisure, 94–6
as metaphor, 43–4, 98, 111
and mindset, 8, 34–6, 37–40, 45
in modern Rome, 152–5
and narrative art, 132–3, 134, 135–42
non-conversational, 88–9
and the *Odyssey* Landscapes, 146
outdoors, 5–6, 46, 80–3, 101
as performance, 52
and politicians, 55–6, 69, 84–5, 152
prudent, 44
and reading, 83, 89
in Roman culture, 4–8, 94–6, 150–2
self-awareness of, 3, 7–8, 157
slaves and, 37, 79
as social activity, 6–7
solitary, 6–7
and status, 8–9, 17–18, 55–6
and talking, 82–9, 93–5
through Rome, 150–1, 156
as universal human trait, 2, 3
see also ambulatio; deductio in forum; gait; Greek philosophers and walking; *perambulare; theoria; and specific philosophers and schools*
wall paintings, Roman, 127, 128, 129, 130–2, 133–4, 148
see also Odyssey Landscapes
water carriers, myth of, 144
weddings, 58
Williams, Craig, 21
Williams, Gareth, 112
wisdom, 97–9
Woolf, Greg, 156
Wordsworth, William, 3, 5

Index locorum

Alexis
  fr. 151 PCG, 92
Ammianus Marcellinus
  22.7.1, 71
Apuleius
  Met.
    9.5, 79
    10.29, 20
    11.11, 20
Aristophanes
  Nub.
    225, 100
    415, 93
Aristotle
  Ath. Pol.
    11.1, 99
Augustus
  RG
    3, 56
Aulus Gellius
  NA
    10.3, 72
    20.5.5, 92

Bellum Africum [anon.]
  22.4, 56–7

Cassius Dio
  56.34, 75
Cato
  Agr.
    5.2, 79
Catullus
  10, 73
  42.3, 22
  42.8, 22
Celsus
  Med.
    1.2.1, 80
    1.2.6, 80–1

Cicero
  Acad. post.
    1.9, 97
    1.17, 92
  Amic.
    1, 17
  Att.
    1.4, 95, 105
    1.6, 95, 105
    1.8, 95, 105
    1.9, 95, 105
    1.10, 95, 105
    1.10.3, 105
    1.11, 95, 105
    1.18.1, 6, 55, 83, 84
    2.23.1, 83
    4.15.7, 87
    7.1.1, 97
    13.40.1, 106
    15.5.3, 47–8
    15.9.1, 106
  Cael.
    49, 24
  De or.
    1.28, 89, 93
    2.12, 93
    2.18, 77
    2.20, 77–8, 93
    3.133, 70, 87
    3.221, 14
  Div.
    1.8, 93, 95
  Fam.
    2.12.2–3, 83–4
    10.31.6, 85
    15.4.16, 56
  Fin.
    2.77, 12
    2.102, 101
    2.119, 93

Cicero (cont.)
  5.1, 93
  5.5, 104
  Leg.
    1.1, 89
    1.15, 93, 110
    2.1, 93
    2.2, 105
    2.3, 89, 108–9
    2.4, 105, 110
    2.6, 109
    2.7, 110
  Leg. agr.
    2.13, 15
  Mur.
    44, 56
    69, 56
    70, 56, 66
    70–1, 60–1
  Off.
    1.131, 19, 28
    1.144, 6, 88
  Orat.
    12, 105
  Phil.
    2.58, 73
    2.106, 72, 73
    2.108, 62
    2.112, 56
    13.19, 62
  Prov. cons.
    40, 57
  Q Fr.
    2.6, 73
    3.3.1, 83
  Sest.
    17, 15
    105, 15
  Tusc.
    1.7, 93
    2.10, 93
    3.7, 93
    4.7, 93
    5.8–9, 99
    5.9, 102
  Vat.
    161, 57
  Verr.
    2.4.67, 61
    2.5.34, 72

Cicero, Q. Tullius
  Comment. pet.
    34, 59–60

    34–8, 66
CIL
  I^2 1211, 23

De physiognomia [anon.]
  74, 22
Diodorus Siculus
  31.25.2, 53
Diogenes Laertius
  6.78, 143
  9.62, 100

Epicurus
  fr. 163 Usener, 144

Fronto
  Ep.
    1.10.1, 56
    229.16–17 van den Hout, 97
Heliodorus
  Aeth.
    3.12–13, 11
    3.13.2, 12
Herodotus
  1.30.2, 99
Homer
  Il.
    13.71–2, 11
  Od.
    7.104, 124
    10.84–6, 136
    10.95–6, 139
    10.100–2, 146
    24.226–42, 110
Horace
  Carm.
    1.22.9–12, 5
  Epist.
    1.2.3–4, 145
    1.2.15, 145
    1.2.17–26, 145
    1.2.23, 148
  Sat.
    1.3.9–11, 36
    1.6.107–15, 55
    1.6.110–15, 7
    1.9, 7
    1.9.2, 7
    1.9.9–10, 7

Iamblichus
  VP
    58, 102
    58–9, 99

Jerome
  Ep.
    22.13, 26
Josephus
  BJ
    7.5.7 (158–60), 113
Juvenal
  Sat.
    1.30–48, 54
    1.37–9, 52
    1.63–4, 54
    1.158–9, 73
    3.236–48, 52
    7.139–43, 54

Livy
    1.48.4, 62
    2.49.3–5, 75
    3.47.1, 59
    29.19.11–12, 90
    32.39.7, 62
    38.50.10, 56, 63
    38.51.12–14, 63
    38.52.3–5, 64
    42.39, 62
    44.43.1, 62
Lucan
    5.508, 39
Lucian
  Dial. meret.
    10.2, 18
    12.3, 18
  Timon
    22, 18
Lucretius
    1.72–4, 100
    3.978–1023, 144
Macrobius
  Sat.
    2.3.16, 19
Manilius
  Astron.
    5.153, 22, 28
Martial
  Ep.
    2.11, 52
    2.14, 52
    2.14.5, 52
    2.57, 51
    3.20, 52
    5.22.5–8, 52
    9.59, 52
Minucius Felix
  Oct.
    2–3, 89

Ovid
  Ars am.
    1.491–6, 28
    3.159–68, 28
    3.297–306, 27–8
  Met.
    11.635–6, 15
  Pont.
    2.10.35–8, 86
    2.10.49–52, 86
    4.5.38–9, 83

*Passio Sanctarum Perpetuae
        et Felicitatis* [anon.]
    18.2, 14
Petronius
  Sat.
    119.1.25, 22
    123.1.204, 39
    126, 28, 35–6
Phaedrus
    5.1.13, 22
Philodemus
  Ep.
    27.6 Sider (= *Anth. Pal.* 11.44.6), 144
  On Flattery
    PHerc 222, 144
  On the Good King according to Homer
    PHerc 1507 col. 43.16–20, 143
  Rhet.
    Sudhaus vol. II, p. 111
        (= *PHerc* 425 fr. 21, 8–14), 142
Plato
  Leg.
    625a–b, 92
  Prt.
    314e–315b, 92
  Resp.
    486a, 100
  Symp.
    173b, 92
    175a–c, 93
    220c–d, 93
  Theages
    121a, 92
Plautus
  Asin.
    403–6, 37
    441, 18
  Aul.
    398, 18
  Curc.
    288–91, 91
    470–84, 70
    475, 70

Plautus (cont.)
Poen.
522–3, 18
Pliny the Elder
HN
9.118, 20
29.19, 73
35.116–17, 134
35.144, 132
Pliny the Younger
Ep.
1.5.8–10, 88
2.14.10, 17
2.17, 87
3.1, 81
3.1.2, 81
3.1.3, 81
3.1.4, 82, 89
3.5, 82
3.5.16, 73
5.6, 87
5.6.5–6, 109
9.36.3, 83
9.36.4, 82
Pan.
22.1, 68
22.5, 68
23.1–3, 68
24.2–3, 69
Plutarch
Cat. Min.
68.1, 82
Cic.
2.2, 87
Mor. (De lib. educ.)
3f–4a, 30
Sol.
25.5, 99
Polemon
Phys.
B39, 21
B40, 21
Polybius
Hist.
6.53.8, 53
6.53.9–10, 53
Propertius
2.1.5, 33

Quintilian
Inst.
5.9.14, 22
7.2.54, 57
10.5.19, 57
11.3.112, 18

11.3.138, 19
12.6.6, 56

Sallust
Cat.
15.5, 20, 36
Scriptores Historiae
Augustae
Hadr.
26.5, 106
Seneca the Younger
Apocol.
5.3, 29
Ben.
5.12.2, 101
Brev. vit.
14.1–2, 110–11
14.3–4, 111–12
Constant.
2.1, 40
Ep.
4.2, 56
8.3, 43
15.6, 83
15.7, 45
24.18, 144–5
52.12, 22
55.11, 86
66.5, 44
66.36, 44
75.1, 87
86.1, 108
86.5, 108
88.5, 143
94.5, 45
94.8, 45
94.8–9, 16–17
94.60, 52
108.3, 92
114.3, 22, 34, 38
114.22, 45
Helv.
8.4–5, 101
8.6, 101
20, 102–3
Her. F.
329–31, 40
Ot.
4, 46
5, 104
5.4, 104
Phaedra
989–90, 38
Q Nat.
7.31.2, 31–2

Thy.
418–22, 38
Tranq.
1.8, 41
1.9, 41
1.10, 41
1.11, 41
1.12, 41
2.2, 43
2.4, 42
2.11, 36
2.13, 5
4.3, 47
4.6, 47
5.2, 46–7
11.1, 44
12.2–4, 42–3
17.4, 26–7
17.8, 46
17.12, 44–5
Tro.
464–8, 16
517–18, 522–3, 40
615–18, 39
1088–91, 16
Vit. beat.
1, 44
1.1, 101
17.4, 101
Statius
Silv.
2.2.42–4, 114
2.2.63, 69–72,
113
Strabo
Geog.
3.4.16, 1
3.4.17, 1
Suetonius
Aug.
26.2, 56, 57
53, 68
53.2, 57
Calig.
35.3, 19
Claud.
4.3, 29
4.5, 29
Dom.
19, 69
Iul.
43.1, 71
52.2, 16
Ner.
7.2, 57

Tib.
15.1, 56
25, 88

Tacitus
Agr.
40.3–4, 67
Ann.
1.14, 65
2.59, 90–1
3.3, 48
11.12, 65
11.32, 65
13.2, 65
13.14, 66
13.18, 65–6
Dial.
33.2, 57
34, 17
Hist.
3.56, 48–9
4.11, 49
Terence
Ad.
376, 18
An.
860, 18
Eun.
918–19, 18
Haut.
249, 18
Tertullian
De cult. fem.
2.1.1, 25
2.1.2, 25
Theagenes (DK8)
A2, 143
Turpilius
fr. 102, 36

Ulpian
Dig.
47.10.15.15, 51

Valerius Maximus
2.10.2, 108
3.6.1, 90
3.7.1e, 56
6.1.2, 58
Varro
Rust.
1.2.1, 97
1.2.3, 97
1.2.4, 99
2 pr. 2, 94

Varro (cont.)
   3.2.2, 99
  Sat. Men.
    fr. 259, 56
Virgil
  Aen.
   1.46, 33
   1.326–34, 11
   1.402–5, 11
   1.689–90, 12
   5.647–9, 12
   6.860–5, 74
   6.863, 74
   6.865, 74

   8.306–12, 150
   8.307–9, 152
   8.345–6, 151
   8.347, 151
   8.348, 151
   8.360–1, 150
Vitruvius
  De arch.
   5.9.5, 80
   5.11.4, 95
   6.5.2, 87
   6.7.5, 95
   7.5.2, 133
   7.5.3–8, 128